3935

The Best American
Travel Writing 2008

GUEST EDITORS OF
THE BEST AMERICAN TRAVEL WRITING

The Best American Travel Writing™ 2008

Edited and with an Introduction
by **Anthony Bourdain**

Jason Wilson, Series Editor

HOUGHTON MIFFLIN COMPANY

BOSTON · NEW YORK   2008

www.houghtonmifflinbooks.com

ISSN 1530–1516
ISSN 978-0-618-85863-7
ISSN 978-0-618-85864-4 (pbk.)

Printed in the United States of America

MP 10 9 8 7 6 5 4 3 2 1

Contents

Foreword

THIS PAST YEAR, we've officially witnessed the emergence of a new subgenre in travel writing, the Travel Writer Tell-All — in which a travel writer can no longer bear the shame and guilt brought on by his chosen profession and must confess his sins. The two most noteworthy examples of this subgenre are Thomas Kohnstamm's *Do Travel Writers Go to Hell?* and Chuck Thompson's *Smile When You're Lying*.

Kohnstamm is a former *Lonely Planet* guidebook author who, in his memoir, admits to — among other things — accepting freebies while on assignment in Brazil, updating a chapter on Colombia without actually setting foot in the country, selling a few drugs to make ends meet, and having sex on a table with a waitress and then writing in his guidebook that the restaurant's "table service is friendly."

Of course, so much outrage ensued. "Travel writer says he made up parts of books," read the Reuters headline. "Travel writer tells newspaper he plagiarized, dealt drugs," said CNN. The *Washington Post* asked, "Can You Trust Your Travel Guidebook?" Meanwhile, travel bloggers fanned the flames and Lonely Planet issued a statement denouncing Kohnstamm.

Only a few months earlier, Chuck Thompson, a former editor at *Maxim* and a veteran magazine freelancer, published his own screed against the travel-writing industry. In his book (which bore the subtitle "Confessions of a Rogue Travel Writer") he disparaged the "breathless cheerleading" and "insufferable hyperbole" and the "kind of chirpy discourse" that "falls back on clichés and fawning descriptions of rooms, views, and meals."

Eventually, Thompson really works himself into a lather:

> As conditioned purveyors of the sell-sell-sell mentality, magazine editors routinely dismiss story ideas if something new to sell can't be attached to them. This limp editorial practice prevents thousands of good stories each year from seeing print and reinforces the contemporary magazine's standing as a cleverly concealed catalog.

"Whither travel writing?" critics have been asking. Is the genre in crisis?

In the end, allow me to sum up the hard-won revelations, insight, and privileged information we apparently learn from Kohnstamm's and Thompson's exposés: (1) You can't totally trust travel guidebooks. (2) Travel writers don't get paid a whole lot for their troubles. (3) A lot of travel writing is driven by advertising and isn't very well written.

Yes, dear readers, travel writing — hold on to your hats — can be shallow and dishonest! And the prose is often bad! And you may never again be able to completely believe it when, according to Thompson, a travel writer tells you an inn is "quaint," a beach is "sun-drenched," a neighborhood is "undiscovered," or a dish is "mouthwatering."

Wow. Allow me a moment to catch my breath. As I do, I am reminded of an entry in Gustave Flaubert's *Dictionary of Received Ideas.* "ILLUSIONS: Pretend to have had a great many, and complain that you have lost them all."

As a service to publishers, free of charge, here are similar ideas for new tell-alls on other aspects of magazine publishing:

- I bet you didn't know this . . . there are some really silly recipes in food magazines. And hard ones too!
- Here's a shocker . . . there are never any trash cans cluttered with soiled diapers in home & design magazine spreads!
- Dirty little secret that golf magazines don't want you to know . . . you don't really need new clubs this year!

My point is, while I don't entirely disagree with the central premise of either Kohnstamm's or Thompson's book, what these books really sound like to me is a lot of whining. And, frankly, there is nothing worse than a travel writer who whines. By Thompson's own admission, he's traveled to more than thirty-five countries, spent a lot of quality time at places most people would kill to visit, and then been paid to write a few hundred words about these places once he's returned home. Boo-hoo. I don't see a lot of sympathy coming from readers who only get two weeks of vacation a year.

The fact is, despite these overheated reports from the underbelly, there is plenty of excellent travel writing that's published each year. Even, surprisingly enough, some of it published in the most commercial, ad-driven magazines on the newsstands. Is there enough of it? Certainly not. If I was a whiner, I might tell you firsthand what it's like trudging through a thousand vapid, dull travel stories just to find one hundred candidates for this anthology. But since I am not, I will tell you that my guest editor and I were able to find — as we have for nine editions now — two dozen travel stories that transcend the type of travel writing that Thompson and Kohnstamm have both committed and now regret and disdain.

Yes, the book you hold in your hands is the antidote to the Travel Writer Tell-All.

The stories included in this anthology are selected from among hundreds of pieces in hundreds of diverse publications — from mainstream and specialty magazines to Sunday newspaper travel sections to literary journals to travel websites. I've done my best to be fair and representative, and in my opinion the best travel stories from 2008 were forwarded to Anthony Bourdain, who made our final selections.

I now begin anew by reading the hundreds of stories published in 2008. I am once again asking editors and writers to submit the best of whatever it is they define as travel writing. These submissions must be nonfiction, published in the United States during the 2008 calendar year. They must not be reprints or excerpts from published books. They must include the author's name, date of publication, and publication name, and must be tear sheets, the complete publication, or a clear photocopy of the piece as it originally appeared. I must receive all submissions by January 1, 2009, in order to ensure full consideration for the next collection. Further, publications that want to make certain their contributions will be considered for the next edition should include this anthology on their subscription list. Submissions or subscriptions should be sent to Jason Wilson, The Best American Travel Writing, P.O. Box 260, Haddonfield, NJ 08033.

I enjoyed working with Anthony Bourdain on this collection, and would like to thank him for choosing the wonderful stories you'll be reading here. I am also grateful to Nicole Angeloro, whose friendship and guidance this year has been essential.

JASON WILSON

Introduction

IT HAS BEEN SAID THAT the more one travels, the more one's attention turns inward. And it is certainly true, in my own experience, that eventually — after years of hotel rooms, bed-and-breakfasts, jungle longhouses, trains, planes, boats, and automobiles of every variety — after seeing so much of the world, even the world's most spectacular vistas can sometimes fly by my window without distracting me from a period of monstrous self-regard. Travel writers seem to seek not just other places, but their own place — as if trying to position themselves precisely in a large and ever-shifting landscape. Travel, when done habitually, when done for a living, changes you in ways mostly good, sometimes bad. On one hand, it is the greatest privilege one can imagine: to see the world in all its flavors, colors, and seemingly infinite variety; to discover firsthand the differences among us on this enormous and complex planet — as well as the things we share. On the other hand, travel can become a compulsion, though it keeps us away from friends and loved ones — sometimes even when we're back. When I'm away, I often yearn for home. When I'm home, I'm listless. I seem no longer to fit. History and literature are filled with characters who see Asia, or Venice, and can never go back to the way they were.

There are slippery moral dimensions as well. Some of the stories in this collection illustrate brilliantly the queasy détente one must sometimes reach with oneself when trying to see and understand the world. John Lancaster's "Next Stop, Squalor," an account of the growing "poverty tourism" sector — in this case a visit to a squatter settlement in Mumbai — is an excellent example of becoming complicit by seeing, or more uncomfortably, recognizing, one's complicity in something very, very bad. How can one take the spanking new, state-of-the-art train to Tibet, as Pankaj Mishra does here, and not, in some way, contribute to a system that crushes its subjects? Phnom Penh, beautifully captured by Ian Buruma, is an example of a place you should by all means visit, but be ready to perform triage with every trip out of your hotel. In every small daily task one must ask oneself: "Which of these people can I or should I help? Which of them will I ignore? Who will get to take me on his motorbike to my comfortable meal? To whom, if anyone, shall I give a dollar? Or an artificial limb?" Is there a theme to this collection? I don't know. Though I'm pretty sure that after all the stories I've read (many, many more than are included here) the ones that spoke loudest and most powerfully to me were usually evocative of the darker side, those moments fearful, sublime, and absurd; the small epiphanies familiar to the full-time traveler, interspersed by a sense of dislocation — and the strange, unholy need to record the experience. If I had to discern — or cobble together — a theme, it would likely read as "Shifting Perspectives." Or "From the Absurd to the Tragicomic to the Simply Tragic."

In my peculiar mode of travel, I must face the unavoidable fact that I am, in some small way, destroying that which I love. My "job," such as it is, is to find authentic out-of-the-way eateries undiscovered by tourists in ugly shorts, to embrace the Mom and Pop hawker stands, the one-chef/one-dish food stalls, and the family-run local joints that I truly love, the kind of places superbly described by Calvin Trillin in his "Three Chopsticks" piece on Singapore's vibrant, food-crazy hawker culture. If successful in my job, I find the perfect little place. I write about my find. I put it on television. In the best case, a successful show or book or article is seen and enjoyed by many, and perhaps inspires others to travel. And the next time I roll through town, the place is packed with Americans. There's a Starbucks next door — and the whole neighborhood is going straight to hell.

In this way, writers are indeed, as Henry Miller suggested, traitors to the human race. We may turn a light on inequity, injustice, and oppression from time to time, but we regularly kill what we love in insidious fashion. As the scorpion with the frog, we can't help it.

It's our nature. We change the charming and unspoiled by visiting and telling others.

In a book of the same name, Gary Shteyngart — whose excellent piece on St. Petersburg's wedding season, "To Russia for Love," appears in these pages — wrote hilariously of the fictitious yet all too real former Soviet Republic of "Absurdistan." As any veteran travel writer knows, absurdity is a regular and often terrifying feature in the life of many who stray off the beaten path. There is a reason that dictators and despots, early in their purges, have always executed writers and satirists and anyone with a sense of humor. Laughter — and particularly ridicule — is dangerous. Recognizing the absurdity of a situation is to recognize that it's simply no good, that it doesn't work, that something has to change. And that can be unpopular thinking in places like Côte d'Ivoire, so atmospherically and dramatically described by Peter Chilson in "The Border," or in the bizarro Dubai of Seth Stevenson's "Looking for Mammon in the Muslim World." The absurdity of the Tongan political system and its royal family are funny to read about from afar in Matthew Teague's "While the King Sleeps," but not so funny, one suspects, up close. And while it certainly seems absurd that a group of wealthy Arab royals regularly career about Bin Laden's presumed backyard, practicing falconry in a war zone, as described in Annie Nocenti's "The Most Expensive Road Trip in the World," it feels somehow like the joke is on us.

It's only right, then, that it took perhaps the greatest of travel writers, Paul Theroux, to capture the menace and terror behind the supremely absurd "Golden Man" of Turkmenistan, Saparmurat Niyazov. The piece suggests that Orwell's *1984* is absurd only until it happens.

Within cultures there are subcultures, often groups that recognize no nation or boundaries as their own. Like some of the authors in this collection, they are frequent travelers or expats, people who left one place and never went back. Many of the people who found a home in the pirate subculture of the Straits of Malacca are merchant seamen of varying provenance. Peter Gwin, in "Dark Passage," makes their lives and chosen profession both thrilling and poignant, painting a full-color portrait of a world that few people have ever seen, much less heard about.

The residents of the notorious Chungking Mansion in Hong

Kong, in Karl Taro Greenfeld's "Hope and Squalor at Chungking Mansion," have constructed their own society just below the surface of the flashy one only a few yards away. The Kabul restaurant scene of Kristin Ohlson's "Kabul Nights" is a subculture of sorts — demanding its own kind of craziness. And as I can tell you from personal experience, the book tours of Thomas Swick's "Have Book, Will Travel" and the dimly lit pretend-normalcy of business class (David Sedaris's "Journey into Night") are worlds unto themselves, a transient population of observers.

And what waits at the end of the road? Two stories suggest a possible outcome for those of us for whom seeing the world is a lifestyle choice: Total immersion — as Peter Hessler seems to have accomplished in his continuing dispatches in *The New Yorker.* Here, in "Wheels of Fortune," he discusses the nuances of car ownership in China. And finally, in the absolutely breathtaking "The River Is a Road," we follow Bryan Mealer all the way into the proverbial heart of darkness and beyond. The story sets the bar almost impossibly high for any writers who care to mine this territory further.

Traditional travel writing follows the author on a voyage with a beginning, a middle, and an end. In between, there are meals, encounters, amusing setbacks, misunderstandings, and helpful suggestions for affordable lodging. I like to think that the stories in this collection have aggressively avoided that formula. Mealer's story, in particular, is everything the "travel" story could and should be at its very best: an exploration of far more than what whips past our windows, a deeper look that, one hopes, will lead to understanding.

ANTHONY BOURDAIN

The Best American
Travel Writing 2008

BILL BUFORD

Extreme Chocolate

FROM *The New Yorker*

ON JULY 7, 2001, Frederick Schilling and his girlfriend, Tracey
Holderman, arrived in New York to attend the Fancy Food Show
and launch Dagoba, an organic-chocolate company. Schilling had
just turned thirty, Holderman was twenty-nine, and the show was
the first entrepreneurial event of their lives. Dagoba had no employees and no orders. It had a lease for a ground-floor industrial
space in Boulder, Colorado (the "factory"), and an investment of
$20,000 (borrowed from Schilling's mother and an uncle), which,
after flights, a hotel, and a fee for the smallest possible booth,
against a dark wall in the basement of the Jacob K. Javits Convention Center, was gone. It also had "launch products" — seven
bars, including infusions of raspberry and mint — an amateur-
ish jamboree, confected and poured into molds by a man who
had never liked chocolate, hand-wrapped by a woman who rarely
ate more than two ounces a year, and tested only by their Boulder friends and roommates, a scraggly crew of ski bums and folk-
singers. Dagoba was more bedroom than boardroom. In New York,
that changed.

"I was overwhelmed," Holderman told me. "The magnitude of
the show, the number of other chocolate companies — I had no
idea." Their venture had begun a few months earlier, on Valentine's Day. Holderman and Schilling were on a chairlift, skiing in
the Arapahoe Basin, when Schilling said he could wait no longer
("I need to do this now!"). He raced down, shopped, got home,
melted two batches of organic chocolate, infusing one with milk
chai, the other with raspberries and rose hips, poured them into

heart-shaped molds, and served them on a silver platter to the hundred friends who came over for a party that went on till the next morning, with guests naked in a hot tub, "praying for peace," as a red sun brightened the Continental Divide.

The Fancy Food Show runs for three days. By the end, Holderman and Schilling's samples had disappeared in a bewildering thirty-six-hour gobblefest, their picture taken so often that they felt like celebrities — the boyfriend-girlfriend team with wacky organics — and Schilling, a self-described alchemist, entered the happiest period of his life. He became a chocolate-maker.

I found Schilling at this year's show slumped uncomfortably in a plastic chair. His face was in a cup of coffee, absorbing steam. He was wearing an oversized floppy cotton shirt, the top buttons undone, a hairy chest on display, jeans, clogs, a discolored shiny leather bracelet. He was wolverine thin, with an unshaven scratchy face, sagging cheeks, and soft round sacks under his eyes, and his breath smelled so powerfully of red wine from the night before that a staff member gave him two sticks of cinnamon gum. He had just returned from a trip to Bali, Java, and Sulawesi, including a stint in the tropical backcountry, and he kept running a hand through his hair, as if to make sure that a soft-tissue creature hadn't made a home there. He wasn't on a New York clock yet, he explained, but realized, counting slowly, that he'd been here five days. He looked up, perplexed, his eyes so red they could have been rubbed with sand.

Schilling is thirty-six, no longer a novice but still not the obvious founder of a manufacturing company with many millions of dollars in sales. His education has been scattershot. He applied to one college, St. John's in New Mexico, didn't get in, prepared to enter a monastery, and, at the last minute, was offered a scholarship by Ohio Wesleyan to play lacrosse. ("I love lacrosse!") He intended to study religion, hoping to satisfy a spiritual need, but, in the summer, attended a music festival "in the sacred valley of Telluride" and never returned. He worked for a record store, the sum of his business experience. He played guitar. He wrote songs, smoked "an insane amount of herbal blends," and was the lead singer in a band. After six years, he moved to Boulder, but, fundamentally, his life never changed.

At the show, Schilling and I walked past the French chocolates of

Michel Cluizel and saw a photograph of the white-haired patriarch surrounded by his offspring: four scrawny young adults, each assigned to a different division of the business. Dagoba is an inverted version. Schilling has no children, but his mother, a soft-spoken sixty-one-year-old divorcée, looks after the front office. She was running the stand that morning. An older sister, unmarried, keeps the books. And his father, a misanthropic ex-I.B.M. corporate manager, retired at forty-nine ("So I could golf, drink beer, bowl, and play blackjack at Indian casinos," he told me), was summoned one weekend to give lessons in how to run a business and stayed for years. "How do I travel so much?" Schilling said. "I've got Papa Jon nearby, Sister Becky doing the accounts, and Mother Mary working the phones." He beamed. His smile was disarming because it was so trusting, confident that the affection it conveyed would be reciprocated, and his manner, despite the hangover and the slouch and the exhaustion, was irrepressibly cheerful. *"Theobroma cacao,"* he exhaled — the scientific name given to chocolate by Linnaeus — stretching out his arms as though to embrace his products in a loving hug. *"Theos,* god. *Broma,* food. The food of the gods."

In the past five years, dark chocolate has had astonishing sales, especially in the United States, and has grown ten times faster than milk chocolate. In 2006, its sales increased by 15 percent. Dark chocolate represents a quarter of what Americans buy, $4 billion last year, and industry analysts, who believe that sales will reach nearly 5.5 billion by 2011, don't see an end. One says that it "will drive the chocolate sector for the next hundred years." An appreciation of dark chocolate is now a sign of a discriminating palate. Most chocolate has no such pretensions. It ends up in a candy bar or a chocolate Easter egg or an M&M-like treat referred to by the trade as "bagged product." But taste is a powerful force — in effect, "taste" is "culture" — which I hadn't fully understood until Schilling introduced me to his high-end hands-on fellow-manufacturers.

They were uniformly earnest. They told no jokes. They seemed to have no interest in selling, wanting to talk only about what they made, bars invariably (anything else — a filled confection like a truffle, for instance — was frivolous), in the compulsive, insistent way that upmarket vintners go on about their wines. The intellectual index was the wrapper, the compact culinary encyclopedia of what was inside. It might tell you where the beans came from. (Madagascar is this year's hot real estate.) It might reveal the varietal. One of the rarest is a Porcelana, from South America; Amedei, an Italian company, sells it for $127 a pound. There were "crus," named after specific farms. Some bars had a harvest year. I got one from an Internet supplier, a 2002, made from Chuao Valley beans in Venezuela, three years past its sell-by date. Suspecting a gimmick, I ate it to confirm its staleness. I was surprised. It seemed fresher than other bars I'd bought. If kept dry, a chocolate with a high cacao content, I've discovered, rarely spoils.

The cacao content is a wrapper's most important datum, and the acceptable benchmark is 70 percent. The figure is a measure of "cocoa mass." (The English language uses "cacao," the Mayan word for the tree, and "cocoa," an eighteenth-century corruption, interchangeably.) The mass is what you get after you grind up the beans, a gooey wet gob. I did this at home. I put old, dry beans in a coffee grinder, and was surprised by the amount of liquid they produced. It is fat, a lot of it, half the bean's content, although the fat is mainly unsaturated, the kind that's good for you, like an avocado's. This benchmark figure is now the heart of contemporary dark-chocolate culture. It provides a confederation of obsessives with a name, "the 70 percent club" (pure chocolate, "no bonbons") — the snobbiest of the snobby, according to Schilling. It is the number on most of the chocolates I saw. Amedei's Porcelana is 70 percent. So is an Ocumare Grand Cru, an award-winning new product, named after a Venezuelan valley unknown to anyone except other fanatics.

I tasted it with Schilling. His face gave little away. "Good chocolate," he said finally.

I had a bite and thought: Harmonic, pure.

"Expensive beans," he added, quietly. "But good." He had another bite. "In fact," he declared, "this is very good." It was too emphatic. I wondered if he had a reservation he wasn't expressing, maybe out of respect to the maker, Art Pollard. In 1996, Pollard had a midlife cacao epiphany and has been on a quest for perfect chocolate ever since. This was one of his three products. It might be years before he produced another. I studied him: pale skin, soft middle, a wife he never sees, talking, talking, talking. His life was this bar.

Schilling took me to the Valrhona stand, the French maker, and we tasted a Guanaja, named after a Caribbean island where choco-late was first seen by a European. Columbus, on his last voyage, in 1502, came upon a dugout canoe filled with brown beans, clearly regarded by their Mayan crew as precious: everyone panicked when some spilled. But Columbus, eager to get on, dismissed them as strange almonds. Valrhona's Guanaja was the world's first 70 per-cent bar, the chocolate world's equivalent of an airplane's breaking the sound barrier. It was released in 1986, after two years of secret testing by pastry chefs and tastings and retastings by a Valrhona jury. Before the Guanaja, most dark chocolate was half sugar, a so-called bittersweet confection.

Since then, Valrhona has followed the same studied approach in launching any new bar. It was founded in 1924 and has ten basic bars. El Rey, founded in 1929, has nine bars. Scharffen Berger has six. The message: serious chocolate is a considered business.

Schilling has twenty-nine bars. He has his dark bars, like every-one else — a New Moon (74 percent), a darker moon (the Eclipse, 87 percent), and the 100 percent Prima Materia, the refined ver-sion of what I produced with my coffee grinder, a brick of intensely complex flavors that can be eaten only in small quantities over a long period. But mainly he has whatever occurs to him. "This seventy-percent thing is a health craze, not a flavor craze. I've had seventy-percent bars that I wouldn't put in my compost pile. Does anyone have any idea what these percentages mean?

"I want surprises in my chocolate," he explained. "I don't want purity. I like peaks and valleys. Good beans, bad ones, the perfect and the flawed. Today, everyone wants the established names, the Ocumares, the Madagascars. I like getting in the truck and driving sixteen hours to a village that hasn't replaced its original stock with the latest hybrid. Every bean is a story."

Schilling doesn't have the patience to conduct tastings over two years. "I prepare a flavor in my mind. Once it's there, I can make the actual physical object quickly." An idea occurs to him, invari-ably at night ("Bottles of red wine essential"), he realizes it in the morning (knife, toaster oven, spice grinder), and manufactures it in a week. He knows one appetite, one curiosity, and one palate: his own.

"What do I want from a chocolate?" he asked. "A beginning and an end. I start with the breast of a woman on her back." He illus-trated with his hand how a breast flattens when a woman lies down.

"That's my flavor curve. You start with the belly." He used his forefinger like a pencil. "You then move up her body, climbing slowly, rising up the flattened curve of the breast, gently, and the nipple pops out suddenly. Have you noticed how a woman's nipple pops out when she is on her back? Then you slide down, an elegant finish." He looked at me. "It always comes back to sex."

He also makes tinctures: "Clarity" for mornings, "Moon Cycle" for a woman's period, and "Eros," a constellation of every tribal moonbeam fringe aphrodisiac he could find. It was foul; it tasted like a drugstore. I asked Schilling if he used it. "Oh, yes." He cited an ingredient, damiana, that he once mixed into a chocolate served at a party. He won't do that again. "People were having sex on a couch."

I stared at the bottle. You took it in a dropper.

"We don't sell a lot of these here in New York," Schilling said. "It's probably a West Coast thing."

He has three drinking chocolates — he brushes his teeth with the unsweetened one — and recently experimented with another, made from raw seeds. I didn't know that this wasn't done — that flavors aren't really created until a seed has been fermented and dried — until I tried it. It was like black dirt. Why make a drink that tastes disgusting?

"Antioxidants," he said. "The benefits are frickin' off the charts. But most never even make it into the product." He offered an example: "Dutching," a process developed in 1828 by Coenraad van Houten, a Dutch chemist. The fats in chocolate are notoriously temperamental and don't like water, and the drink had always been grainy. Van Houten figured out how to squeeze out most of the fats with a heavy press, and then pulverize the cakey leftovers into a powder: better, but still silty. He then added an alkaline, sodium carbonate, and rendered the smooth modern cocoa. But alkaline destroys antioxidants.

"You will never understand cacao until you see it in the tropics," Schilling said one day. He mentioned Diego Badaró, a "spiritual brother" who farms it in the rainforests of Brazil. We should go to Bahia, Schilling proposed. And I agreed.

A few weeks later, Badaró at the wheel of a Land Rover, Schilling and I entered cacao country at five in the morning, an hour before a tropical dawn revealed green, foggy wet hills, the landscape of the Mata Atlântica, the rainforest of the Brazilian coast. A banner of welcome was stretched above the road, Highway 101. We'd been driving south for six hours, having set out from Salvador, Bahia's capital. We ate cacao beans to stay awake. We stopped at a twenty-four-hour tapioca stand. We passed a muddy market square, with posts to tie your horse. A monkey ran across the road.

"*Jupara,*" Badaró said.

Jupara was the mythic animal that introduced cacao to the rainforests here. It is said to have entered Bahia bearing a pod, which it broke open, eating the pulp, discarding the seeds, and sowing the first tree, having run from the Amazon Basin, two thousand miles away. Most botanists believe the fruit originated in the Amazon, and they continue to find new varieties there — more than anyone can count, each an expression of a unique microrainforest spot. Bahia is the Amazon's geographical next-of-kin: the same climate, forest canopy, diverse floor. But there is no wild cacao; the tree was introduced, most likely by a Frenchman, Louis Frederick Warneaux, who, in 1746, sowed seeds near one of Bahia's large rivers.

By then, the fruit, which grows in the shade in warm, wet latitudes — the "twenty-twenty zone" — had migrated from the Amazon Basin, adapting and cross-pollinating along the way, west and north through Venezuela, Panama, southern Mexico, where it was cultivated by a succession of Mesoamerican civilizations. The Olmecs, on the Gulf Coast, were the first, around 1300 B.C. They called it *kakawa*. You still find semiwild trees in Mexico's humid lowlands, and some of the world's fruitier blond-brown chocolate comes from family holdings there. Mayans were next. By 1519, when Hernán Cortés and his army attended an Aztec feast on the island capital of Tenochtitlán (now Mexico City) and witnessed the seed in a beverage, cacao was a profoundly sophisticated food.

The Spaniards had seen nothing like it. The "beans," as dried seeds were called, were roasted over a fire; crushed into a paste; flavored with flowers, chilies, black pepper, and vanilla; diluted with cold water; poured between vessels until a froth formed; and served in a lacquered gourd, by a train of solemnly reverent women, to Motecuhzoma Xocoyotzin. Montezuma drank it all night — fifty cups, by one account — and *cacahuatl,* when later presented in

Europe as *chocolatl,* would have two specific associations arising out
of the high theatre of its introduction: as an elitist food (only the
ruler drank it) and an erotic one (the suggestive female attendants). It had more rarefied associations among the Aztecs. For
them, it was a divine food: the gift of a deity, Quetzalcóatl, and used
in the worship of Xochiquetzal, a fertility goddess. It was consumed
at births, sacrifices, and funerals. It was a trading currency — three
beans bought you a fresh avocado, one an overripe one — and
hoarded in storehouses. (Nine hundred and sixty million beans
were counted in one stash, according to Sophie and Michael Coe
in their "True History of Chocolate," the best account of cacao in
Mesoamerica.) The Aztecs couldn't grow it — they had the wrong
climate — and, like others, depended on colonies of rainforest
farmers.

Among them were the Kekchi Mayans, in Guatemala. In 1544, a
group was invited to Spain by Dominican priests and, in an audience with Prince Philip, the future king, made Europe's first recorded chocolate drink. Commercial shipments began in 1585,
arriving in Seville, and by the early sixteen hundreds the beverage
— the Aztec preparation, served warm, with European flavorings
(sugar, cinnamon, nutmeg) — had its own high-society rituals, including ornate serving vessels and a *molinillo,* a stirrer to make the
froth. The beans were probably from Guatemala, the blond-brown
variety prized today. Spaniards call it *criollo,* the "native."

In London, the first chocolate shop opened, on Gracechurch
Street, in 1657. Two private clubs, White's and the Garrick, got
their start as chocolate houses. By 1664, when Pepys was writing
about the new beverage ("To Mr. Blands and there drank my morning draught in good Chocolatte, and slabbering my band sent
home for another"), he was a representative European consumer.
He didn't understand what he was drinking, had no idea how it was
made, and knew only that it came from the New World and that he
wanted as much as he could get. In the face of a global shortage, an
equatorial panic set in, and prospectors and opportunists fanned
out across the tropics, looking for wild trees and planting new
ones. Spaniards started finding a darker, more bitter variety in
South America, an immigrant cousin of the Amazon Basin's original bean, which they called *forastero,* the "newcomer." By the end of
the seventeenth century, the Spanish had found trees in Venezuela

and Ecuador. They planted some in Trinidad, the French planted in Martinique, the English in Jamaica. Jesuits finally discovered the original *forastero* along the Amazon, the wild breed that had started everything, an astonishing bounty. But it was deep in the backcountry, and their harvest often rotted before reaching a port.

The Rio de Contas, a wide, almost deltalike river, was startling, a sudden big sky and a feeling of openness, and very bright. It was noisy with birds. The rainforest houses most of the earth's plant and animal population. I hadn't anticipated it would be so loud. The effect was unexpectedly welcoming: you felt isolated but not alone. Badaró's property was called Monte Alegre, and was some miles away. The road was flooded, not really a road but a shallow bog, with giant holes that seemed deep enough to sink the vehicle. The air smelled of burning wet wood. We passed a house, once white, now moldy black and fighting off the forest, its front door long gone, five small children in front, a cloying, damp smoke coming out of a chimney. We passed another, with a sliding roof, the drying area for cacao beans, built to close up when it rained. There were monkeys, hawks, and toucans. There were pigs, chickens, and a mule. An old man was out for a hunt, followed by his wife. He looked cantankerous and unhopeful, carrying a musket and a bag of homemade ammunition.

The road climbed a hill. A cacao plantation is a *fazenda,* and four hundred acres seemed large enough to fit the American sense of the word. But most of it was thick and impenetrable, cacao trees scattered throughout. It seemed to invert normal real-estate economics: *not* to use the land efficiently.

Badaró stopped the vehicle at his gate and got out. He was wearing high black boots and forest green rain gear. He was tall, with some bulk, and had thick eyebrows and jet black hair, parted in the middle. A machete was strapped to his belt. He was twenty-six but had the deliberate, unexcitable manner of an older man, and a deep baritone, referred to by his family as "the voice." He used it to speak to officials. In his bearing, he could have been sixty, with a dozen children. Instead, he had a thirty-four-year-old stepson. His wife, Luiza, a dark-haired artist, was fifty-five, the same age as his mother.

He had eccentricities. On the journey down, he had turned off the headlights — despite curves, blind hilltops, other vehicles — in order to see the stars better. He drove at bewildering speed. He lost control once, the Land Rover snapping back and forth in a succession of extreme hydroplaning skids. He often prayed: to Ewa, a god of serpents; to Oxossi, the hunter god (Badaró's personal deity); and to a dozen others, West African in origin. One night, I accompanied him to a worship service in Salvador — an airless room, chanting, drums, members working themselves into a trance, throwing themselves about, jabbering — and met his mother, Katia. A warrior woman — helmet, dagger, breastplate — grabbed Badaró, made battle cries, and grunted.

At the *fazenda,* Schilling spotted the first cacao. It was like a toy football, green and unripe, attached to a tree trunk as though it had been stapled on: a hulking pod defying gravity and seeming to invite you to take a swipe at it. He saw more, full-size footballs, bright yellow, mainly, but also red and orange-yellow, looking even more preposterously pendulant.

Badaró twisted a pod off a trunk and lopped off the top with his machete. The inside was creamy wet. It smelled of honey and orange and perfume. This was the pulp surrounding the giant seeds. The seeds looked like wet white maggots. Nothing suggested chocolate. Badaró stuck his fingers inside, pulled out some seeds, and tipped them into my hand, and I ate them. They had a slimy, sweet zing, more liquid than substance, and as I rubbed them against the roof of my mouth the pulp disintegrated. I was left with four seeds — still a mouthful. I bit one gently. It was bitter, awful. I spit it out.

The spitting is everything. Cacao has peculiar rainforest dependency. If the pod is not removed, it shrivels and the seeds die. It needs to tempt whatever happens by — monkey, man, squirrel, rat — to stop, wrestle it off its stubby stalk, break it, drink the nectar, eat the pulp (or try to), and cough out the seeds. No creature likes the seeds; the fruit's future is in its immediate ejection. The seeds that end up on the rainforest floor sprout within hours of exposure to the air.

Badaró lopped off another pod. I raised it over my head like a canteen, hoping to get a taste of *miel de cacao,* the honey. It is what remains after the seeds have been drained, but it keeps for no more than a day. You never see it outside the twenty-twenty zone. In Bahia, it is a specialty, drunk in the shade of the trees that made it.

We climbed back into the vehicle and followed a two-track road into the trees, where we found four men sitting on the ground, surrounded by yellow fruits, thwacking them rhythmically with their machetes, digging out the pulp, and tossing the empty pods to the side. The pulp was heaped into a white, gooey mound, and a viscous liquid trickled down into a receptacle. Badaró poured some of it into a discarded pod.

It had the same bright citrus flavor that made the pulp so startling. How could there be citrus notes? I identified acidity and sugar; I thought of grapefruit, qualities associated with a sun-ripened fruit: a translucent skin, exposure to direct light. But a cacao pod has a white, inch-thick shell, like a chunk of Styrofoam.

Badaró poured more into my gourd. It seemed to balance sweetness and acidity, weight and liquidity, mouthfeel, and perfume; if not universal in its appeal, it was clearly irresistible to all but a few palates. In effect, the tree had made a monkey out of me so I could help it along by spitting out the seeds.

In Bahia, the cacao business started slowly because the rewards came so slowly: you stuck a sapling into a wild, uninhabited land and waited. It might be ten years before you saw money from the fruit. Offspring of the Frenchman's first tree may have been growing since the eighteenth century, but no cacao was harvested until the demand from Europe was great enough to make the labor worthwhile. By the middle of the nineteenth century, the Dutch had reinvented chocolate as a beverage, and the cacao butter extracted in the process had been used by the Cadbury brothers, in England, to make their first bar.

By 1850, chocolate was being made in factories, on a much larger scale. By then, farmers in Bahia had developed the *cabruca* system, a way of cultivating a wild tree in a wild forest by thinning out the understory — trunks, dwarf palms, vines — planting in the cleared space, and preserving the canopy for protection: the rainforest disturbed but basically intact. (The earth is almost sterile; nutrition comes from the trees.) By then, the Bahians also recognized that their harvest had a better chance of reaching port than anything hauled out of the Amazon. The forest wasn't less impenetrable; it just grew right up to the sea, and deep rivers led out of it.

But it wasn't easy, even by 1920, as Roy Nash, an ex-army adventurer, observed in the three years he spent in the region. On a visit to a cacao plantation on the Rio de Contas, Nash came across an Olympian effort: a gang of workers driving mule-led pack trains, trying to get their harvest to a rail depot and then to port, "troop after troop struggling with their precious cargoes through mud that ate the very heart out of the beasts and through water that ate much cash value out of the beans. Two days to the railroad, two days back, two weeks for the animals to recuperate!" Nash's account, "The Conquest of Brazil" (1926), is a rare contemporary document of what was becoming an unusually secretive land visited by few foreigners, mainly because, as Nash saw firsthand — in flight from a cacao gang of two hundred "with Winchesters across their saddles" — this giant territory was simply not governed. He witnessed a shooting at a dance, a stabbing on a train, a private army stopping an election, another in a battle with the governor's troops, a gangster's "game of raid, rape, and run," hired gunmen, and "colonels" everywhere — landowners entitled to make their own laws and enforce them with armed deputies.

By then, Badaró's family had been producing cacao for thirty years. The family knows nothing of the first Brazilian Badaró, except that he was born in Sicily and arrived in the eighteen-fifties. Of the second generation, they know of a son, Antônio, a man of visionary industry, who cleared the understory along the Rio Almada, twenty miles of a famously fertile tract where cacao thrives, and planted millions of trees. We drove over the river during the night. By the time Antônio passed the enterprise on to his oldest sons, Juca, Senhor, and Domingos, it was one of the largest in Brazil, hundreds of thousands of acres on one bank. Another family, the Oliveiras, were on the opposite bank.

Now there was not enough cacao in the world to meet demand. Chocolate had become a wholly different food — a mass-market global confection — because a way had been found to make it with milk, previously impossible, owing to the fats' absolute intolerance of anything with water in it. (People had been trying to mix chocolate and milk since cacao beans arrived in Seville; the model was probably coffee.) The trick was in manipulating the boiling point. In 1867, Henri Nestlé, in Vevey, on Lake Geneva, trying to create an infant formula that wouldn't spoil, put milk in a sealed container, removed the air with a crude pump, and heated it until the water content evaporated. In a vacuum, milk boils at a lower temperature and doesn't curdle. Nine years later, Daniel Peter, the town's chocolate manufacturer, fed the formula to a newborn baby and understood an essential implication: a dried milk would not be rejected in cacao. Chocolate now had a populist formulation, its intensity diluted and dulled by sweet fats. It was an indulgence (fat + fat + sugar) and it was cheap (because milk was the principal ingredient), and by the time Peter's Chocolate won a gold medal at an Amsterdam exhibition in 1883, people couldn't get enough of it. By 1901, Peter's Chocolate had a U.S. distributor and an unobstructed horizon to expand to. No American had figured out the boiling trick, although many tried, including Milton Hershey, whose milk kept curdling, until finally, after years of experiments, Hershey settled for what he could get: milk chocolate that was slightly soured but not entirely ruined. (To this day, American milk chocolate makes Europeans gag.) By 1905, Juca, Senhor, and Domingos were running Antônio's estate. The same year, Hershey opened his new chocolate factory.

The sons had never seen a northern chocolate factory. They didn't know how to make chocolate. They didn't eat it. But they had seen booms before: a raw resource is discovered (diamonds, gold, rubber) and is wanted on the other side of the earth — and many people had become rich. Even the Rio de Contas had been mined for diamonds. Cacao was just the next thing. There was a rush to get to Bahia before others got there first.

In twenty years, the region went from producing almost none of the world's cacao to most of it. Ilhéus — a provincial port in 1885 (sugar, coffee, timber) — became a boomtown, with gaudy baroque mansions, cacao barons, nightlife, a celebrity prostitute, towering warehouses, harbor congestion, brokers, lawyers, tax inspectors, the agencies and excesses of sudden wealth.

All of this appears in the work of Jorge Amado, the region's chronicler. Amado's family moved to Ilhéus in 1914, when he was two, after a major flood destroyed their plantation; he died in 2001, at eighty-eight, after generating thirty-two books, seven movies, and a soap opera watched by twenty-five million. At the heart of Amado's region is the high drama of a flawed squatter's right: all property had been acquired by possessing, then defending — possibly a reasonable practice in 1850, definitely a dangerous one later, when desperate arrivals believed chocolate would make them rich. Claims had been filed at the Cartório de Ofícios, in Itabuna. Between 1905 and 1910, it burned down: no records, anarchy, and everyone at war with everyone else. It was rebuilt; new claims were received; it burned down again. Cacao made Amado into a writer — and in an introduction to "The Violent Land" (1943) he expresses his debt. He doesn't thank the Badaró family, although it is their stories he tells, using their real names, a dizzying feature to come upon for the first time, as if the novel were a history, and maybe it is. The Badarós, too, were at war. Their adversaries were the family across the river.

At Monte Alegre, Badaró revealed that he had learned of a ninety-three-year-old Oliveira survivor, his head and neck still laced with hacking scars. He had retained a heavy bell that had been rung when his home was under attack, and he still spat when he heard his rivals' family name. We made an effort to visit him — Badaró nervous, gravely imagining a reconciliation across generations — and then discovered that the man had died. A granddaughter owned a restaurant near Ilhéus called Tocaia Grande, where she displayed the family weapons as trophies. In Bahia, *tocaia* has a historically specific sense, referring to a particular kind of isolated rainforest assassination: a hired gunman, lying in ambush, in a land too big ever to hold him accountable. Amado's father had been the target of a *tocaia;* it may have been partly why he fled the *fazenda* with such dispatch. There would have been no negotiation. You want a neighbor's land? You kill him. Or you pretend to buy it, visit, bear a gift, and kill him. Or you offer property to a man who has never had it, often an ex-slave, provided he clears and cultivates it, and five years later, never having filed the claim, you kill him: an efficient way of planting trees.

Katia, Badaró's mother, growing up on an isolated cacao farm, had been kept ignorant of family history by a protective father, who died when she was sixteen. That year, she made a friend in school, Paloma Amado, the novelist's daughter, and "the bell jar I had been living in shattered," she told me. I met her brother, Badaró's uncle, who had notions about the number of fatalities, but vague ones, because he, like other members of the family, had learned what he knew from Amado's book. In it, two of Antônio's sons are shot: Sinhô in a fight, Juca by *tocaia*. The third son is not a character. This was the uncle's grandfather and the man he was named after, Domingos: the pacifist, a quiet farmer and peacemaker, who, on New Year's Day, 1910, ended the violence by marrying a member of the Oliveira family, Anita. According to Badaró's uncle, she was a "remarkably ugly woman," but one who "genuinely loved him. She was courted clandestinely — our own Romeo and Juliet — and their marriage ended the cacao wars."

Diego Badaró didn't read Amado's novel until 2003, the year he decided to devote his life to cacao and needed to understand the burden of his family's legacy. By then, most members had abandoned the rainforest, in the aftermath of witches' broom.

Witches' broom appeared in 1989. It is a fungus that attacks the tree and its fruit, often as it is about to be harvested (overnight, the pod shrivels into a stick and the leaves go brown — hence the name). There was no cure. Cacao is a monoculture crop in Bahia and has always been vulnerable to a sudden disease. The fungus, indigenous to Latin America, could have come from anywhere — a ship's hold, the flatbed of a pickup truck, the bottom of a boot.

Once the blight appeared, it spread with baffling efficiency, in all directions. In the second year, ten million trees were infected; half the harvest rotted and was thrown away. By its fifth year, the disease had reached forty-five million trees, 80 percent of everything ever planted. Five billion dollars had been lost. There were suicides. People wanted out but had no exit. Banks had inventories of foreclosed properties that they couldn't sell. The warehouses by the pier in Ilhéus were abandoned and now teeter dangerously, the windowpanes gone. The pier is closed, and access to it is roped off for fear of collapse. A hundred and fifty thousand people lost work. In a region so rural, they have no prospects and live on scavenged manioc root. You see the people on the mournful wet road to the sea, the stumps and trees of the original forest cleared a century ago to get the cacao to port, every few miles a plantation, once brazenly Brazilian, a bright turquoise or yellow, now faded to a ghostly pastel, overrun by packs of scrawny animals and occupied by barefoot families boiling water over fires on floors of manor house bedrooms, the doors kicked out, the windows gone, the walls dissolving from exposure to the constant rain. The owners never appear. They can't get rid of the land, and they can't make money on it. The farms that haven't been reclaimed by the forest are run by aging managers who were left behind.

Badaró is the exception, and one of the youngest people to return to the forest. He looks after land abandoned by an aunt, by his mother, and his own Monte Alegre. By now, you can get a cacao rootstock that is resistant to the fungus. The forest has almost recovered by itself, although I still saw affected trees everywhere, including on Badaró's property, the seeds of the pod black, cobwebby, and spoiled-smelling.

One morning in Salvador, Badaró took me to the market of São Joaquim. The bounty of Brazil — bananas, cocaine, diamonds, rubber, gold, coffee, vanilla, teak, nutmeg, mahogany, sugar, cacao — has always passed through the port city. At the market, you see some of that bounty — the plenitude of an extreme, tropical botany.

Badaró introduced me to hundreds of fruits, aisle after aisle of them. I bit into a bulbous *caja-umbu,* with so much juice it squirted me from head to foot, a long, curving, herbaceously fragrant yellow arc. I delicately ate my way around a *caju,* red like a tomato, pulpy like a mango, and with a pod on the outside that was fatally poisonous. A yellow berry, a *caza,* was so sweet and complex that it excited an entrepreneurial fantasy: should I try to export it? There were remedies: A leaf rubbed into a wound was an anti-inflammatory. A seed made into an infusion treated a headache, an unwanted pregnancy, a brain injury. "Ah, *catuaba,*" Badaró declared, affectionately holding up a piece of wood. "I love this. It is very powerful!" *Catuaba* was an aphrodisiac.

I asked about a thick rope, rolled up like a sticky black snake on the ground. It was wild tobacco, a wholly different species from the domesticated Virginia leaf. "The most effective natural insecticide in the world," Badaró said. "I dust my plants with it." I bought a three-inch chunk, scrutinized it — wet like motor oil — and popped it into my mouth. I sucked, recognized the flavor of aniseed, and chewed. The chewing released a heat not unlike a chili's.

It was a warm afternoon. We made for an exit by way of a butchers' aisle — in a nose-to-tail art, the cuts, hanging graphically, were principally of the art's nether regions. A girl with a basket of lemons abruptly stopped in front of me and poked one of the items, displayed on a tray of black-rimmed eyeballs. I'd kept chewing, and an interaction of some kind had occurred between the juices in my mouth and what had been released by the wild tobacco. My tongue had gone numb and the roof and inner cheeks were very hot. Sweat cascaded from my eyebrows, suddenly, as though a valvelike gland had been opened, and my pulse increased. I was also producing an unfamiliar saliva, which filled my mouth. I spit it out. We reached the street. Badaró, in white linen, crossed in front of me, his bright sleeves swelling in the breeze. My mouth filled again.

Wild tobacco is toxic; in some countries it is banned. The toxin is an alkaloid, a bitter-tasting compound formed by the plant as a defense against being eaten by insects and animals. A plant defends itself in many ways. An alkaloid is the most extreme, principally a response to big threats, and of the twelve thousand alkaloids known to science — quinine, codeine, cocaine, caffeine, ephedrine, strychnine, and nicotine among them — most come from the tropically wooded twenty-twenty zone. Many, like wild tobacco (*Nicotiana rustica*), originate in Brazil. An implicit dynamic was at work; every fruit, bark, seed, and root had a complexity you didn't find in a temperate climate. It was defensive.

In the dynamic, I understood cacao, the best-defended fruit in tropical botany. Its sugary seed lands on a rainforest floor, exposed. It is subjected to the most congested predator traffic (and the highest concentration of microbes, fungi, and possible bacterial attack) on the planet. Cacao contains, unusually, not one alkaloid but several, including caffeine, found in many tropical plants, and theobromine, found in few. It has more than five hundred other chemical compounds, also mainly defensive in purpose. Their benefits were first described by Andrew Waterhouse, in a study, published in *The Lancet* in 1996, that examined polyphenol content. A polyphenol is an antioxidant. Red wine has plenty: two hundred and ten milligrams. A forty-gram bar of dark chocolate has nine hundred and fifty-one. "There is such a concentration," Harold McGee, the author of "On Food and Cooking," told me, "that they create much of chocolate's uniqueness — the bitterness, the astringency, the edginess, and other sensations that we don't know about."

I discovered some of them during the all-night drive from Salvador. I had eaten one bean after another, hoping to find in it a version of what I believed to be the ultimate flavor of chocolate, when, unexpectedly, I experienced a flat-out, unmitigated euphoric stimulant buzz.

Badaró nodded, knowingly.

What had happened? Was it the caffeine? I'd asked.

No, too little. (A dark-chocolate bar has the equivalent of one cup of coffee.) Theobromine, he said.

Although theobromine can cause cardiac arrest in dogs, it appears to affect the human nervous system in only modest ways. It creates a few undisputed physiological symptoms. It makes you pee, for instance. Cacao has pharmacological ingredients, including serotonin, the mysterious neurotransmitter of well-being; a cannabinoid component, similar to what is found in marijuana; and a neuromodulator, phenylethylamine, an amphetamine-like antidepressant. But the conventional view is that the quantities are too small to be significant. I felt unsupported by the science. But Badaró understood. So did his uncle Domingos. They ate the beans. Domingos sometimes ate nothing else for days. On the drive, Badaró had also offered me kola nuts, one of the original ingredients in Coca-Cola. "It will also make you alert." Kola also has theobromine.

Fermentation has been around forever. It is older than cooking. It was probably the first method of food preparation. Fermentation transforms grapes into wine, grains into beer, wheat into leavened bread. It transforms a raw ingredient, often valued for its nutrition, into one valued for its taste. It yields vinegar, yogurt, sauerkraut, cheese, prosciutto, vanilla, and pickles. It occurs most readily in fruits, because they have, in abundance, the two essential elements: sugar and yeast. A yeast is on a leaf or a branch or in the air. It is the fine white powder on the skin of a grape, like a dust that you should wash off. At its most basic, fermentation is how sugar becomes alcohol.

In the long history of the rainforest, every hunter-gatherer familiar with the cacao pod would have seen evidence of fermentation. The seeds, in their sugary envelopes, ferment effortlessly. But only Mesoamerican culture understood what to do with them, because it had been using fermentation to prepare foods and alcohols for thousands of years, possibly as early as 7000 B.C., and knew how to control it. Badaró's process was fundamentally no different.

He conducted it in his "laboratory." It was a concrete shed. It had door frames but no doors, an overhead light that had burned out, a temperature alarm that didn't work, a digital thermometer that was broken, and five large wooden troughs, like pigpens. It was the responsibility of Pedro Jardin, who had been running Monte Alegre for four decades.

Jardin was now seventy-two, evanescently thin, with high cheekbones and sad eyes. He rarely spoke and seemed never to smile. Jardin had grown up with cacao. By day, he was wrapped, from cap to bright rubber boots, in rain gear. One night, he surprised me. He was barefoot and stripped to the waist, bearing an old Winchester. A Colt revolver was tucked into his trousers. He also had a sawed-off double-barrelled shotgun with a Tommy-gun-style grip. He walked the river before bedtime, a stealthy patrol, tiptoeing in and out of the trees, and returned to lock everyone in for the night — a claustrophobic touch, I felt, until I was wakened by something hurling itself against my door. Each time the door was struck, it lifted off its hinges slightly — four or five times, a ferocious force — until whatever it was (animal? man?) went away.

Jardin was waiting for us at the lab. It was late in the afternoon, a still, equatorial twilight about to turn dark, in the sudden way of the tropics. You could smell what was going on from fifty feet. It was a brewery.

Inside, the room was shadowy and hot. The smells multiplied instantly, a sudden olfactory cargo: a brewery, but also a winery, a vinegar factory, a dairy. It could have been an exaggerated version of an English pub. There was a gas, mildly disconcerting. It singed the lungs but felt strangely pleasant.

Schilling inhaled. "Aaah, get those acetic acids up your nose."

One trough was full. The beans, about chest-high, were covered with banana leaves, a gently heaving green blanket, wrapped tight, an oven on high. The yeast plus sugar produced carbon dioxide, plus heat and alcohol. There were plenty of yeasts on the banana leaves, a rich source, an additional insurance that could kick-start a fermentation if it hadn't already begun, or else add to it. There were yeasts in the slats of the trough, the natural ones in the wood as well as those left over from previous fermentations. The beans had yeasts. The humid tropical air had them. The forest had them. I thought about the yeast in bread. This approach seemed less about control than about attack.

Badaró pulled back some leaves. The beans instantly released a more intense hit of everything we'd been smelling. It was alcoholic and vaporous.

They were in their third day of fermentation, and were now purply, the sweet pulp almost entirely gone, although still gooey. "A ton," Badaró said.

"A ton?" Schilling and I both asked, and looked again, feeling compelled to do the banal calculation. "Two thousand pounds?" The beans were so compact.

The full trough was separated from other empty ones by wooden slats. Badaró removed one so that he could shovel beans into the next space. No matter how tightly everything was wrapped, the beans on top were cooler than the ones at the bottom. By shoveling everything next door, Badaró was turning them over. Normally, Jardin would then hop inside, shuffling beans under his boots, poking a toe into corners, to insure that every bean was equally fermented. Other foods are not fermented in this way. In wine, yeast converts the sugars in grapes into alcohol.

No one worries if some haven't fermented. At the end, they, and the mashed skins and stems that remain, a shapeless purple sponge, are thrown out. With cacao, an infantry of yeasts converge on the pulp around a seed and convert it into alcohol — plus acids and carbon dioxide and heat, none of it important, because none of it is the point. The liquids drain away; the alcohol evaporates. The attack doesn't stop. The seed is heated to a temperature rarely seen in the natural world. The shell is savaged and penetrated, until the tissue inside is invaded. At the end, the bean is the equivalent of the grapey mash. It has been reduced in size. It smells powerfully of vinegar. Its proteins have been disfigured. If you open one up, its insides look as though they'd been obliterated. In the devastation, the extreme intensities of cacao are converted to flavors.

Badaró, meanwhile, was trying to fix his thermostat. He wanted to keep the temperature from exceeding 122 degrees Fahrenheit, but he had no way of measuring it. The beans in the trough seemed hotter than that. I stared at them, trying to gauge how hot they might be, and then I did a thing that seemed strange at the time but was really just a misunderstanding. I took off my shirt, shoes, and pants, and, with my boxers on, I swung myself over the side and sank into the beans. They really were very hot.

I had wanted to get a sense of what you went through to complete cacao's strange fermentation, and had assumed that most people wouldn't be wearing many clothes. Jardin stared at me with a look of apparent horror.

Then Schilling removed his clothes, slipped into the beans, and was jubilant. "Yoni juice," he said. "Yoni of cacao juice." He filled his hands with beans, looked up, and poured them down on his face.

Badaró then removed his clothes. He landed with an awkward splash. Three of us were in a trough that might comfortably accommodate an adult pig, and the fermenting cacao was up to our necks. Badaró had taken to invoking some god, humming in his deep voice. "We must immerse ourselves and connect to the Aztec gods," he said. He disappeared, sinking below the surface. When he reemerged, he was covered in goop: beans behind his ears, stuck to his eyelids, clinging to his hair.

When Schilling and Holderman returned to Boulder from their first Fancy Food Show, in the summer of 2001, he knew they had a winner. According to Holderman, he also had a plan: five years to build the company, then sell it. "We'll be rich!"

"In those days, it was still a 'we' thing," Holderman told me. Dagoba was owned by Schilling, his parents, his uncle, and Holderman. (She is unsure how many shares she had.) "That was 'our' goal — 'rich' in five years. He doesn't remember saying this. But I do." (And he doesn't: "I am very confident I didn't state this. I'll take a lie-detector test.")

They had a division of labor: he made; she sold. Her calls were done cold. "'Want to try a new chocolate?' No one said no. I was peddling a legalized drug." Schilling filled the orders, pouring each one with a measuring cup, eight hours a day, the easy rhythm of a repetitive task, fuelled by vast quantities of marijuana.

One morning, he got a call from an East Coast distributor, his first, who wanted ten thousand bars. "I was excited," Schilling said, "and then thought, Oh, shit, I have to pour each one." For ten eighteen-hour days, he did nothing else. His mother, who lived in Minnesota, flew in to help. She arrived on a Friday, wrapped bars until three in the morning, dizzy from the glue stick used to seal them, and returned to the airport on Sunday night. After the first distributor, others followed. ("They could now trust the neophyte manufacturer with his odd chocolates.") The orders meant success, but also chaos. Schilling forgot to order wrappers. The air conditioning broke. Chocolate was compromised. The basement flooded. The accounts were bad lecture notes. "We were winging it. We needed Papa Jon."

Schilling's father was, in Holderman's description, single-dimensional and myopic: "We were just going for each other." He was a threat. To the father, she was just the girlfriend. He never disliked her ("She was, above all, an absolutely gorgeous, stunning, vivacious young lady"); he just didn't rate her. He never imagined her as a partner in the future business, even though she was a cofounder and a shareholder. The son was the project, "a visionary," but with no register of risk, no future tense. "He couldn't even spell the word 'business.'" They had issues. The father didn't "get" organics. "They argued constantly," Holderman said. "Every day, over morning coffee, at lunch, it was nothing but the business. I wasn't interested in business."

There were fights, hysterics. "The females in my life, both personal and professional, have been very emotional," the father observed. "I don't think I will ever understand their psyche."

Holderman began, in her words, "acting out in a mild way and then not such a mild way." She told Schilling: Marry me and take me away.

He gave her a ring and they moved to Ashland, a town of twenty thousand people, in southern Oregon. They found a space with a large walk-in refrigerator and tables for packing. It was thrilling, according to Holderman, a "bona fide chocolate factory." But the father followed. Then the mother moved there from Minnesota; the sister from California. "At least, I was still his business partner," Holderman said. If she hadn't been, she recognizes, she would never have seen Schilling, because, astonishingly, he was still pouring bars by hand. In the summer of 2002, the company made its first million dollars in sales, but Schilling was in the back with his measuring cup, "smoking a big stick during the lunch hour," convinced that anyone buying his chocolate would know he had personally made it. He couldn't keep up. By Dagoba's second anniversary, he finally bought a small depositor, a machine that fills molds. Sales tripled by the end of the year, reaching $3.5 million. They then bought a huge machine, costing $250,000, paid for by selling 5 percent of the company to his mother's six siblings (putting its worth at probably around $7 million). But in Holderman's view nothing was changing. Her mother came one weekend and was put to work. "We wrapped bars until we could no longer stand, went home, passed out, got up, did it again. My mother wasn't unhappy to help. I was unhappy she had to."

In fact, there had been a change. Schilling had had a "visitation." A woman had appeared to him in a waking dream.

The predawn visitor was Xochiquetzal, a goddess of cacao. Schilling recognized her. He had been studying Mesoamerican religions, and believed cacao to be a sacred food. The reverence had been evident in the naming of his company, originally Gadoba, a temple, because eating a chocolate should be like a moment of prayer, "each bite a personal *gadoba*." He then wondered if Gadoba sounded too much like Godiva, the Belgian chocolatier. So he switched the "g" and the "d." "He just liked the sound," Holderman told me. He discovered later that a *dagoba* was a Buddhist shrine, and that worked, too.

The goddess asked Schilling to accompany her, and they flew over North America, across the Atlantic, and into West Africa, a first stop. As a child, Schilling hadn't liked chocolate because, like most of us, he had grown up eating what was made in West Africa, and he didn't like the flavor. Eighty percent of the world's cacao comes from there, principally the Ivory Coast, where trees were planted in 1905, the year that chocolate became industrial and global.

West African cacao is cultivated by the "pioneer" method and has few of the vagaries of a rainforest. The plantations are tightly managed and mechanically irrigated, with close plantings and little shade, and exposed to an intense direct light that makes the trees hyperproductive. Schilling and Xochiquetzal watched what would happen next. ("You were hovering above on what — a carpet?" I asked. "No, just floating.") The trees quickly become exhausted, the farm is closed, a swath of forest burns, and the business starts over. Land is cheap, labor is cheap, the beans are cheap. There are problems: "black pod rot" (with the trees so crowded); a dependence on pesticides; accusations of child labor and slavery.

Xochiquetzal and Schilling flew east into Sri Lanka. Then Bali, Java, Malaysia, the Philippines — all developed to meet modern needs. They flew across the Pacific and reached South America, and found patches of parched earth, once a rainforest, the origins of cacao, now blighted and infertile, "dead brown, like a scab." They inspected the Amazon Basin, on fire and with trees in flames. They flew up through Central America and paid a solemn visit to a Mayan tomb. Schilling was then returned to his bed. Xochiquetzal had a mission for him. He understood and swore an oath of allegiance.

He was shaking. The visitation had lasted forty-one minutes. It was 5:23. He woke Holderman and described what he had seen. "I didn't tell her I was now pledged to a goddess — I didn't want to hurt her."

Holderman sleeps deeply. "A dream?" she said, when I asked her about it. "Really? No, that one eludes me. A dream, you say?"

The couple broke up. "We had to," Schilling said. "I couldn't be unfaithful." Holderman returned to Boulder, married one of Schilling's good friends, and is now a massage therapist. Schilling hasn't had a serious girlfriend since ("I can't — I'm married to cacao"), now lives by the Mayan calendar, and began a life of manic tropical travel: in the past year, Costa Rica (twice), Panama, Venezuela, Nicaragua, Mexico, Ecuador, Peru, the Dominican Republic (three times), and Brazil (three times).

Last year, on October 19, Schilling may have had another visitation. He remembers nothing, but he woke in a condition of heightened clarity. By then, he had fifty employees in Oregon. He was helping to sustain a cooperative farm in the Dominican Republic, a family in Peru, an enterprise in Guatemala. He made bars sold in Whole Foods, hippie pharmacies, organic markets, and beside the cash registers of independent bookstores.

He had an immodest vision that he couldn't stop thinking about. It involved all the stripped, torched, desiccated, denuded, barren land of the ruined tropics. Why couldn't he figure out how to buy it up, most of it worthless anyway, and replant it with cacao, and, in effect, reforest the planet with chocolate bars?

I had been advised about Schilling's ambitions. "He has no limits," Holderman had told me forcefully. She described a trip the two of them once took to visit her family in Pennsylvania, passing through the town of Hershey. She was silenced by the scale, memories of a childhood visit, the wonder of it all, and, turning to Schilling, was alarmed by his focus and what he appeared to be thinking: he seemed to be measuring his future against Hershey's achievements. Schilling wanted to be a player, and not just a normal high-stakes player but an ideological one: someone who could change the world.

On the morning of his clarity, Schilling called his father. For months, Papa Jon had been working out the details of a sale ("Frankly, I just wanted to get a good chunk of change"), even though it had never been approved by his son. "Let's do it," Schilling said, and by nightfall a deal was done — so quickly it seemed like a spontaneous act — and Hershey became Dagoba's owner. The price was $17 million. Schilling was retained as a consultant.

That night, Schilling met friends, broke down, and wept uncontrollably for twelve hours. He spent the next month defending himself from charges made by organic colleagues that he was a "sellout." "How could I make a difference at Dagoba, working on such a small scale?" he said repeatedly, an incomprehensible argument to people who had no idea that he wanted to plant two or three billion trees and that he had the support of a goddess. Holderman, who got the news by group e-mail, was one of the few friends who were not surprised. "It was right on time, wasn't it?" she said. Five years, give or take a month or two, since the first Fancy Food Show.

IAN BURUMA

Phnom Penh Now

FROM *Travel + Leisure*

WHEN THE INVETERATE nineteenth-century French traveler Xavier Brau de Saint-Pol Lias first saw Phnom Penh, he declared it to be unlike any other place he had ever been: the red-tiled roofs; the white and gold-leafed temple domes; the Phnom pagoda, constructed by a wealthy woman named Penh as a tomb for her husband; the houses on stilts; and the boats bobbing up and down at the confluence of the Mekong, Bassac, and Tonle Sap rivers. What a splendid port this inland city might be, he wrote, for the entire Mekong Delta, from Siam to Indochina.

But it was only a dream. Many centuries ago, he continued, Cambodia had been the seat of one of the greatest civilizations in human history. Now the region seemed dead, a desolate, impoverished place "ravaged by war and piracy." Yet there was hope, for "a country does not simply die; its inhabitants renew themselves, and the eternally fertile land will give up its treasures to those who know how to possess them."

So the traveler observed in 1885, when Cambodia was ruled by the French. He might as well have been describing the same place in 1985, when the Khmer Rouge, after committing genocide on its own people, were still terrorizing the areas near the borders of Thailand, and Phnom Penh had barely been repopulated after being reduced to a ghost town in 1975. At that time, all the city dwellers were forced to march to remote country areas, where they were made slave laborers, and around two million people, more than 20 percent of the entire population, were murdered or left to die of starvation. One of the few remaining functioning buildings in the city during the terrible years between 1975 and 1979 was a school that had been turned into a torture center, whose name, Tuol Sleng, still makes Cambodians shiver. Of the approximately fourteen thousand known inmates, fewer than twelve survived.

Since I have a morbid curiosity about such things, I tried to find traces of the city's recent past as soon as I arrived by plane from Bangkok. The old French colonial–era Hotel Le Royal, where I put up, is on the corner of Monivong Boulevard, along which the Khmer Rouge soldiers, in raggedy black uniforms, mostly peasants and many of them teenagers, entered the city with their mouths agape. The buildings, the stores: they had never seen such urban splendor. A ten-minute walk from the hotel is the wall of the former French Embassy, where more than eight hundred petrified foreigners were holed up for a month before they were allowed to leave the country. I stared at the spot where French diplomats, forced to hand over the Cambodians who had sought refuge there, did so knowing that they would probably be killed. I tried to imagine the terror that had once hung over this place. But of course it is unimaginable. Monivong Boulevard is now crowded with young people on scooters and motorbikes and lined with hotels and fine restaurants — French, Japanese, Vietnamese, Chinese, and Cambodian. The French Embassy is just an embassy again, and Hotel Le Royal, restored by Raffles International, is one of the most elegant places to stay in Southeast Asia. The city's population now stands at close to 1.39 million.

On the surface, then, all looks normal in Phnom Penh. At the Russian Market you can buy almost anything, from twelfth-century ceramics (if you're very lucky) to a bowl of noodles with chilies and frog's legs. A five-minute taxi ride away from the Russian Market is another, the Central Market. One of the architectural sights of the city, Central Market has a beautiful 1935 art deco dome in what's known as "colonial yellow," vaguely modeled after one of the temples near Angkor Wat. Inside, a hive of traders peddles jewelry, clothes, flowers, tropical fruits, vegetables, electronic goods, and more. And the National Museum, next to the Royal Palace, has been restored to a better-kept treasure trove of Buddhist and Hindu sculptures than its shabbier Thai counterpart in Bangkok. Some of the finest freestanding Khmer sculptures from Angkor Wat can be seen there, as well as an eight-armed Vishnu from the seventh century and a ninth-century statue of Shiva, the Destroyer of Evil.

Although they're not quite as raunchy (at least not openly so) as some of the entertainment areas in Bangkok, Phnom Penh also has plenty of places that offer massages, ranging from a pedestrian foot massage to a more exotic menu. Poverty has boosted a sex industry that was at its height in the 1990s, when the city teemed with UN officials trying to bring some security to a still-fragile society. But even now, as a young British entrepreneur put it to me with brutal frankness, "most people come here to get laid." As he spoke, I spotted a motorized rickshaw with an advertisement written on the back, trumpeting what are presumably the city's three chief attractions: ROYAL PALACE, KILLING FIELDS, SHOOTING RANGE. Sex, mass murder, and gun sport, a winning combination.

Many of the bars and restaurants in Phnom Penh bear French colonial–sounding names like Le Deauville or La Croisette, but also more Anglo-Saxon ones like the Hope & Anchor and the Jungle Bar. Instead of men in white linen suits and pith helmets, the typical foreign clientele in these places nowadays adopts a style that might be called Lonely Planet chic: women in Tibetan ankle bracelets and men in ponytails and Indian shirts. The most popular hangout in the evenings is the Sisowath Quay, on the Tonle Sap River, near the National Museum and the Royal Palace (built in 1917 and 1866, respectively, along the same "traditional" lines — with elegant spires, golden roofs, and eaves held up by mythical figures — that were favored at the time by French administrators). One of the more pleasant places to eat on the Quay is the Foreign Correspondents' Club (FCC), a lovely colonial-style building that is neither a club nor a place to find many foreign correspondents. But the service is friendly and the food, Western with a smattering of more local fare, is excellent.

While the tourists sip their drinks at the FCC and other waterfront bars, Cambodians sit in the grass by the river, fanning themselves, loosening their shirts — anything to feel the river breeze as the humid heat stubbornly refuses to relent, even in the late fall. Families picnic in the gloaming. Couples kiss and cuddle in the shadows. Others have their fortunes told by dubious-looking characters installed in front of a shrine enveloped by clouds of sweet incense. Teenagers drink beer and soft drinks and casually toss the empty cans into the lazy river current.

A typical Southeast Asian city, then. And yet, there is a melancholy about the place that still speaks of recent horrors. Phnom Penh is a city of survivors. Everyone has a story. A journalist I spoke to over a cup of coffee told me about his family's forced evacuation, when they were stuck in his father's car on Monivong Boulevard in a sea of human traffic. A young boy at the time, he would never forget the sight of a terrified woman on foot, who offered all of her money and jewelry to his father if only he would let her into the car. The car soon had to be abandoned anyway, and money would be useless in the slave labor camps. He remembers the blood-stained clothes that came back on the empty trucks that had taken away fellow citizens in the morning. Only dumb luck stopped his family from sharing their fate.

I had an introduction to Youk Chhang, director of the Documentation Center of Cambodia, which collects documentary evidence of the Khmer Rouge years, not just for the historical record, but to help surviving victims seek legal redress. Chhang is a handsome man who, after the fall of the Khmer Rouge, studied in the United States and worked for the city of Dallas. I met him in his office, which used to be part of a grand family house, whose owners never returned from the carnage. There are many such houses, now used as offices or restaurants. We talked about the difficulties in getting reliable witnesses; some were too frightened to speak, others wanted compensation. Most of the perpetrators, prison guards and the like, were very poor.

Chhang and his family survived because they were helped by their maid, a poor village woman whom Chhang had treated brattishly as a child, but who loyally shielded her former employers after she had joined the Khmer Rouge. Chhang smiled as he told me this story. I asked him, Did many people still speak of the past? He replied that children born since the 1970s often resented it when their parents told them about their suffering: "They feel that it is used to pick on them." And yet the subject cannot be avoided.

The Hungry Ghost festival, in the fall, is one of the most important holidays in the Cambodian calendar. People leave food and drink at their local pagodas to feed the spirits of their deceased relatives. If there is not enough food or water, the spirits will curse those still alive. "Most of the spirits belong to people who died under the Khmer Rouge," Chhang said. "When people remember starvation, they get very emotional, more so than when they recall torture or even murder. That is why this festival is such an emotional occasion."

He smiled again. And then he told me something even more chilling. On festival days, he said, Phnom Penh is half empty, almost like it was in the 1970s. The majority of people return to their native villages. The citizens who lived in Phnom Penh before the onslaught of the Khmer Rouge are almost all dead.

When his project is finished, Chhang may go back to the United States. Phnom Penh, to him, no longer feels like home.

Unlike the Chinese Red Guard during the Cultural Revolution, the Khmer Rouge did not actually destroy many buildings. Far more have been pulled down by developers in recent years than by the revolutionaries of the 1970s. Some of the most interesting architecture in Phnom Penh, apart from several fine colonial buildings, was built in the 1950s and 1960s in a kind of tropical-modernist style known as New Khmer Architecture. The clean, unadorned lines of Bauhaus-type design were adapted to the Southeast Asian heat. Vann Molyvann's National Theater, for example, is a masterpiece of this era — an airy gem in concrete and brick. It caught fire, alas, in 1994, but there has been no effort to rebuild, and developers are poised to tear it down. The new Cambodian elite is more interested in copying the grandiose style of contemporary China: big shiny buildings done up with lots of glass and marble, sometimes topped with quasi-traditional roofs.

I was told about Molyvann by a remarkable couple, John Shapiro and Sophiline Cheam Shapiro, who live in a village just outside the city. He is an American; she is Cambodian, and a classical dancer. Up to 90 percent of the country's classical dancers died in the 1970s, since the Khmer Rouge associated their art with the ancien régime. Sophiline was one of the few survivors. Across the road from the Shapiros' house is an open-air theater with a backdrop in the shape of an Angkor temple. It was built by the former culture minister, a man of great refinement, who evaded the Khmer Rouge by posing as a cowherd.

Sophiline studied in both Cambodia and the United States after the Khmer Rouge fell from power but returned with her husband to help keep her art alive. We watched her put about two dozen young women in classical costumes through their paces, adopting dance poses that reminded me of both Khmer sculptures and Thai boxers — balanced on one knee, for example, while lifting the other ankle, and similar impossibly graceful movements. They were rehearsing a Cambodian dance, but it had been inspired by Mozart's *The Magic Flute*. While his wife was rehearsing, I asked John about the state of traditional culture. It had been liveliest in the 1980s, he said, when people were thirsting for a return to beauty and tradition. Dancers would perform in villages, where some people mistook them for divine apparitions, having "never seen anything so beautiful before." On some nights, unknown to the dancers, rogue Khmer Rouge soldiers would come down from their mountain hideouts intending to kill the intruders but become so entranced by the performances that they abandoned their missions.

Now that people have television, however, and DVDs, and karaoke, it is a lot harder to hold on to tradition. To make a living, dancers have to perform in hotels for the tourists, or at official functions for rich politicians, where they are little more than exotic ornaments, part of the opulent décor, like the faux-classical roofs on the flashy postmodern skyscrapers. On some occasions they are not even required to dance, just to pose with trays of party favors. "The problem," John said, "is no longer how to recover from the past, but how to recover from the present."

It is an all-too-common story, of course. The same thing has happened in many parts of the world. Traditional culture is for the poor, who know nothing else, or for the cultivated rich, but it is not to the taste of the newly prosperous. That even those working in textile factories or selling souvenirs to tourists can afford a pirated DVD with the latest movie starring Brad Pitt is progress of a kind. It would be patronizing to deplore such access to the wider world. But I am filled with great admiration for Sophiline and her dancers, struggling against the odds.

I asked our driver, a rather dour man named Vessna, what he thought of the classical dancers. He was born in a village but had moved to the city with his wife, who worked in one of the textile factories along the road to the international airport. He liked the dances well enough, he said, but he preferred more modern entertainments, such as television and MTV. Vessna was a man of few words. He had learned English in the 1990s in order to drive UN personnel around town. When he did speak, he came to the point quickly.

We drove to Tuol Sleng, the former torture prison, now a museum. Vessna had been there countless times but never wanted to go inside. It is located in a posh neighborhood, in what had once been a good high school. Outside the prison, still fortified with barbed wire fences, are several guesthouses and cafés with that Lonely Planet vibe: Eric Clapton songs, fresh fruit juices, silks in time-honored designs. I saw expensive-looking houses behind gold-painted gates. "Government officials," Vessna said. Then, after a short pause: "Many were in the Khmer Rouge before."

The architecture of Tuol Sleng is sober but not unpleasant, an example of the modernist optimism of the 1960s: four three-story white concrete buildings with balconies, set around a spacious garden with palm trees, plants, and an exercise bar. The old schoolrooms are bare, with brown-and-white-checkered floors. Some of the rooms on the third floor were divided into tiny brick cells, not high enough to stand up or wide enough to lie down in. Inside the bare schoolrooms are steel bed frames, rusted around the edges, and enough bolts for shackling several people at a time by their feet. Various instruments of torture are exhibited in these cells: pliers, whips, manacles, hammers, water tanks. On the walls are photographs of corpses, some barely recognizable as human. There are also paintings by the Cambodian artist Vann Nath, showing scenes of torture and killings. These were painted from memory. After being tortured to the brink of death, he was put to work on portraits of Pol Pot, the Khmer Rouge leader. His artistic skills were the only reason he survived.

Despite all the photos and grisly exhibits, the mind is unable to conceive what it must have been like to have been a prisoner in Tuol Sleng, being forced to make detailed confessions that corresponded with the paranoid visions of the jailers before being killed. The most haunting images are not the torture pictures, but those of the victims' faces, like passport photographs from hell. Most of the people put before the camera, and subsequently killed, had themselves been in the Khmer Rouge and fallen victim to one of the periodic purges. Many were young, a few of them children, like the vicious guards who were barely fifteen. Most look numb with terror. Some Khmer Rouge peasant cadres, who had been suddenly accused of spying for the CIA, just look bewildered. And others smile, perhaps to ingratiate themselves, to buy time, or perhaps as a vestigial reflex, smiling for the camera.

As at many of these atrocity sites, tourists go in giggling, or chatting about last night's barhopping adventures. They take souvenir photos of each other. And so on. But by the end of their time there, silence prevails. Even the unimaginable can be difficult to bear. I was certainly not in the mood for visiting a shooting range or a massage parlor. So I went to the Russian Market and bought myself a plain, beautiful bowl with an earthy light green glaze. It was probably not more than a few hundred years old, if that — not a rare find in this ancient land. But it expressed a human sensibility far removed from bloodlust or fanaticism. In its simplicity it offered comfort.

Even though the Khmer Rouge left most of the buildings in Phnom Penh intact, there were other places that were destroyed in a kind of class rage. There is a seaside resort, a few hours' drive from the capital, very close to the Vietnamese border, called Krong Kep. From the early 1900s through the 1960s it was where the Phnom Penh elite, including the royal family, built their holiday retreats, often in interesting modern designs. The main attractions are the empty beach, the beautiful sunsets, and, above all, the juicy crabs plucked straight from bamboo traps in the surf and prepared for picnic lunches. Kep was not left untouched by the Khmer Rouge — who maintained control of the resort town well into the 1990s — after they had wrecked the holiday homes.

I decided I wanted to see this place. So Vessna drove me out there one morning, past the textile factories, through many villages, past emerald green rice fields dotted with white bullocks, past temples and spirit shrines, past a river where farmers bathed their horses, until we reached the hills beyond which lay the Gulf of Thailand. "Khmer Rouge," said Vessna, pointing at the densely wooded hills, "Khmer Rouge were all around here."

There is a pretty hotel in the hills overlooking the sea called the Veranda Natural Resort, where you can stay in a thatched-roof villa.

Nearer the coast, once you enter Kep, you see the concrete shells of Bauhaus and art deco houses. Some are more ruined than others, but altogether they leave the impression of a modernist ghost town — except that the ruins are all inhabited. Inside the shells live peasant families, with tethered goats, people cooking food, and children sleeping in the shade. A small urban enclave has been reclaimed by rural Cambodia. But reflecting on this sight, as I ate my lunch of fresh grilled crab (for a few U.S. dollars) at one of the little restaurants built on the beach, I did not find it depressing. The image was no longer one of violence, but of human survival and renewal. I thought of Xavier Brau de Saint-Pol Lias, the French traveler. He was right: countries don't die, they keep on being reborn.

JAMES CAMPBELL

Chasing Ghosts

FROM *Outside*

I'M LYING in a bark hut surrounded by strange men. One sits
smoking pungent tobacco rolled into a long, fat spear, a caricature
of a Rastaman's joint. Two others chew betel nut, their mouths a
bright, frothy red. Curled up in the corner, my friend George
Houde is sleeping the sleep of the dead while rats play at his feet.

Sidelined by a steep, muddy trail and a bad fall, we're here because I tore my ACL while attempting a 130-mile trek across Papua
New Guinea. Now George, a reporter on leave from the *Chicago Tribune* and part of our eight-person team, and I are back in the inland village where we started our trek on foot. My goal of following
in the footsteps of a group of World War II soldiers via what they
called the Kapa Kapa Trail (a mispronunciation of Gabagaba, the
coastal village where the route begins), which runs across Papua
New Guinea from its south coast to its north, is in serious peril. It's
the first day of the trip.

In October 1942, during a march considered one of the cruel-
est in modern military history, twelve hundred ill-equipped, un-
trained American troops from the Thirty-second Infantry Division
endured more than a month of suffering on the Kapa Kapa en
route to the north-coast battlefields at Buna, where the Imperial
Japanese Army was waiting. At least two men died of exhaustion
during the crossing, and the rest were physically shattered by the
trek. Remarkably, after nine weeks of fighting in stinking, hip-deep
swamps full of floating corpses bloated by the heat, the Allied
troops finally dislodged the Japanese from Buna. But the victory
came at a cost. According to General Robert Eichelberger, the

commanding officer, fatalities "closely approached, percentage-wise, the heaviest losses in our own Civil War battles."

The soldiers' memories are still searing. "If I owned New Guinea and I owned Hell, I would live in Hell and rent out New Guinea," says Buna veteran Bob Hartman.

I'm beginning to see what he means. Three years ago, while researching a book on the soldiers' experience, I hatched the idea of repeating the World War II march. If the trek succeeds, it will be the first time in sixty-four years that a team from outside Papua New Guinea has hiked the trail in its entirety. I'd visited New Guinea four previous times, the last trip just ten months ago, when I came to scout the area. I was advised then by former Australian colonial patrolmen, the Papua New Guinea Defense Force, and a number of trekkers familiar with the New Guinea bush not to attempt the crossing. Even if the route had not been consumed by jungle or erased by torrential rains, I was told, it was at best nothing more than a narrow hunting-and-trading trail that traversed some of the country's most formidable territory. One villager looked into the mountains and whistled through his teeth, "Long way too much." A former government patrolman challenged my sanity. "You're delusional," he said.

The Australians had counseled General Douglas MacArthur against sending men on this route, too — the mountain passes were too high, the terrain too rough, the rivers too fast, the tribes unpredictable.

But they went, and now so have I. The sun drifts below the mountains, and the evening is stifling. Dela, the hut's owner, inexplicably refuses to prop open the thin bamboo boards that serve as windows. When I persist, he explains in a mix of English and Motu that there are sorcerers who roam the hills at night, cast deadly spells, and will try to kill me. Just then I hear soft voices outside the hut. Dela opens the door and villagers file in with bowed heads, as if in prayer. They begin to sing, in two-, three-, four-part harmony. It's as if angels have descended.

Perhaps our luck is turning, I think. The next morning, George and I walk out of Dela's village to a rutted road and jump in the back of a truck. After a series of bone-jostling rides we arrive back in Port Moresby, Papua New Guinea's capital city, where I buy anti-inflammatories and painkillers and plot with George about how we can continue the trek. Could we meet up with the rest of our group by plane? "Impossible," a pilot we approach tells us. With a helicopter, though, he thinks we stand a chance.

Seventy-two hours later, as we hover in a chopper over a vast jungle canopy broken only by rivers spilling out of murky mountains, the sight of so much raw wilderness has me second-guessing my decision. I've never seen the likes of the Kapa Kapa Trail.

Despite its proximity to Australia, New Guinea is geologically a much younger land. Shaped by the explosive tectonic forces of the Pacific Ring of Fire and carved by near constant rain into a tangle of swamps, trackless ravines, and twelve-thousand-foot mountains, it is one of the most rugged and mysterious places on earth.

The world's second-largest island, New Guinea is divided between two countries. The western half, originally colonized by the Dutch, has been part of Indonesia since 1969 and is called Papua (the name was changed from Irian Jaya in 2002). Since gaining its independence from Australia in 1975, the eastern half, roughly the size of California, has been an independent nation called Papua New Guinea (PNG). Though tourism is still in its infancy, adventurous travelers visit PNG for wreck and reef diving, sea kayaking along its incredible coastline, and the chance to see birds found nowhere else in the world. For the ultra-adventurous, New Guinea offers challenging treks, mainly on the Kokoda, a sixty-mile World War II trail, forty miles northwest of the Kapa Kapa.

Still, vast swaths of the island remain unknown, and it's hard to imagine what World War II soldiers might have encountered here. In 1942, the Japanese landed eleven thousand troops on the Papuan Peninsula's north coast, hoping to use New Guinea as a steppingstone to invade Australia, or at least to disrupt the supply lines from the United States to the South Pacific. MacArthur, who had been spirited out of the Philippines in March 1942 to command the Allied forces in the southwest Pacific and lead the Army effort against the Japanese, sent in Australian soldiers to stop them. Two months later, with the Japanese gaining a stronger foothold on the peninsula, MacArthur ordered a battalion of the American Thirty-second Division to cross the treacherous Owen Stanley Range and fight them at Buna. None of the men had spent a single day in the jungle.

Nor had I, but our team contained no slouches. I had logged hundreds of miles on foot and snowshoe through Arctic Alaska while researching my first book, and had been hiking with an eighty-pound pack for eight months prior to this trip. Besides George, a fifty-eight-year-old long-distance runner and biker, our expedition group consisted of Dave Musgrave, fifty-four, a wilderness expert and professor of oceanography at the University of Alaska–Fairbanks; Philipp Engelhorn, a fit thirty-seven-year-old Hong Kong–based photographer; Lee Ticehurst, a fifty-five-year-old Aussie expat living in Port Moresby and an accomplished jungle trekker who has completed the Kokoda three times; a young three-man film crew (Cal Simeon, Jack Salatiel, and Kenneth "Samu" Pasiu) from Port Moresby–based POM Productions, there to shoot a documentary; and teams of porters hired in various villages along the way to carry our food and camping gear.

It took the World War II soldiers seven weeks to reach the north coast. They walked for more than half of those days; the rest of the time, they recuperated in villages and waited for food and supply drops. The Army's decision to let the men rest seemed practical at the time, but it backfired. The soldiers were already suffering from dysentery, trench foot, and jungle ulcers when malaria hit them like a bomb. Eventually, 70 percent of the division would contract the disease. We decided to walk considerably faster, even if it meant putting in ten- and eleven-hour days on the trail. Concerned about malaria and battery power for the film equipment, our plan was to reach the end at Buna village in two to three weeks, limiting our exposure to the jungle.

It is impossible to avoid superlatives when talking about New Guinea. Four days into the trek, the team enters a rainforest whose biodiversity is nearly unmatched worldwide. Among its avian species is the bird of paradise — approximately thirty-eight of the world's forty-odd species live here. It is also home to more than three thousand species of orchids, the world's largest butterfly, its largest moth, the smallest parrot, the largest pigeon, and the world's longest crocodile. The jungles of New Guinea's Papuan Peninsula, in particular, support such an astonishing assortment of trees, ferns, mosses, bromeliads, frogs, butterflies, and rare, night-loving marsupials that the World Wildlife Fund has submitted a proposal to UNESCO to include the entire Owen Stanley Range on its list of World Heritage sites.

Joining our team to guide us over the mountains is Berua, a bone-thin, jungle-wise man whose parents served as carriers for the GIs on the Kapa Kapa. Only seven years old at the time, Berua struggled with them across the spine of the Owen Stanleys en route to the remote community of Jaure. Berua's tattooed sixty-five-year-old wife, Bima, and his hunting dog also join us.

With Berua at the front, we follow the rushing Mimani River into the sodden heart of the rainforest, where sunlight dimmed by a dense mesh of trees, leaves, vines, and fronds has turned the jungle into an immense boiler room. If I was worried about Berua and Bima keeping pace, I shouldn't have been. Papua New Guineans spend their lives walking. For most, it is their only mode of transportation.

We bivouac at the river's edge. Our bush camp consists of a large, blue plastic tarp thrown over a ridgepole, supported by two more poles and tied down to ground pegs. We clear the area of sticks, rocks, and roots and then lay large leaves over the moist ground. I can see George, who is playing the role of expedition skeptic, eyeing the shelter, wondering what is going to keep the snakes out. Twenty-foot pythons and "one-cigarette" snakes like the taipan — whose bite will kill you before you have time to finish a smoke — lurk on the Papuan Peninsula.

Soon darkness presses in, tight and coal black. As if to underscore our vulnerability, the forest becomes an opera house as millions of crickets, cicadas, frogs, "singing" worms, and other strange, boisterous insects and animals wake from their afternoon slumber. As we place our sleeping bags under the tarp, Dave stumbles out of the bushes. He's spent the past twenty-five years exploring Alaska's remote wilderness areas, but he's never seen a night like this. It is so dark, he says with a laugh, that he couldn't find his pecker to piss with.

Concerned about my knee, I begin walking early the next morning while the team breaks camp. We face a grueling hike to the 9,500-foot summit of what the locals call Mount Ororo. As I climb, a maze of spider webs tickles my hands and face. Massive trees, with trunks the size of silos, adorned with lianas and wrapped in a swarm of vines resembling large pythons, reach for the clouds. Less than an hour into the hike, though, I am incapable of admiration. I'm on all fours, pushing through the mud, grabbing at roots, trees, ferns, bushes, leaves, anything I can clasp with outstretched fingers to keep from falling backwards down the steep, slippery mountain. In a cruel twist, everything I reach for is equipped with spurs, thorns, tiny sharp bristles, or swarms of red ants, and my hands sting and bleed.

The porters approach behind me, calling to one another in excited, high-pitched voices, and skip by as if their forty-pound loads weigh nothing. They are off-trail, jumping over downed trees while trying to locate Berua's dog. They do all this without shoes, on broad, thick-skinned feet that make a mockery of my new jungle boots.

Entering the cloud forest, I encounter a scene that inspired the spooked American soldiers to dub Mount Ororo "Ghost Mountain." In the heavy fog, the huge, moss-draped beech trees look like apparitions. Ghost Mountain is soggy, sunless, and silent, suspended in perpetual twilight. The team has caught up with me, and we crest the mountain together. At the top, George quickly notices that the trail catapults down the mountain alongside a steep cliff. "That's comforting," he says. "We might as well throw ourselves off right now."

Cal, one of the young cameramen, apparently takes this as a cue. He grabs a vine as thick as my arm, lets out a deep-woods yodel, and swings out over the cliff and back. He beams. I decide he's been driven mad by the jungle.

To lessen the punishment of the descent, I ride the stream of mud on my backside. Tiny leeches attach themselves to any bare skin they can find and gorge on my blood. Even the porters are tired when we make camp late that afternoon on the slopes of Ghost Mountain, but it's clear they don't want to stop here for the night. It's cold, the wood is wet, fires are hard to start. What's more, they believe that high mountain regions are populated by *masalai*, or evil spirits. Through the night I wake periodically to find the porters smoking tobacco out of flutelike bamboo pipes, unwilling to sleep.

By day ten we're nearing Suwari, the most remote mountain village we will encounter. Our 1:100,000 scale topographic map shows a dense jumble of contour lines and three large white patches that read OBSCURED BY CLOUD. The map was compiled by the Royal Australian Survey Corps more than three decades ago and has not been updated.

As we walk through fields of sweet potato, corn, and banana trees, a sentry spots us and blows on a conch horn to announce our arrival. Drums boom, rattles cackle, and in a small dirt opening a group of people begin to dance. The men are decorated in elaborate bird-of-paradise headdresses and necklaces of pigs' tusks, their bodies rubbed with black oil; they lunge at us with wooden spears, their tongues shooting serpentlike from their mouths. The women dance bare-breasted in woven grass skirts, shrieking as they swing axes over our heads. The soldiers never got to see such a display. In fact, American World War II maps list Suwari as deserted. When the villagers saw the soldiers coming, they fled to nearby caves.

One of the dancers approaches and introduces himself as Giblin. In broken English he explains that the village had learned that a group of *taubada*, or white men, was on its way, and they had organized the ceremony in our honor. At one time, he says, the dance was performed as a celebration after a successful raid. Having captured or killed their enemies, warriors would return to dance and to feast on human flesh. Smiling, he assures me that his people have no intention of eating us.

That night, crowded into the open-sided "house of wind," Giblin lights the village's only lamp, a sure sign that we are honored guests — kerosene is a four-day walk away. We are, he says, the first outsiders to visit Suwari since 1975, when Papua New Guinea gained its independence. Prior to '75, Australian colonial patrols used to make infrequent visits, imposing on the distant mountain villages a Western economic structure and the British system of law. The patrolmen occasionally doled out harsh justice, but they also brought medicine, tools, and contact with the outside world. Now the village is suffering — no school for the children, no employment opportunities, and a high incidence of malaria, tuberculosis, skin diseases, and infant mortality. Had Suwari been more accessible, Giblin's people might have sold their pristine forests to logging operations. Because of its location, though, Suwari is putting its hope in the Kapa Kapa Trail. Perhaps it will bring *taubada* with money.

After years of promotion, the Kokoda Trail, on which the Australians fought the Japanese, now draws two thousand trekkers a year to Papua New Guinea. The World Wildlife Fund and the Kokoda Track Authority have joined forces to begin turning the trail into a model of sustainable ecotourism. Though there have been problems — erosion, siltation, the clearing of forests for firewood — and though the track authority worries about the loss of cultural identity among the people of the Kokoda, the trail has been a success. A new plan calls for the training of guides in expedition skills, English, history, environmental stewardship, and the promotion of native culture, architecture, and craftsmanship.

Giblin is not aware of any of this, yet he already has a plan for the Kapa Kapa. His village will build a guesthouse, the young men will make money as carriers, the women will sell fruits and vegetables, the villagers will take trekkers on birding expeditions, they will don traditional tribal costumes and dance and sing. The question is, will the *taubada* come?

Giblin tries to convince us to stay an extra day. It is mating season for the bird of paradise, and soon the gaudy males will be dancing on their forest perches, courting females. Although tempted by the chance to see one of the world's rarest birds, we press on.

George has all of us worried. He has developed dangerous skin ulcers on both legs. Despite the pain, he insists on trying to complete the remaining three days of the trek, but we need to get him out of the jungle fast. Jack isn't in great shape either. His feet are cracked and bleeding. Cal's knee is giving him trouble. Lee looks pale and tired (is it the onset of malaria?). For all intents and purposes, I'm walking on one leg. Only Dave, Samu, and Philipp are holding up, but if the trail lives up to its reputation, their turn is bound to come.

The thing about the jungle is that often you can see nothing but more jungle. But on day fourteen, having negotiated the fierce currents of the Musa River and the crumbling, volcanic slopes of 5,512-foot Mount Lamington — which erupted in 1951, killing three thousand people — we reach the Girua River. The clouds have lifted, and we look up the river valley, getting our first glimpse of the territory we've covered. Ahead, the flat coastal plain sprawls north under a battering tropical sun. Though the worst is behind us, from here the trail slices through fields of head-high, razor-sharp *kunai* grass and wanders back and forth across the river. It will not be easy, but the end is in sight.

Two days later, after sixteen days in the jungle, we reach Buna.

The Kapa Kapa, which we've renamed the Ghost Mountain Trail, is, as Lee concludes, "the Kokoda on steroids." For the weary soldiers and the hundreds of New Guineans who served as carriers and scouts for the Army, the end of the trail was the beginning of a long nightmare. When they arrived in Buna, they entered tangled, tea black swamps and a battle that General MacArthur described as a "head-on collision of the bloody, grinding type."

Papua New Guinea tourism officials told me that they hope to promote this history and, in light of our success, turn the route into something like a national historic trail. The World Wildlife Fund currently has plans to incorporate the Ghost Mountain Trail into its blueprint for conservation and tourism in the Owen Stanley Range.

For their part, the World War II veterans can't imagine anyone ever choosing to walk across Papua New Guinea. "Are you kidding?" Thirty-second Division member Stanley Jastrzembski said to me. "I would have taken an enemy bullet before going back into those mountains."

But none of us regretted a mile of it.

PETER CHILSON

The Border

FROM *TheSmartSet.com*

IN ZEGOUA, a town in southeastern Mali, I stand on the patio of my hotel where the border — between Mali, a country at peace, and Côte d'Ivoire, divided by war — bumps the concrete. I am the lone guest in this two-story, whitewashed building with a top floor that resembles the bridge on a steamboat. The flags of Burkina Faso, Mali, Côte d'Ivoire, and France hang above the hotel entrance, stuck in the heat.

A Malian named Hamidou Sakara, who runs the hotel, and I are listening to a call-in trivia show on Radio Bamako, broadcast from the capital city. The program's topic is African geography. The host tosses out a question. "What physical feature marks Mali's border with Senegal?"

"It's the Falémé River," Hamidou says.

A man calls with the same answer.

"Well," says the host, "the River Falémé forms nearly the entire border with Senegal, but a section wanders east of the river. That leaves part of the river and a small piece of land in Senegal." He laughs. "A bit of Mali is in Senegal."

Hamidou slaps the table. "Yes, Mali *is* in Senegal."

The mystery dates to 1895 and may be linked to a French officer who wanted a hunting ground in his district along the river. The story goes that he altered the border with French Sudan, as colonial Mali was called. I'd heard this before and checked it with the director of the National Archives. "It's a story we know but cannot prove," the director told me.

I explain this to Hamidou. He throws up his hands. "Who cares? You carved us up like cake."

A few days before, Hamidou and I had stood on the patio, looking south over fields along the dry bed of the Danboro River, the seasonal drainage that marks the border. It was afternoon. I'd been waiting since 10 A.M. for an interview with Ousmane Coulibaly, a commander of rebel forces controlling the north of Côte d'Ivoire, torn in two by civil war. His job was to oversee Côte d'Ivoire's northeastern border with Mali. But he hadn't shown for our appointment.

"I can't wait, Hamidou. I'm going to Niélle in the morning."

He ran into the field. Facing me, he shouted in English, his "favorite" language: "Welcome in Ivory Coast!"

I wasn't sure what country Hamidou was standing in: Mali — a country without coastline, trapped in the Sahel between desert and forest — or Côte d'Ivoire. The patio aligned with a guardhouse on the road a few hundred yards west. The building looked empty, the Malian guards gone to shade. All around us villagers worked their fields.

This town — fifteen miles from the tri-point where Mali, Burkina Faso, and Côte d'Ivoire meet — is Mali's gate to the Atlantic and the seaport at Abidjan, Côte d'Ivoire's economic capital. Mali begins or ends here with concrete pillboxes painted pink against fierce heat. For days I'd been asking around about the border and the rebels. I interviewed Zegoua's mayor, merchants, truck drivers, customs officials, and police. I hired a car for trips along the border, often not knowing which country I was in, and met villagers who didn't care about nationality.

And why should they? In 1904, France organized 1.8 million square miles of coastal forest, inland savanna, desert, and millions of people from countless tribes into the eight colonies of French West Africa. Then they recut the region dozens of times, dividing land by stability and wealth and suitability for cotton, coffee, and cocoa. They never planned for independence. Where the borders lie now is mostly guesswork. On the Michelin map of West Africa, the Mali and Côte d'Ivoire border runs a jagged 350 miles from Burkina Faso to Guinea. Mali's national tourist map, made by the Institut Géographique Nationale in Paris, shows the same. But both maps use disclaimers. "The positioning of frontiers," notes Michelin, "in no way implies official recognition or acceptance," while the tourist map reminds us the borders are not "legally veri- fied."

In Zegoua, Hamidou introduced me to Ousmane Coulibaly's lieutenant, an ex-Malian army officer who lives here with his family. Mornings he dons combat fatigues and drives his blue Renault compact with broken headlight over the border to Niélle. He wouldn't answer questions but promised an interview with his boss. "Wait at your hotel," he said. Some mornings I'd stand on the road and wave down his Renault for news. He'd wave back.

I looked at Hamidou standing in the sand. "Come with me," I said. "I need an interpreter."

He shook his head. "I must stay here."

"But I'm your only guest."

Hamidou was twenty-two, tall and lithe. He raised his hands, fingers splayed against the "wall" in mime.

"The border is here," he said. "You just cross it."

At dawn, I pay a boy fifty cents to take me by motor scooter across two miles of spongy vagueness between nations. We leave Mali un- challenged, but at the first Ivorian checkpoint, red-eyed, unarmed teenagers in tattered uniforms wave us down. I hand out packs of Winston cigarettes and ride on with a passport no one cares to see, stamped with the visa of a government these boys despise. Minutes later I'm left in a village at a yellowing concrete building with the national tricolor painted above the entrance beside the words:

HALTE! DUANES!
CÔTE D'IVOIRE.

Inside, men and boys — soldiers of a sleeping rebellion — sit on desks and windowsills. Some play cards on the floor. They wear camouflage looted from Niélle, a town twenty miles south, where I hope to interview their commander, Ousmane Coulibaly. A boy, about sixteen, leans against a wall, eyes closed, cradling a boom box playing music distorted by low batteries. I recognize the sad rolling melody of Bob Marley's "Redemption Song" and look around, hands in my pockets. In French I ask, "May I speak to someone in charge?"

It was May 2006. Without guaranteed safe passage, I wanted to avoid this crossing into the stateless territory of northern Côte d'Ivoire. But nine days in Zegoua negotiating to interview Ousmane — calls to rebel officers, messages passed through Malian officials, and broken meetings — have left me here, on my way to see him *sans rendezvous.*

A soldier knocks on a door to an adjacent room. He pulls it open and tells me to speak to his sergeant.

Inside, a shaven-headed man in desert camouflage hunches over a desk across from two men in green fatigues and caps, sitting in wooden chairs. Gray stubble covers their faces. A bookcase stands behind the sergeant, empty except for a plastic bucket. Above that hangs a framed image of a white dove.

I greet these officers of the rebel New Forces. They've cast their fortunes against the government in Côte d'Ivoire and its policy of denying northerners a stake as citizens and in the southern coffee and cocoa farms that made Côte d'Ivoire rich. But coffee and cocoa prices collapsed, and a failed coup in 2002 and civil war split the country between the south, loyal to President Laurent Gbagbo, and the rebel-held north, with close ethnic ties to Mali and Burkina Faso. Fighting has lulled under various peace accords and Côte d'Ivoire remains divided.

The sergeant, broad-shouldered with a broken nose, offers me a seat. He leans back in a faux leather office chair, fingering a maroon beret as he speaks to the two men in French. "I paid them each five hundred francs [about a dollar] yesterday," referring, I think, to the soldiers outside.

One replies, "There will be trouble."

Now they look at me. "I'm a journalist," I say, and explain my interest in this border across tribal lands. I tell them I know Ousmane Coulibaly by reputation: commander of this border zone and former noncommissioned officer in the Ivorian Army. He is Bambara, majority ethnic group in Mali and northern Côte d'Ivoire, where he was born. His men call him "Bin Laden" because he's Muslim and wears a long beard. But Malian officials say Ousmane is "a reasonable man."

The sergeant looks tired, the skin around his eyes puffy. "We are not tribalists," he says. "We are Ivorian, one hundred percent."

I nod. "I'd like to interview the commandant in Niélle."

He purses his lips. "I cannot guarantee your safety. The govern-

ment employs South African mercenaries against us. You might be
misunderstood."

"You think I'm a mercenary?"

He sighs. "You should not go, but I cannot stop you."

Through the window I see a blue Mercedes bus arrive. I thank
the sergeant and hurry outside. The driver says he's headed to
Niélle and I buy a seat on a hunch that the sergeant is lying and
Ousmane is in Niélle.

Inside are mostly women in colorful head cloths and wrap-
around skirts called *pagnes,* laughing, chewing sugarcane. Burlap
sacks beneath their seats burst with onions and carrots for market.
I sit on the aisle beside an old man in a brown tunic and skullcap.
He tells me he's going to Niélle and then Abidjan.

"I will collect my pension. I drove a bus in Abidjan for thirty
years."

"But there's a war. You're not frightened to travel?"

The brakes hiss. We begin moving. "This is my country," he says.
He shows me his identity card, revealing his nationality (Malian),
ethnicity (Fulani), and profession (bus driver).

We race past people on foot, bicycles, scooters, and donkeys. I'm
certain we'll arrive soon and I'll talk my way to Ousmane's headquarters. After a mile the bus slows. Barrels and logs block our
path. Uniformed men loiter at the roadside.

The old man shakes his head. *"Les enfants,"* he says.

Three men board the bus, unarmed. The women carry no papers and the men scold them gently, accepting mangoes instead.

I show a soldier my passport.

"American!" He smiles. "Can you offer something so we can
eat?"

I hand over two 100-franc coins.

The old man offers coins, but the soldier shakes his head. *"Non,
mon vieux.* Keep your money."

I nudge my new friend. "Guess we're not through the border
yet."

"We aren't in Côte d'Ivoire," he says, meaning we're in New
Forces territory. He adds, "This is Africa."

Five rebel checkpoints mark the eighteen miles from the border to
Niélle. At the fourth, three hours into the trip, the women on the

bus are annoyed. A soldier in canvas boots, red beret, and mirrored sunglasses walks the aisle with an exaggerated frown, snapping his fingers and plucking money and identity cards from raised hands. He is tall and strong, holding cards in one hand, dropping money in a leather pouch on a cord around his neck with the other.

After I give him coins, he snaps his fingers at a woman across the aisle from me. She raises her hand to his face and snaps her fingers. The other women laugh.

The soldier persists in French. Maybe he believes French makes him sound official, or maybe he's not Bambara. He barks, "Your identity card."

She shrugs.

He shouts, "Get off the bus!"

She rests her head on the seatback. A crescendo of voices rises from her friends. "Oooooooooo OOOoooooooo OOOOoooooo." The woman smiles at him.

The old man bows his head. He whispers, "The women call him 'little boy.'"

The soldier spits on the floor.

She rolls her head back and forth. He raises his hand as if to strike but she grins, pulling up the edges of her wrap and spreading her thighs. Her friends laugh and cluck their tongues as if to remind the soldier they're watching. She lies down on the seat, spreading her thighs again with her feet up against the windows, head hanging in the aisle, against my knee. The soldier snorts and walks off the bus, leaving the blow hanging in the air. The women clap and cheer as their friend sits up and straightens her clothing. She catches me staring at her and smirks. The women make more noise and whoop it up, "*Le blanc, le blanc.*"

Children clear the roadblock and we roll on.

At the checkpoint outside Niélle, a soldier in green camouflage and a black policeman's beret offers a ride on his motorcycle, provided I buy him extra petrol. Ousmane keeps his office at the old gendarmerie and when we arrive, dozens of soldiers stand about. A couple of toughs demand my purpose, but my driver fends them off.

"He is an American journalist," he says. "He wants to see the commandant."

"He left this morning," says one man. "He is in Zegoua."

"No, he is in Bouake," says another.

"May I see his lieutenant?" I ask. "I know him."

"He travels with the commandant."

"When will they return?"

More guesses. I take notes. They complain of empty peace agreements and corrupt leaders.

"We have no work."

"Côte d'Ivoire is shit now."

My escort and I settle on a new fee and ride back to Zegoua, breezing through the roadblocks. At the border, he greets the Malian guards by name, exchanging hugs and kisses on the cheek and news of family and friends.

"We are cousins," he explains.

"Welcome back," a guard says. He stamps my passport and signs the page.

In the morning I'm sitting on the patio with Hamidou when the blue Renault with the broken headlight arrives. It's the car Ousmane's lieutenant drives, the Malian soldier turned mercenary.

Hamidou jumps up. "Ousmane is here!"

The lieutenant — his name is Dialla — steps out from behind the wheel. Another man, balding and heavier with a black beard, shuts the passenger door. His purple cotton tunic falls to his knees over leggings and leather sandals.

Ousmane shakes my hand while Dialla smiles, dressed in gray trousers and a collarless shirt, with yellow and green flower patterns.

Ousmane says, "Dialla thinks it's a good idea if I talk to you."

"You're an important man."

We sit at a table in the restaurant, I across from Dialla and Ousmane, who offers an apology. "I am sorry if anyone troubled you at our checkpoints."

"No trouble at all."

"You have thirty minutes."

Hamidou brings Cokes and sits. He listens, eyes on Ousmane as if memorizing his face. The commandant pinches the skin under his chin through his beard. He talks for a while about his twenty years as a soldier stuck in rank because he is an ethnic northerner. He massages a wrist with his thumb.

"Our struggle is for identity," he says, "as northerners and Ivorians. I was born in Korogho (a city in northern Côte d'Ivoire), but because I am Bambara the government says I am Malian. That is the tragedy of Côte d'Ivoire."

"So, why don't the New Forces take the north of Côte d'Ivoire and join Mali and Burkina Faso?" I ask.

Ousmane frowns. "My homeland is Côte d'Ivoire. Eventually, the borders will dissolve, but for now . . ." He shrugs. Dialla crosses his arms.

"So, you fight?"

He tugs at his beard. "I want no more fighting." He looks to Dialla, who nods.

Ousmane says, "We must go."

"What about you, Dialla?" I ask. "What nationality do you choose?"

"My friend," Dialla says, his smile gone, "I am not important."

SIMON DOONAN

Brighton Beach Memoir

FROM *Travel + Leisure*

LAST FALL I BOUGHT one of those super-trendy Moncler puff
jackets. *This will really wow the folks,* I remember thinking as I in-
serted myself into this somewhat age-inappropriate garment and
hopped onto the platform at Brighton Station. I was home for
the holidays in style, or so I thought. Later that same day: Terry
Doonan and I are taking a wind-lashed constitutional along the
Brighton Esplanade. Terry, an eighty-two-year-old World War II vet,
is my father. I have called him Terry for as long as I can remember.
I was originally motivated to do this by a desire to limit the scope of
his parental authority. Now I call him Terry because I think of him
as a good friend.

"Nice jacket," says Terry.

"Isn't it just?" I reply, affecting a couple of smug *Zoolander* model-
ing poses.

SPLAT! A direct hit. Half a gallon of seagull poop.

"They say it's lucky!" says Terry, with undisguised amusement.
After cleaning my jacket with paper napkins cadged from a fish-
and-chips shop, I toss my unsalvageable cashmere scarf into the
nearest trash bin. Seagull poop and cashmere. What a perfect metaphor for Brighton — the ultimate combination of elegance and
grunge!

Like an aging socialite who has done something ever so slightly
common, Brighton has, and always has had, a high-low chic. This
city has been a louche getaway ever since the Prince Regent (later
George IV) and his mistress, Mrs. Fitzherbert, were cavorting round
the Royal Pavilion two centuries ago. Clandestine shenanigans are

as much part of the Brighton landscape as the dreamy terraces of white Regency town houses that line the seafront. The doilies-and-scones gentility normally associated with British south-coast resorts such as Bournemouth and Worthing is totally missing from Brighton. In 1920, when T. S. Eliot was looking to inject a bit of moral decay into his masterwork, *The Waste Land,* he didn't have to look further than Brighton. Even as a sixteen-year-old schoolboy I understood that, when the unshaven Mr. Eugenides asks the protagonist "To luncheon at the Cannon Street Hotel / Followed by a weekend at the Metropole," he means the Hilton Brighton Metropole. A bit of slap 'n' tickle. A bit of hanky-panky. Playwright John Osborne said he could never have lunch in Brighton "without wanting to take a woman to bed in the afternoon." Keith Waterhouse, another Brit scribe, went further: he said that Brighton looks like a town that is "helping the police with their enquiries" — an age-old tabloid euphemism suggesting that the unsavory person in question is guilty of every crime under the sun and will probably burn in hell forever.

My visits to Brighton are never unsavory. They are, in fact, quite relentlessly savory. Literally. This is due to the fact that I spend the majority of my recreational time gormandizing with Terry Doonan. Having both been raised in the grim pre-gourmet Britain of bubble and squeak, we are anxious to take advantage of the full-throttle Nigella-ization of the Brighton food scene.

Terry's sardonic view of contemporary Britain makes him a stimulating dining companion. He grew up poor in Cardiff, then at fifteen ran off and joined the Royal Air Force. After World War II and for the next forty years, he worked for the BBC in the news department, monitoring Radio Moscow throughout the Cold War and beyond. His gritty journalistic background gives him carte blanche to say things like "What the bloody hell is truffle foam!" wherever and whenever he feels like it. After taking the redeye from New York, it is my custom to drag Terry to the Real Eating Company, where fresh ingredients are slapped together with a Jamie Oliver-ian laissez-faire behind a gorgeous white art nouveau façade. Terry likes to linger over the fish cakes (providing, of course, that the waitress can secure some kind of cushion for his bum, which is bonier than of yore and dislikes being plonked on the ultra-groovy Bauhaus seats). I order the risotto, which the chef obligingly prepares *sans beurre.* "Fifty-five years old and worrying about your cholesterol! How the hell did that happen?" Terry says.

Sunset often finds Terry and me dining with my sister Shelagh — a Brighton resident of long standing and the reason the widowed Terry moved here from Belfast five years ago — at a fab place called Al Fresco. This reliable Italian joint is located in and around what appears to be a converted art deco lifeguard station. Dangling as it does over the pebbled beach, Al Fresco has staggering views of the world's largest kinetic art installation. I refer to the blackened and crumbling remains of the grand old West Pier. After almost one hundred and fifty years of war, fire, and salt air, this charred and collapsing skeleton now resembles a massive Louise Bourgeois crustacean emerging from the sea. Portions of it tend to drop off in front of your very eyes while you're enjoying a bit of local bream. Ominous, much photographed clouds of swirling starlings add to the Gothic visuals.

On my most recent visit we ate at Blanch House, a preposterously cool boutique hotel in Kemp Town. Located near the other, nondisintegrating pier, Kemp Town is the Williamsburg/SoHo/Chelsea of Brighton. This is the kind of neighborhood where it's not unusual to see a gay woman walking a dog with one hand and rolling her own cigarette with the other, or a tranny in full sequined regalia bursting proudly out of a doorway. My sister lived in Kemp Town for many years, above a gay disco called the Zanzibar. (Whenever I hear the throb of a distant nightclub I think of those long nights spent above the pounding Zanzibar, wondering whether I would die or go insane or both.) The Blanch House bar is chock-full of *Wallpaper*–reading media types. These are the monied young moderns who have fled London in recent years, driving up real estate prices and making Brighton one of the top ten most expensive places to live in the U.K., with residential properties running to $1,700 a square foot. The Blanch House restaurant is topnotch. The service is incredible and the all-white *Clockwork Orange* décor — hilariously incongruous in the context of the rest of the town — reeks of contemporary Las Vegas. The cuisine is a tad contrived in that wacky Vegas-y way, causing Terry to morph into Lady Bracknell, as in "Cardamom *fritters?*" "Earl Grey *ice cream?*" "A *handbag?*"

For a more down-to-earth repast, head to the Forager. "The ingredients are foraged from hedgerows," I had made the mistake of telling Terry before our first visit. "I'm not eating badger roadkill with boiled privet," he had said. This humble gastropub serves contemporized, organic-y versions of English Sunday lunch — they build it all up into a wobbly Gordon Ramsay tower, with a Yorkshire pudding on the side — in an authentic environment. The foraged components are (much to Terry's relief that day) limited to things like fungi and dandelions. Unlike many gastropubs, this one has made a conscious effort not to lose its original pubbiness: housewives in halter tops showing off their Tenerife tans chat for hours about God knows what with blokes with pipes and dogs. Best news of all: by the time you read this, the new smoking ban will be in effect and you, dear reader, will not emerge from the Forager, as I did, smelling like a smoked kipper.

While Terry is a Forager fan, my favorite eatery is the Gallery Café at the Brighton Museum. Yes, they do a lovely organic chicken sandwich, but the real purpose of coming here is to check out the Moorish-inspired interior and the costume and art exhibits, which are invariably fabulous and, most importantly, rather minuscule. (Large museums always leave me feeling ignorant and overwhelmed.) After a quick skip around this idiosyncratic permanent collection — Alma-Tadema to Frank Stella — I feel like a total genius. And I still have plenty of energy left to attack the Royal Pavilion, which is right next door.

The Royal Pavilion is so totally insane — Queen Victoria thought it was unsuitable and was always trying to sell it to the town — that it makes every other monument in the world, from Neuschwanstein to Versailles, look pedestrian and boring. It is quite simply the most over-the-top publicly accessible building there is. Attempting to describe this orgy of hallucinogenic chinoiserie and exoticism is a complete waste of time. Just go!

History tells us that the Prince Regent spent so much time lolling around the Pavilion and amusing his *bouche* that he became hideously fat. He relied on massive amounts of corsetry to maintain even the suggestion of a normal shape. The same would happen to me in Brighton if I did not jog. To offset the gastronomical indulgences I take a long run every day along the Esplanade. There are two trails to choose from: I call them the Cate Blanchett and the Heather Mills. The Cate Blanchett involves running — or walking or biking or even skipping — east as far as the notorious nudist beach and the Brighton Marina. Cate Blanchett's former house — I'm not exactly sure which one it is, but I know it's there somewhere because it was pictured in the tabloids when a crane was delivering a massive marble bathtub through her front window a couple of years back — is located in one of the beautiful crescents on your left. The Heather Mills leads west, past the crumbling West Pier and miles and miles of gorgeous architecture until you reach a cluster of white houses with direct beach access and can run no farther. You are now at the Malibu of Brighton, the former home of former happy couple Sir Paul McCartney and Heather "Dancing with the Stars" Mills McCartney. Heather still spends time in Brighton and is frequently spotted riding a bicycle along the Esplanade. (One of the great pleasures of visiting Brighton is getting to say the word *esplanade* over and over again.)

Between eating and jogging there is little time for shopping, which is just as well, since there is not much to buy. This does not mean that you should not take the time to slog through The Lanes and the North Laine, with their charming alleyways of bijoux boutiques and art galleries. Though the strong British pound and the globalization of retail have sucked the fun out of vacation shopping, there is no denying that wandering around the stores is still the best way to mingle with the locals and catch those great snippets of Joe Orton dialogue. The best eavesdropping can be done in Café Revive (you'll find one in almost every Marks & Spencer, including the one here, opposite Churchill Square). Two of my recent overheards: "I draw the line at digging out me own corns, don't you?" and "Our Lilly had it all taken away last week, bless her."

When is the best time to visit Brighton? Much as I love Terry and Shelagh's adopted city, I have to admit it's a bit grim in the winter. May is my preferred month: a visit will coincide with the Brighton Festival and related arts events and carnivals, one of which prominently showcases a mysterious troupe called the Lady Boys of Bangkok. I have yet to visit Brighton in the spring without being assaulted by ubiquitous posters adorned with images of bejeweled Lady Boys. When I asked my sister who the target audience for this show was, she replied, "Hen nights. It's the new Chippendales."

Where to stay? If you are a high-maintenance Four Seasons–

loving kind of person, you may prefer to commute from a luxe hostelry in London. (The trip from Victoria to Brighton takes less than an hour and provides endless opportunities for cell-phone eavesdropping.) Less demanding tourists may happily opt for T. S. Eliot's Metropole. Be sure to ask for a front room with a sea view, or you'll end up staring into a car park. If you are a big Thatcher fan, there's always the historic neighboring De Vere Grand. (Remember the IRA bombing that nearly did Maggie in?) Glamour-seeking, boutique-hotel lovers should stay at Drakes, on Marine Parade, which has those oval bathtubs like the one Cate Blanchett was craning into her house, or the aforementioned Blanch House, which offers, among other accommodations, a themed room called Boogie Nights.

What to wear? Despite its penchant for questionable behavior and flashes of cheek, Brighton has always been a stylish town. A dollop of fashion panache is much appreciated. Just make sure you bring a Windex-able outer garment. You never know when the seagulls are going to show their appreciation, too.

J. MALCOLM GARCIA

African Promise

FROM *The Virginia Quarterly Review*

THE THROBBING MUSIC EMANATING from Le Carnivore Restaurant behind our hotel grows tinnier with each tortured beat, the voices rising to ever higher levels of screeching, and although Darren and I feel exhausted from the twenty-four-hour flight from Boston to here, N'Djamena, the corrupt capital of the ruined African country of Chad, the merciless pulse of distortion refuses us sleep. We have no choice but to immerse ourselves until we are inured to the shrill bombardment and find, if not sleep, at least an accommodation with the noise.

Darren and I seat ourselves at a round table that tips beneath the weight of our elbows, sinking into the soft dirt floor. Ravenous cats dart about devouring meat scraps. We squint in the pale candlelight at murals of pink camels advancing ponderously through purple sand dunes. Dwarfing the murals are the jagged, lunging shadows of the singers. Players of trumpet, saxophone, banjo, and guitar sit ringed beneath a plastic valentine heart of colored lights and a neon wreath snapping on and off, on and off.

U.S. oil workers shout over their sauce-smeared plates, on which a few French fries lie untouched. Their shadows bob, entwined with those of the singers in a crazed copulation. The singers themselves gyrate without expression as if they have lost all connection to the stage, as if they no longer exist except as a manifestation of the dead weight overwhelming me that in time might pass for sleep — when suddenly, amid trails of exploding static, their estranged voices are diminished to broken barks.

Women in bright orange and yellow dresses strut past the stage

— unbidden and not the least distracted by this new failure in the sound system — to troll the oil workers. They escort them into the street one by one where the night absorbs them just beyond a fringe of blinking lights.

A young woman asks to join us and sits down without waiting for an answer. She orders a beer. Our dime. She introduces herself. Princess. A hairdresser and, she adds, a great soccer player. Perhaps she will leave for London and turn professional. What do we think?

Of course. Makes perfect sense.

"Do you want to go to a club?"

"No."

She strokes little labyrinth swirls through the sweat-dampened hairs on my arm. I shake my head no.

She asks Darren to take her to our room for a back rub.

"No."

Princess shrugs and finishes her beer.

"Where will you go from here?" she asks.

"Abéché."

"And then?"

"The border."

"With Sudan."

"Yes."

"We think of the Sudan border as people trying to solve an ethnic problem. It's a private problem."

She stands, pulls the plastic tablecloth from her hot arms, then kisses me on both cheeks, turns, and dissolves into the crowd. The thin scent of her hovers about my face until it, too, passes.

I ask a waitress for the bathroom and she points outside. Soldiers and security guards lounging on the backs of pickup trucks watch where I go. Not a star in the cave darkness of the overcast August sky that deepens ever blacker with storm clouds in this the last month of the rainy season. I slosh through puddles, disoriented in the gloom. I recognize one of the oil workers and ask him directions to the bathroom before I realize that he stands naked from the waist down, pants pooled at his ankles before a kneeling woman. She pauses in her ministrations, bloodshot eyes barely discernible in the depthless shadows, and pleasantly points the way toward the toilet.

"Thank you," I say.

I retreat toward a dimly lit hall, abandoning her to her transaction in the secluded corner of a broken cinderblock wall. The damp imprint of my boots indicates that I, too, had fleetingly passed this way among supplicants seeking relief from the rigors of their exploitation.

"What do you do?" a man on our flight to N'Djamena had asked Darren.

A photographer for Getty Images, Darren answered only, "Journalist."

"Oh. I do something counterproductive. I'm in oil."

Back in Le Carnivore, I watch an oil worker prance on stage, exposing his buttocks to us bleary-eyed pilgrims, the boards quaking beneath the heavy clomp of his boots. Darfur and Chad and the plight of thousands of people lie lost somewhere beneath the abundance of money dispensed for drinks and whores and whatever other tawdry commerce might come available this night. Darren and I wave off the servers, mutely mesmerized by the obscenity of that jiggling white ass blurring before us as, slumped in our chairs, our eyes closing, sleep finally comes.

Since 2003, millions of dollars' worth of oil has been pumped out of Chad and neighboring Sudan, putting huge profits into a few well-connected hands.

In Chad, little if any of that revenue has benefited the country.

The Berlin-based organization Transparency International conducts an annual survey of the abuse of public office for private gain and measures the degree to which corruption is perceived to exist among a country's public officials and politicians. Chad is tied with Bangladesh for most corrupt in the world.

In January 2006, the corruption became so apparent that the World Bank, which helped finance Chad's oil boom, suspended $124 million in loans and grants, and stopped payment of an additional $125 million in oil royalties after the government resisted pressure to invest its oil profits in projects to aid its impoverished people, who survive on an average income of $30 a month. Chad's president, Idriss Déby, threatened to shut down the country's oil production unless the World Bank released the funds. The World Bank stood firm. Déby then demanded that Chad's oil consortium, led by U.S. oil giant ExxonMobil, pay at least $100 million to tide the country over until the World Bank released Chad's royalties. U.S. diplomats acted on behalf of American oil companies. Déby received his money, thank you very much, and the roads, hospitals, running water, schools remain little more than dusty dreams.

There could be no better symbol of his corruption than the one Déby himself has chosen for his political party, the so-called Patriotic Salvation Movement. The logo features an AK-47 assault rifle (the weapon that has ensured Déby's power) crossed with a hoe (what better emblem of the poverty of those scratching out existence in rural villages?). Above it all floats an eternal flame, fueled by the oil that virtually assures the strong-arm tactics and fiscal dishonesty will never end.

Making matters worse is the unstemmed tide of refugees from Sudan. Divided between its Arab heritage in the north and its African heritage to the east and south, Sudan is cleaved along linguistic, religious, racial, and economic lines, resulting in civil war and ethnic cleansing in the Darfur region. More than 250,000 people, the majority of them civilians, are believed to have died in Darfur, and the United Nations estimates one million people more have been displaced. Already ranked the world's fifth poorest country, Chad has in the past three years absorbed about 235,000 Sudanese refugees.

In April, a new twist came in the bloody, three-year-old conflict in Darfur. Sudan announced that its ABCO corporation — which is 37 percent owned by Swiss company Cliveden — had begun drilling in Darfur, where preliminary studies showed there were vast quantities of oil. A China-owned consortium already pumps over 300,000 barrels of oil a day from Sudanese wells. What might Darfur yield? Washington and the European Union had all but ignored the atrocities taking place there for three years, but now that the crisis threatened to disrupt the opening up of Sudan's lucrative oil fields to Western companies the United States started waving the threat of UN sanctions against Sudan.

As it is, there is no love lost in Chad for the government of Sudan. At the start of the Darfur war in 2003, Sudan armed Arab militiamen called the Janjaweed, many of whom came from Chadian Arab tribes, to quash a political uprising by Darfur's black villagers who wanted increased autonomy — but the Janjaweed heeded no borders and occasionally led raids into eastern Chad. To this day, about eight thousand Chadian rebels maintain a camp in Darfur; earlier this year they fought with Chadian government forces sixty miles south of the strategic border town of Adré.

Last summer, to head off further fighting after the discovery of oil, the Sudanese government signed a peace agreement with the strongest of the rebel groups, but since the agreement was reached Darfur has grown more chaotic and violent. Meanwhile, Darfur rebel groups that did not sign the peace agreement have splintered and realigned, creating new ties and divisions that have made the conflict more complex and dangerous. Most importantly, a faction of the Sudan Liberation Army (SLA) and the Justice and Equality Movement (JEM), an Islamist group, have joined to form the National Redemption Front (NRF), which claims to have gunned down Sudanese military aircraft. Some humanitarian experts worry that oil will only increase Khartoum's resolve against the NRF in Darfur and encourage a scorched-earth policy against rebels' communities.

"No one doesn't see oil as not a big element in all this," a Western diplomat told me, his words twisting into a careful knot of negatives. "Chad broke relations with Taiwan and sided with China. China has oil markets in Sudan. Is Chad trying to get China on their side so that Sudan will stop supporting Chadian rebels? What we do know is the Chadian people are not seeing any benefit from oil."

In the morning, Darren and I wander out, following rolling breaks of daylight in a desperate search for coffee. Mud clings to our boots. Women with their children sit on the ground hawking trays of cigarettes. Men fan mobile-phone cards in our faces, exhorting us to buy. Clouds gather. The air turns gray, cool, then still. Boys selling corn hold out their hands, look skyward, and run.

Curtains of rain sweep down upon us. The soft ground explodes beneath our feet, and dirt paths suck in the rain until the ground can absorb no more and the water rises back up through the saturated earth and stands in pools, spreading, consuming whatever patches of dust remain. The rising pools become streams, rage into torrents, sweeping up piles of garbage, sending it spinning past us. Harder and harder it rains, and the water rises and rises. Women with bundles of clothes strapped to their backs hold on to parked cars against the pull of the thick water. We stand on railings and watch, our weak coffee splashed by rain, clumps of curdled cream like bobbing islands.

After half an hour, the rain finally falters, then stops. We emerge from beneath a tin overhang and make our way back to the hotel past sodden vendors who peer with doubt at the still sky. Boys mince through the water holding their shoes above their heads. Mosquitoes spin madly in the gauzy sunlight. Almost immediately, the sun begins to burn the water off.

I call Djimte Salomon, a spokesman for the aid organization World Vision. He offers to drive us to the ministry for public security and immigration. We need permits to travel within Chad, a bit of red tape begun after an April coup attempt prompted an already paranoid dictatorial government to track all foreigners within its borders. The failed overthrow followed months of rising tensions between Chad and Sudan over the Darfur war. Chad's President Déby comes from the same Zaghawa tribe as many Darfurians and has been accused by Khartoum of secretly backing rebels opposed to the Sudanese government by allowing them sanctuary in Chad.

"I am from the Sara tribe," Salomon tells us, his car swerving on the slick mud streets. "If I killed a man, I would have to pay a fine. But if I was Zaghawa, I would pay nothing. Déby would protect me."

Someone, however, wanted Déby to pay for interfering with Darfur. Chadian rebels attacked N'Djamena on April 13 but were defeated. On national radio Déby declared the situation under control, but residents, diplomats, and journalists reportedly heard shots for days afterward. Chad accused Sudan of backing the eastern-based rebels, some of whom appear to have been joining in Janjaweed attacks.

"They came early morning," Salomon recalls of the rebels. "It was nothing planned. They had never seen N'Djamena. They had been too long hiding in Sudan. They got lost and asked directions for the presidential palace. The people were excited. Fed up with Déby. The rebels got confused and attacked the parliament. At one point the rebels' truck died. They ran away and left mines and other ordnance in the truck. People came out to loot the truck and blew themselves up.

"Rebels, we don't know what's in their minds. I think if they get in power they will think, now it is our time to get rich. Just another cycle. The best thing, keep Déby and ask him to help all the people."

He turns down a narrow street. Burlap stalls, drooling with rainwater, stand beside flooded fields where shacks slant in the unstable ground. Salomon says his job does not pay well enough for him to live like Déby and his henchmen, but at least he does not have to live underwater like the families outside our windows. He drives off the road to make room for a shiny Hummer barreling toward us.

"Stupid World Bank," he mutters. "Can they not see? How does a man who earns less than five hundred dollars a month afford a Hummer?"

He rubs his fingers together, kisses them, and gestures toward a billboard of grinning Déby, beside Muammar al-Qaddafi, promoting oil development.

"That's how."

At the ministry, a drab cinder-block building where women sweep ankle-deep water out the door and into a flooded courtyard, a clerk tells us our papers won't be ready until the afternoon. If then. Unless of course we pay additional fees. We refuse. The clerk shrugs. Chickens run down the hall past the clerk's supervisor, a large woman with a pendulum walk who thrusts herself into the office and spills folders onto the desk. She asks our business and we tell her.

"What is the problem?" she asks.

"Nothing," the clerk says. He gives us our papers. We walk back to the car.

"When do you leave for Abéché?" Salomon asks.

"Tomorrow."

He starts the car. Rain begins falling.

"Don't cross into Sudan. Journalists used to do that. Now they are arrested."

Darren and I arrive in Abéché aboard a fourteen-seat propeller plane courtesy of the United Nations. We wait outside the empty airport for our ride. Dusty streets. A few mud-brick buildings where dogs pant and soldiers in T-shirts and khaki pants sit with AK-47s balanced against their legs. Turbaned nomads with scarves across their faces ride their snorting horses like characters broken free from some myth to wreak havoc. A UN Land Rover maneuvers around the riders and stops beside us. We get in.

Our driver, Matt Conway, has been the UN flack in Abéché since February. The rain has kept things quiet, he says, but we can expect the fighting in Darfur and skirmishes between the Chad army and Chadian rebels to resume when the rains stop.

We turn down a rutted street toward the UN compound. Nothing on either side of us but aid organizations. A circling of the wagons against what lies beyond this alley.

"Journalists from *National Geographic* were jailed for crossing into Sudan from Chad earlier this month," Matt says. "They probably went in with the faction of the Sudanese Liberation Army that signed the peace agreement."

"And were betrayed by them?"

"Yeah."

"To score points with Khartoum?"

Outside a pair of towering spiked gates Matt brakes the Land Rover and honks. A guard opens a panel and looks at us. Then the doors open and Matt drives through. All that's missing is the moat.

"Everyone is just out for themselves, man," Matt says. "It's all about survival."

Matt's office. Paper-strewn desks. Computers humming off generators. Maps on the walls. Circles indicate "areas of concern" in eastern Chad.

Abéché, where we are: "Degradation of the security situation in town ongoing."

Bahai: "Presumption of recruitment by Sudanese rebels in the camps."

Guereda: "Permanent Sudanese and Chadian rebels' or bandits' threats."

Farchana: "Permanent risk of military confrontation."

With my fingers I trace the arrows and circles and small dots for towns. Tomorrow we leave for the Farchana refugee camp. Mustapha Mohammad, a thirty-five-year-old man whom Matt recommended as an interpreter, stands beside me, his shaved head tipped back as he contemplates the map. He was born in Abéché, speaks English, studied in Khartoum, and knows Arabic. He worked for the Chinese-owned Great Wall Drilling Company in the oil fields of southern Chad. A radio operator. He still has his ID tags, shows them with pride.

"Bad?" I ask.

"No, nice map."

"I mean going out to the camps. Too dangerous?"

"No, not too dangerous. Not for me."

"And me?"

"For you, little bit dangerous."

I tell Mustapha to meet us at eight o'clock in the morning.

"I give you African promise."

"What is that?"

"You tell me to meet you at eight o'clock, African promise means I will see you no later than nine o'clock."

"Meet me at seven."

We can't leave, however, until we register our travel permits with the local chief of police, still referred to, in this former French colony, as the "commissar." His secretary sits behind a wobbly wood desk. A broken, dust-covered typewriter and an ink-cartridge box take up a corner. He looks at our papers, mutters, reads them a dozen times, asks when we arrived. He takes a stamp from a drawer, presses it into an ink pad. He grinds our papers with the stamp so thoroughly he leaves a stain on the desk, examines his handiwork, blows on the ink. Satisfied, he advises us to wait for the commissar.

We stand outside, on the windblown road where beggars lie in ditches and raise wrinkled arms to all who pass them. Empty oil cans collect rainwater. The commissar pulls up in a Suzuki Jeep. We follow him into his office. Dank, white walls, dirt floor grimed with chicken droppings. He tears into his secretary for not having our papers numbered correctly. He reviews the stamps and signs his initials. He points out the Louisiana flag he has on his desk. He studied at the Baton Rouge police academy. He gives us our papers, on which the ink is still damp. He warns us against going out at night. Bandits. He asks if we like jazz.

"Yes."

He smiles and nods and follows us to the door. Through the rear window of the Land Rover I watch him. He grows smaller waving the Louisiana flag.

We begin the three-hour drive to Farchana with Claude, a retired Canadian marine in charge of overseeing the "gendarmes" — Chadians hired to provide security for refugee camps. The UN pays the gendarmes a monthly incentive fee of $150 to offset their paltry $64-a-month government salary. This arrangement was intended to motivate the gendarmes and provide a firewall against bribes from rebel forces. Unfortunately, the plan has backfired. The gendarmes effectively hold the UN hostage for ever-increasing incentives, and the UN has little choice but to pay up, if it wants to maintain camp security and ensure the safety of its personnel. The Déby government happily encourages this lopsided relationship, as it allows the government to avoid spending oil profits on maintaining the cronyism that passes for loyalty within its ranks.

Meanwhile, the gendarmes do little more than escort UN personnel — without raising a finger to actually protect them or the refugees in their camps. Before Darren and I arrived in N'Djamena, Chadian rebels kidnapped four thousand men and children from a UN-run refugee camp near Goz Beïda in the south. The gendarmes did nothing. Thirty-five NGO vehicles have been stolen since November of last year; UN personnel have also been assaulted in carjackings and burglaries. Again, the gendarmes have done nothing. So all travel, even under supposed guard, is understandably tense.

We follow a dirt road out of Abéché and into the brush toward Farchana. Our driver stops at checkpoints where our papers are inspected and laboriously stamped again, our names recorded on curled sheets of paper dusted with the ancient import of the old men writing on them. Scavengers had passed this way before us and dug up the bones of cattle and goats and camels and other animals whose shined skulls leer at us in the glare. We turn north on a narrow dirt road crushing scrub brush under our wheels.

Claude talks without end, his voice amazingly steady despite our being tossed about by the deep ruts we hit and our driver's insistent speeding. "The camps are better organized than the towns around them," Claude says. He raises his hands against the roof for balance against the bumps. "They are jealous, these towns, but they don't understand. This is not home for the refugees. They can't work. They have small living quarters. I'm going to see how the police are doing. Sometimes there are small problems. Like they beat people."

We stop at a soupy brown wadi — Arabic for a dry riverbed — filled with roiling rainwater. Boys whip donkeys with switches and the donkeys bellow their protest and refuse to cross the frothing waters. Nomads on camels pause at the edge of the water and let their mounts drink. Toll keepers ask us for money to grow grass and keep the shoreline stable. I look at the crumbled ground without a hint of greenery.

Okay.

Boys shovel dirt into the sandy craters swallowing the wheels of another Land Rover ahead of us. Our driver drops a Central African franc, worth about twenty-five cents, out his window to them. The boys scamper after the limp paper bill, swinging their shovels at one another. The wind teases the bill just out of reach until it vanishes in the mottled dusty air and drops invisibly into the water.

The toll keepers advise us to drive straight, don't stop. Our driver backs up, guns the engine, and, picking up speed, takes a running start toward the wadi. Water explodes in all directions and we're thrown against our seats and the Land Rover plows forward and we feel the resistance of the water against the grille and we feel our tires spin madly and we see the muddy slough rise to the doors as we sink, brown geysers jetting outward like wings of a bird, and we pass another Rover roped to complaining mules in the middle of the wadi, and we pass naked men lined chest-deep in the water, encouraging us, and we grind on, humping up the opposite bank sluicing water and mud, emerging triumphant onto land.

"We don't have much time," Claude says, inspecting the sky. "See those clouds. They are nothing now. But tomorrow. We have until tomorrow afternoon or we'll be stuck for days by rains, because the wadi will be too deep."

Five-year-old Mukhatar Ahmad stares at me from his parents' hut in Farchana refugee camp. His right eye protrudes white and glassy from its socket. He does not talk. He will not tell Mustapha how his eye was damaged. Perhaps playing with other boys, one woman suggests. Perhaps he was born like that. Flies suck at the eye. Mukhatar does not blink. Faces balloon and shrink, huts curve, reflected grotesquely in his eye.

Three years he has been in this place. The weight of time, the slow drain. He pours water from a heat-swelled oil jug.

I am here because of war. I saw fighting, killing by helicopter, by guns. Militia of Janjaweed. I saw dead. I can't describe it. Because of this problem we left Darfur.

Mukhatar moves his head and I follow his dead eye, the world turning in its silent orbit. Mountains green from rain. Women carrying buckets of water on their heads. Goats kicking at the dirt.

They shoot people in the head. I stayed in my village. Hid in my room. Saw through window. Many killed. I hope I return. The situation is worse here. No money. Not enough food.

A child takes my pen, tries to suck the ink from it. Boys drag toy trucks made from the rusted tin of sardine cans. Toothpicks as axles. Tires of mud. Putrid heat within the tents, where they play despite their parents' apathy. Pallets of dirty blankets. The boys hold their toys for me to see.

War came in three ways. Some war by helicopter. Some by the Janjaweed on camels. Some by soldier in trucks. They attacked in the morning. Many times come with guns and shoot. We were in school. Some escape, not all.

"We must go," Claude says.

The UN has rules. All of its people inside by 4 P.M. He stands to leave, and I step out of Mukhatar's compass, leaving the globe of his eye to the flies. He watches me go, his hand raised, outstretched fingers ready to clasp my hand if I offer it to him. *Take me with you,* he seems to say, but his lips do not move. Just that eye in its blindness following me. *Take me with you.*

We make the three-hour drive back to Abéché the following afternoon and beat the rains by just under an hour.

"This would have stranded us at the wadi," Claude says.

We sit in a screened-in building that serves as a cafeteria. I nod, pick at my plate of rice and beef liver.

"Oh, that would have been awful," tut-tuts Rodolphe, another security man who monitors the gendarmes in northern Chad. He served more than twenty years in the French foreign legion. He looks well into his sixties. Shaved head, trim and taut as a wire.

Rain slashes through the screen. I wipe the water off a map Darren and I are consulting. We want to drive north to Guereda, spend the night and continue to Iriba and then Bahai in the Sahara Desert. Then drive south to the border town of Adré.

"Impossible," Claude says. "No roads from Iriba to Adré. And what about water, what would you do about water?"

"Carry it."

"You'd have to carry a well. That's the Sahara, man."

He traces a dirty fingernail from Abéché to Guereda. The road is bad, he explains. It will take us at least five to six hours. He cannot say that it is safe. In the past few days, more than one hundred Chadian soldiers were deployed in Guereda. The drive from Guereda to Iriba would be very bad. Even UN convoys do not follow that route.

"Bandits, man, when you pack your gear they know where you're going," Claude says. "Why do you think you fill out all that paperwork? Information is passed along."

"At first," Rodolphe adds, "they won't know when you leave here. But when you check in at Guereda, then they'll know. Travel with others. Don't discuss plans with your driver or translator. What's their tribe?"

We shrug.

"My God, you don't know! Always know people's tribes. The president is Zaghawa. If your men are Zaghawa nothing will happen to you because they are part of president's tribe. But if they are Tama don't go. A Sudanese tribe. No one likes them."

"Why?"

"They were strong once like Zaghawa."

"Any other tribes that would be bad?"

"No. Just Tama. Give me your names."

I write them down. He scowls at my handwriting.

"I will notify the *prefe* in Guereda you are coming. Villages are still run on the French administrative system. The *prefe* is the administrative leader. He will protect you once he knows you are there."

He examines our map.

"Bahai is a hot spot. The main road from Sudan to Guereda goes through Bahai. A rebel route. At night many things happen. Four people on camels shot up Kounougo camp in Guereda two nights ago."

"Why?"

"Why not? It's a war, man."

In the morning, we sit outside the cafeteria and wait for Mustapha and Abdullah, the driver we hired. Rodolphe stops in for bread and cheese. He flies to Guereda in a few days to organize security for a visit from U.S. Senator Barack Obama.

"That senator must be an expert on Chad," he says. "Two hours in Guereda and he will know everything. I wish I could work for him. Maybe I will see you, eh?"

He stuffs bread in his mouth, interrupting his laughter.

Mustapha waves to us from the gate. I call him over.

"What is your tribe?"

"Masalit."

"Abdullah's?"

"Masalit."

"Not Tama?"

"No. Why?"

"No reason."

We drive through the rain-cooled desert. A thin layer of green scrub grass stretches across the sand. The seething, clay-colored waters of wadis carve the land into an irregular patchwork of dunes and bare trees.

Men and women pause to watch our passage, moving between their morning cook fires. We wave and they raise their arms and the children chase our dust, shouting for candy.

"Is that a baboon?" I ask Mustapha and point to a red monkey squatting below a tree.

"No."

"What kind is it?"

"We have three kinds of monkey. Small, bigger, biggest. That one is small."

"Thank you."

A flock of gray African quail crosses the cattle trail that serves as our road. Abdullah accelerates. The quail scurry and begin squawking and I hear one of them thump beneath our Land Rover. Abdullah takes a knife off the dashboard and runs back a few yards looking at the side of the trail. He pauses at a clump of weeds, knife raised, then makes a slashing motion. He looks up smiling and carries the dead pheasant by its feet.

"Dinner," Darren says.

The administrator of the Guereda compound is out, a guard informs us, so we decide to check in with the chief of the gendarmes. We ask directions of some men on the street. They look inside the Land Rover without answering. They look at us, reach with their hands but decide against touching our clothes. Finally, one of them points down the road to a clot of square mud buildings.

The security chief paces behind a desk, above which hang pendulum-shaped beehives. Black wasps circle our heads. An aide sleeps on a cot. The security chief examines our papers upside down, lips moving. He stamps them with heavy deliberation, applying his whole body as he leans over the stamp. He blows on the ink, signs his initials, holds it out as if determining its suitability for framing. He tells us to return to the UN compound. He will bring the *prefe* to us momentarily.

Emmanuel, the compound administrator, meets us at the gate. His red-rimmed eyes speak of sleepless nights, of nerves on edge.

"How did you get here? Drive?"

He doesn't let us answer.

"How long will you be here? My God, you came through the jungle. Since January, rebels have been attacking Guereda. Since April NGOs have lost six vehicles to road bandits. We have had attempted carjackings on two cars. A policeman was killed, another injured."

He pauses, breathing hard. A Rwandan, he survived the genocide there by escaping into the compound of an aid organization. All of his family was killed. He survived only to be kidnapped here in February by rebels. They held him for forty-five minutes before he was released. Looking at him, I realize he lost more than just forty-five minutes. He must have thought Rwanda had finally caught up with him.

"We don't talk of curfew, but after four o'clock we enter our no-movement phase. We don't leave the compound. Six hundred soldiers arrived two days ago. They were promised since April. Maybe they are here because of the U.S. senator. I don't know."

He fusses with paper on his desk. A fan scatters the papers and his hands scramble after the fleeing memos and lists of protocols.

We step outside the compound, look at our watches. Where's the security chief?

Two men lounging on the ground beside a blanket buried under pots and pans tell Mustapha that rebels came through yesterday, but did not bother them. They were after soldiers.

We walk away, but I feel the two men watching us.

"They won't tell you, but there is much violence here," Mustapha says.

"How do you know?"

"They are Tama tribe. This was Tama territory. Before, each family of Tama have two hundred to three hundred cows. They were destroyed by Zaghawa. Before, you would see hundreds of camels and cows on the road to market. Now nothing."

We tire of waiting for the security chief and decide to see the *prefe* ourselves. The two Tama men point us down a rock-strewn road toward a building that resembles a mosque. Giant vultures perch in vast nests that consume the tops of the trees. They stare down at us with their red faces and featherless necks.

The brown-robed *prefe* sits alone in a room equipped with only a rug.

"Go back to the UN and make your plans," the *prefe* tells us in a voice somehow disconnected from his jowly face.

Outside the vultures have roused themselves and circle overhead.

"The *prefe* knows nothing," Mustapha says under his breath. "He is a stupid man. He can't read, can't write, but he is of Déby's tribe."

An hour later, Mustapha comes to our room. The security chief came by. Pissed off. We should not have seen the *prefe* without him. Now, he informed Mustapha, we cannot visit the camps.

Middle of the night. Lights out. Our breathing in the dark. Darren complains the pheasant was tough. Mosquito net heavy on my face. I hear the little fuckers buzzing, wanting me. I need to piss but dread the outhouse. The fetid stink. The flies. The lumbering black beetles.

Pop, pop, pop.

"You hear that?"

"Gunfire."

"AKs."

"Maybe."

Pop, pop, pop.

"More."

"Yeah."

"I have to piss."

"Can't help you."

*

The security chief meets with Emmanuel in the morning. Darren and I sit with Mustapha and Abdullah. We wait to see if he will relent on grounding us. I understand we bruised his ego. By meeting with the *prefe* without him, we effectively said he doesn't matter. The *prefe,* too, was insulted. We violated protocol, cut around the chain of command and strode without escort into his inner sanctum.

"You should not have seen the *prefe,*" Emmanuel scolds us. "I have spoken with the chief of security. He understands you are new so you won't be punished."

"Punished?"

"Jail, thrown out. It doesn't matter. He will escort you to Mile camp."

An armed convoy of Toyota pickups filled with gendarmes holding rocket-propelled grenade launchers and machine guns waits outside the compound.

We reached Mile camp by midmorning. I see women and children swarming to a hospital tent for free milk. Most young men were either killed in the flight from Darfur and Chad border towns or have joined a rebel militia.

A boy with SLA printed on his sandals stops me. Slung over his shoulder is a butchered goat. Blood runs down his back. He looks at the soldier-filled pickup, just feet away, and laughs.

"We have no security in the camp. Sometimes at night the Janjaweed attack doctors. Sometimes shoot guns. In all of Chad there is no security."

He points to the letters on his sandals.

"Before we are refugee we are Sudanese. We support the opposition to the government. After the rains, there will be fighting. We wait for fight."

He walks away, the head of the goat flopping. I tell Mustapha we should leave. We need to return to Abéché for the night and then in the morning drive to Adré, an hour east of Farchana, where we will spend the night. No roads run from Guereda to Adré so we must backtrack. No hurry. Leave in about an hour. African promise. I laugh, slap him on the shoulders. Mustapha nods but doesn't smile. His eyes follow the goat's blood trail.

"There is no promise," he says. "Especially in Africa."

*

"Mustapha, tell Abdullah to slow down."
 "What is the problem?"
 "Those are goats."
 "It is good."
 "I can handle birds, no goats."
 "Maybe one."
 "We are close to Abéché. We'll eat there."
 "Abdullah, drive slowly."

After a night in Abéché, we return to Farchana on the way to Adré. We stop for bread and sardines. Mustapha and I drink tea. I lean against the wall of the tea shop. Suddenly my back burns. The pain increases. I take off my shirt and my back has exploded with welts and red slashes as if I'd been whipped. No one knows what has bitten me. I fight panic, feel my heart race. I want to spin in circles and slap at my back. Mustapha applies across my back a mud poultice mixed with wet tea leaves. It helps. The welts recede. We need to continue to Adré. My back itches. I swallow a fistful of Benadryl tablets.

In Adré, road signs fallen in the soft sand point the way to Sudan. Across a wadi where children splash in the water, we see the rough hills burned brown in the sun, and cattle spot the hills close enough that I can see their bent heads scouring the ground for grass.
 "El Geneina," Mustapha says. "Sudan."
 "We can't cross over," I remind him. "Always know where the border is. We'll get arrested."
 Abdullah drives into the town center. Armed soldiers expressionless behind their sunglasses monitor the roads. People stop what they are doing to watch us. The vendors selling car tires. The women washing clothes in buckets. The boys chasing one another down the narrow streets. Sheep stand behind a butcher stall and the butcher watches us, too, sharpening his knives.
 We drive past walls cluttered with faded oil-company advertisements. Children and goats stand by mud stoops, and vultures observe the commotion from the branches overhanging vendor stalls. Rap music carries faintly from cassette players. We pass a herder of goats, the animals wide-eyed due to the clanging of metal coming

from one of the huts; there an old man beats shapes out of metal that is orange from the light of a forge fire.

We stop at Adré Hospital. Guards lounging within the crevices of broken walls rouse themselves and lead us to the main office, where we meet Dr. Autid Adam.

"Patients live under trees. Many injured. Many refugees. No medicine, no doctors. Shooting injuries. Situation not good. It is too difficult. All is lost."

He calls an orderly to escort us through the halls. The soles of my boots stick to the floor. Flies collect on discarded bandages. Women sit outside dimly lit rooms, passive to the flies scrambling across their faces. One of them grabs my hand. Her boy. There. On the plastic brown mat where dirty sheets peek out from beneath a mosquito net. That boy. He fell from a tree, fractured his left leg. The cast won't dry in the humidity.

Across from him lies another emaciated boy with a gunshot wound to his left hip; it is clotted with flies. My stomach turns. The funk. Soldiers shot him in June or July. He can't remember. Shot here in Adré while working in a grain mill. Janjaweed attacked his village in Darfur in 2003 but it was here he was shot. He smiles. I clamp my hand over my nose and mouth against the smell, try to convey with my eyes that I appreciate his sense of irony.

Another boy. Shot in the buttocks in January by the Janjaweed. He lies on his stomach, urine bag spilled on the floor. A nurse steps on it, shakes it off her foot.

A fat bandage covers the boy's wound. It hasn't healed. The doctors don't know why. Perhaps the heat. Perhaps the lack of medicine. Perhaps it is just bad luck. They shrug, helpless.

"What are you doing here?"

I turn and face a doctor with Médecins Sans Frontières. We don't have his permission to be here. This part of the hospital belongs to MSF, he says. Do we not understand the danger we are in? Have we not seen all the soldiers? Everyone is watching everyone. Even now, as we speak. My God! No one is safe. MSF cannot be seen associating with us. What if we offend the Chad government? What would happen to his work then? If we want to talk to "the blacks" we must go over there.

He points to a collection of dejected buildings, a courtyard where fowl nod in the afternoon heat beside men and women sprawled beneath gnarled, leafless trees.

"I don't know what they do there," the MSF doctor says. "The blacks operate that. It is not MSF. You can go there if you must."

"Even if we offend the Chad government?"

"This is very dangerous. A war. You put yourself and us at risk being here. You must leave our side. I will talk to Doctor Adam."

He spins around and stalks down the corridor, trailed by a nurse. Black orderlies in white coats follow at a respectful distance.

We leave the hospital and follow a rutted street draining sewage. Our windows open, dust blowing in. Wide-eyed children stare from open doors that lead into darkened halls wet from mop water. Squatting men eat with their fingers from tin bowls. The air stands heavy with the funk of cows and goats and sheep that have passed this way to market. Many of the mortared huts provide empty reminders of the dozens of families who lived here once.

Abdullah parks outside the compound of Secedev, a Chad NGO that provides agricultural assistance. We get out of the Land Rover dust-covered and sore. Inside the gates, a man scoops pasta onto a large plate. He inserts spoons all around the plate and the staff and we sit in a circle on the ground and dig in. Flies ignore the food, descending instead on us.

"Janjaweed come together in great numbers and attack and take the animals of farmers," Ndoyengar Narisse says after I tell him about the MSF doctor. "It is very insecure. The SLA is in Adré. Sudan troops are in the hills across the wadi. This morning we go to Goungour, less than a mile from the border. The security there is okay, but villages near it have been attacked and all the people flee to Goungour."

We drive forty minutes through the bush, following Ndoyengar, the soft sandy ground sucking at our wheels. Some spots are lushly green from rain. Goats rise up on their hind legs to graze in leafy trees, and farmers till the ground in fields of sorghum.

In Goungour village, fencing made from twisted branches encloses empty corrals; dust churns up from the bare feet of children fleeing our advance. A generator hums through the warm, wet air. An old man lays straw mats on the ground. We sit and he pours mud-filmed water from a plastic National Diesel Oil jug into a bowl.

"This is our water," Ndoyengar says before he drinks. "Taken from the wadi."

The village elders join us to share the water, their cheeks drawing in like the gills of a fish with each sip.

"This is the biggest village in this area. We had a police station but the police left for Adré."

"There's no security now."

"Yesterday the Janjaweed took twenty-six cows."

"In July they took one hundred fifty cows and eighteen camels."

"They always come back."

"On horses and camels. White turbans. Sunglasses. Khaki pants. Rifles."

"They look for villages with animals."

"We miss our cows."

"We miss our land."

"We miss the people who are dead."

The afternoon creeps up on us without warning. We leave Goungour, return to Adré then Farchana before nightfall. Ndoyengar takes us by another route he says is faster. My stomach turns. Perhaps from the water. The sun swims in the sky, rainbow rings throbbing from it with each hole the Land Rover strikes. I drink from my water bottle, which I left too long in the heat. I'm woozy from the Benadryl, mouth pasty. My back itches. I bounce from my seat, flopping like a marionette as we hit another hole.

What is that? A ravine? We dip into it, drive ahead. Or is this the border wadi? Are those hills Sudan? Where the fuck is Ndoyengar taking us? The heat. I'm burning. I drink more water. I don't know Ndoyengar. Is he taking us to Sudan? More rainbow rings. Oh shit, what's going on? How much can he get for us? Yellow sky, Arizona desert, except those are not Apache warriors on the sunned buttes. No, they're Janjaweed. Oh Jesus, TV fucking Westerns, what am I thinking? The skull of a cow. Its sightless eyes hold the sky and me in it. Jesus, is he taking us into Sudan? Why can't anyone hear me? Where are we? *Where are we?*

"Stop, stop! Stop the fucking car!"

Abdullah stops, looks uncertainly at Mustapha, who reaches for my hand.

"What is wrong?"

Ndoyengar drives on then he stops. He gets out and walks back to us.

"Where are we?" I ask, my voice coming out in gasps. "Why are we crossing the wadi into Sudan?"

Ndoyengar scowls.

"Sudan is a mile away. What is the problem? I have work to do."

He walks back to the Land Rover. Abdullah starts the engine. I sip more water. Hot wind dries my face. I'm sweat-soaked. My back itches. I pop a few Benadryl and close my eyes. Day-tripping. Let the land take me where it will.

We spend the night in the Farchana compound and then return to Abéché in the morning. After we stow our gear, Darren and I join Claude in the cafeteria. There's a bottle of beer on his table.

"The gendarmes say they need an increase in their incentive pay," Claude tells us. "The UN has approved a 6 percent increase. We're worried it will become a subsidy. It's already more than their salary. We're not sure how much of the salary they use. They might just sock it away."

Darren and I buy beers.

"The UN voted to deploy troops to Sudan. But Sudan won't accept them. So . . ."

Claude throws up his arms.

"There're rumors of a new offensive in Darfur," he continues. "Who knows what will happen now on the border. Will the rebels flee into Chad? Will Déby let them? Does he have a choice? The border guards and rebels are all from some tribe. If Déby lets them stay, will Sudan support another coup attempt?"

He pauses to sip his beer.

"It's about oil. There's oil in northern Sudan, oil in southern Sudan, chances are there's oil in the middle. Move out black Africans and put Darfur under Arab chiefs and the oil is theirs.

"It's about Arabs versus black Africans, herders against farmers, Darfur population versus Khartoum leadership. But don't forget the oil."

In the morning we fly to Bahai, where the Oure Cassoni refugee camp was established in 2003, literally feet away from the Sudan border in the Sahara Desert.

Beneath the wings of our plane the land transforms from a thin layer of green to rolling sand dunes. We land on a rock-strewn runway and stop beside a shack with a torn tin roof that is rattled by bursts of hot wind. A UN Land Rover awaits our arrival.

An African gazelle, a gift from the village elders, sits in the sandy lot of the Bahai compound and watches with wide dark eyes as we swing by it and park in front of the administration building.

The compound's administrator, Comlan Spero Guy, offers us chairs. He asks his assistant to provide us with a security briefing.

The people of Bahai are Zaghawa. The camp is twelve miles from here and less than a mile from the border. We travel in convoys only, at least three Land Rovers. A 6 P.M. curfew is in effect. Be careful of looking at Zaghawa women. The men will harm you if you approach their women. If you kill a woman, you will pay at least one hundred camels. A man, you will pay countless camels. Understand?

"Where would we get the camels?"

"Please, just try not to kill anyone."

"Right."

"It is very hot. The winds are dangerous here. Sandstorms cover the sun. What else do you wish to know?"

"You tell us."

"It is not easy to distinguish rebels from soldiers. They have the same guns, wear the same uniform. But no one will admit this to you. Chad and Sudan have an agreement. Chad is not to support the rebels, Sudan is not to undermine Chad's government. We will see, eh? Just on Sunday we saw Sudan forces deployed on the border, watching the camp. There may be some Janjaweed there as well. Questions?"

After lunch we drive to Oure Cassoni through a treeless desert landscape like the bottom of an ocean. Diesel-spewing jeeps loaded with armed men pass us. Some of the men wear desert military garb, others T-shirts and khaki pants. Rebels? Soldiers? Both? Who can say?

The camp sprawls for miles, the tents so covered with sand that at first I mistake them for dunes. Unlike in the other camps, I smell nothing. Instead the still air feels as vacant as the stares from families who sit immobile outside their tents in the harsh light.

We stop at the market where the Shell insignia glints off aluminum siding used on some of the stalls. An elderly man offers us tea.

Beside him other men take off their argyle socks and pour water over their feet in preparation for the time for prayer.

"My tea shop is called Gahwatu Alatilleen," the old man tells us. "It means if you have no work, come here."

He laughs. A young man approaches, asks where we are from.

"America."

The old man is his uncle. The young man, twenty-five-year-old Izeldeen Khacter, shows us a business card from Brigham and Women's Hospital in Boston.

"I have worked with doctors from this place."

"I want to talk to the rebels," I tell him. "I want to know what is happening in Darfur."

"Yes, you can do this. Come."

We follow him out of the market toward his tent in Zone C, Block L. The camp is divided by villages and tribes; Zaghawa, Fur, Masalit, Grron, Dagno.

In Zone C live families from Furawiya, Sudan; Zone A, Korunie City, Sudan; Zone B, Awmrow, Sudan.

Izzy left Furawiya with his parents days before the Janjaweed attacked it. From the road to Oure Cassoni camp, he could see Furawiya burning.

"I have no work papers. I only have refugee card for food. People say, Since you are Zaghawa won't Déby help you? In New Orleans, people were American like your President Bush. Did he take them in?"

We stop at a tent that serves as a small library. Izzy manages it every morning. He attended university in Tripoli where he learned English. Inside, he retrieves a Thuraya satellite phone.

"Tonight I will call people in Sudan to speak with you tomorrow."

"How do you know the rebels?"

Izzy shrugs.

"Are you a rebel?"

"If I support George Bush and another man supports John Kerry is that man a rebel? That is me. In America I would support John Kerry. I don't support Sudan government, but I'm not a rebel."

Evening at the Bahai UN compound. Vast blue-gray sky tinged with the rust color of an approaching sandstorm. I play with the gazelle, its black tail wagging like a dog's as I tug on its horns.

"We have three kinds of this deer," Mustapha says.

"This one is biggest?"

"Small."

The wind increases, stirring the sand at my feet. Sheets of burlap toss in the air and twist away toward an obscured moon.

"Do you know we have Janjaweed in Chad?" Mustapha says. "I see them, know them. They leave their problems in Sudan. Their generals rob them. They get tired of fighting or join the Chad army for better pay."

"Why would Chad let the Janjaweed come in?"

"The defense minister and minister of foreign affairs are both Arab. Déby says nothing so they don't try a coup."

"Why doesn't he buy them off with oil money?"

"All the oil money goes to war; war with Sudan, for rebels, to generals protecting Déby. What do you think?"

"It makes sense."

"Yes. Because none of it makes sense."

Mustapha laughs. We shield our eyes against the wind, so much sand now in the air I cannot even see the compound walls. Then Mustapha disappears. The wind howls.

In the morning, we wait for Izzy outside the library tent. We pass the time by visiting with a man chained to a tree. He is crazy from war, we are told. There are about fifty people in the camp like him. He lives on a moonscape of rocks and boulders, the skulls of animals. Children observe him at a distance. Dressed in red rags, his sister swings a metal pole and talks to herself. Warns us away.

Izzy finds us, excited that he just sold a goat. He tells us he called rebel commanders the night before. There is heavy fighting in Darfur, they told him. They were too far away to meet us. But he will call them again so I can speak to them on his Thuraya.

I want to see the border. Our UN driver takes us toward a water tower next to Wadi Hawar, which separates the camp from Sudan. He radios the dispatcher at the compound and gives our position. His voice shakes. I hear frantic talk from the dispatcher.

"What is he saying?"

"Don't get killed," Izzy says.

We park by rubber tubes connected to the water tank. Sparse shrubs thrive in the wet ground around the tubes, but beyond the tubes little else grows, except in the wadi where tall, grassy weeds wave above the water.

Across the wadi, we see Sudanese jeeps, machine-gun mounts and soldiers. A Sudanese soldier follows us with a telescope. Izzy points to a hill where he says rebels once camped. A soft wind ripples the water. Long-legged birds strut through the weeds.

"I lived in that direction," Izzy says and points over the wadi, a short distance that is as far from here as the moon.

He calls Abdallaha Xaya Ahmad, a spokesman for the NRF, and interprets.

"The Sudan government is killing everyone. They are attacking us even now. Three days ago they bombed Umseeder village. Right now Umseeder is still smoking. Many killed. I don't know how many. Yesterday, Janjaweed attacked people between the villages of Kutom and Disa and killed seventeen persons.

"At this moment all civilians can't move between Kutom and Disa. Fasher University was attacked. Many students killed because they support rebels."

Izzy hands me the phone.

"He wants to talk to you."

I press the phone against my ear. I hear gunfire.

"What is your name?"

"Malcolm."

"Malcolm," he says struggling with his English, "we stay and defend our rights and people even if we are killed. What kind of name is Malcolm?"

"I don't know," I shout above the noise on the other end. "Scottish. My mother gave it to me."

"Very nice to meet you, Mr. Malcolm. God's blessing to your mother. Call anytime."

Then nothing but the silence on the other end of the phone and the quiet breezes blowing over the wadi.

When I lived in San Francisco and counseled Salvadoran and Cambodian refugees, I thought I learned from them the meaning of war and loss. But what I've seen here confounds my sense of earned expertise. Chad swirls around me, a seething waste of lost souls where years of war have shaken its steady heart, its proverbial moral compass — its way out.

Refugees live hopelessly in the camps. Government officials, aid workers, gendarmes, all of them alike are out for themselves because nothing and no one represents anything larger — especially American diplomatic globetrotters who dance the dance of nonintrusive intervention, urging other countries to stand up against the war, knowing none of them will without U.S. leadership.

I came here suspecting that oil companies were war profiteers, cynical oppressors of an already impoverished people — the obvious scapegoats, the villains. I don't hold them blameless, but they may be the most honest among the dishonest. They arrived to find a moral vacuum, a willing bureaucracy that places more emphasis on titles and courtesy calls and the stamping of travel permits than governance and prefers personal gain to the protection of its own people.

While we were in the bush, President Déby accused Chevron and Malaysian state-owned Petronas of failing to pay taxes totaling $486.2 million. When Chevron produced official agreements, showing the amount they owed had been paid, Déby suspended the underlings who signed the documents and publicly denounced the taxes as mere "crumbs." Chevron and Petronas, along with ExxonMobil, have already promised to invest $4.2 billion in an underground pipeline from landlocked Chad to the Atlantic port of Kribi in Cameroon, but that's no longer enough. Now Déby wants another half billion dollars in taxes. Now he is demanding 60 percent of their profits. And what can even the petroleum giants do? If they refuse, Déby will boot them out, and another company will fill the void.

Long ago, oil executives must have discovered, as I have, that one's position here determines rank and place in the pecking order of trickle-down payoffs. There's no obvious way to fix it, only a way to work it. Because it's not what you do but where you stand in line — and if you want to improve your standing, you have to do it by force. So strongmen set up shop and make their own rules and take what they can before the next coup. The American companies didn't make these rules; they're just willing to play by them in order to get the precious oil that you buy to fuel your car.

So acknowledge your own place in this order. Step in line. Be ready to change allegiances with chameleon speed. Play along and pray you don't get trapped in the middle.

*

The music drumming into my brain from Le Carnivore has improved little since Darren and I were here three weeks ago. The sound system has been repaired. A few U.S. oil workers sit in folding chairs. One of them apologizes to a waitress for his behavior the previous night.

"You're back," Princess says.

We offer her a seat but she demurs. She wears a pink blouse, tight jeans, and impossibly high platform shoes. She sits alone until a man kneels behind her and puts his hands over her face. She grins and turns around.

With luck, he will carry her away to England where she can become the soccer player of her dreams. With luck, he will offer her more than ten dollars afterward. As someone who sits here pleasantly plastered after too much time in the bush, knowing that I will fly out to Paris in a day, I can indulge in optimism.

Just an hour earlier we had taken a cab to the airport to check our luggage. A sticker on the windshield read, USAMA BIN LADEN. MAI GASKIYA YANA TARE DA ALLAH. "Osama bin Laden. Praise be to God." Darren tipped the driver a dollar and the man smiled and pumped Darren's hands with both of his.

"That's how we defeat terrorism," Darren said. "One goddamn U.S. dollar at a time."

I gave the driver a dollar too. Just for backup.

Princess and her escort get up together. She pauses at our table, holding his hand.

"How was your trip?" she asks.

"The fighting continues."

"Yes."

Princess and her man walk away to pursue their tryst in the alley, a pickup, some rotten hotel room. She doesn't give us so much as a backward glance. Soon, Darren and I will do the same, put the whole lot of it behind us. The music, the oil workers, the hovels of refugee camps, the killing. All of it. Let it be gone with the daybreak, gone with the rains. What else can we do but wish it away?

There is no promise, Mustapha. You got that right.

KARL TARO GREENFELD

Hope and Squalor
at Chungking Mansion

FROM *WorldHum.com*

CHUNGKING MANSION is the only place I have ever been where it is possible to buy a sexual aid, a bootleg Jay Chou CD, and a new, leather-bound Koran, all from the same bespectacled Kashmiri proprietor who can make change for your purchase in any of five currencies.

It is also possible, while wandering the alleys, hallways, and listing stairwells of Chungking Mansion, to buy a discount ticket to Bombay, purchase two thousand knockoff Tag Heuer watches, or pick up a counterfeit phone card that will allow unlimited calls to Lagos, Nigeria. Need a tattoo? Piercing? Dental work? Yellow fever vaccination? Cialis? No problem, just don't ask to see a pharmacist's license or medical school degree. Or, if your schemes have all run aground and truly desperate measures are called for, you can sell your passport and order up a forged new identity. You can disappear here. Thousands have. Most of them by design.

I was twenty-four when I first visited the Mansion, stopping en route from Tokyo to undetermined points west. My friend Trey and I, encouraged by a blandishing Delhian dwarf wearing an NWA T-shirt, had boarded a shuttle bus from Kai-Tak Airport that deposited us before the dizzyingly busy entrance. He guided us to a fifth floor, B-block guest house, assuring us, "You will be stupendously pleasure with this accommodation," before opening the door to a minivan-sized chamber strewn with loose electric wiring and a sort of fecal mildew staining the walls.

There was a sit-down toilet, on which the previous tenant's footprints were still visible on the plastic seat, and a working hand shower of sorts. Plus, it was hard to beat the price in famously expensive Hong Kong — about five bucks a night. Within two hours, we'd fallen in with a Canadian man who described himself as a "Leftenant-General" and told us he knew where we could get injected with a mixture of one part snake's blood and one part Demerol.

"Wouldn't that kill us?" we asked.

"Demerol?"

The Leftenant-General shook his head. "Best painkiller in the world."

"No, the snake's blood."

"Hasn't done so yet," he assured us, thumping the chest of his safari vest.

For hundreds of thousands of visitors and immigrants to Hong Kong, Chungking Mansion provides the first way station into what has been known since the 1997 handover to China as the Special Autonomous Region. Take everything that Disney's Epcot Center represents — the squeaky-clean, child-safe, good-natured cheer of painless globalism — and then cover it in mutton fat, dope resin, and human excrement and you'll get Chungking Mansion. Known as "The Armpit of Asia," Chungking Mansion is the claustrophobic home for about twenty thousand residents from all over the globe. Yet the Mansion also provides a glimpse into one possible overpopulated, multiethnic future for all of us. This seventeen-story bazaar of curry stalls, discount electronics vendors, pirated CD and video CD stores, brothels, meth dens, and guest houses provides a glimpse of a dystopian, posttechnology future where tribes, cultures, and races coexist in bustling, jumbled squalor.

Think *Blade Runner* or *The Matrix*, set up by a Bollywood production company and recast and reshot by John Woo. It's not just the tiny rooms and dim halls and perpetual damp and the wires and phone lines running up and down and across every vertical surface; there is also a sense of displacement and a vague anxiety that wash over you as you thread your way between Pakistani businessmen carrying bulging suitcases stuffed with pirated video CDs and a trio of over-made-up, platinum blonde Russian working girls squeezed into impossibly tight red and black leather catsuits. Here are the turbaned and beaded and mustachioed masses, displaying everything that is glorious and terrifying about a truly multiethnic world. The cliques of barrel-chested Nigerians hanging out beside the traffic-jammed road, the gangly Bangladeshi touts on the stairs, the Chinese hookers by the money-changing queues talking on cell phones — it is exhilarating and confusing all at once. Yes, you discover, we can all get along. But it will take every ounce of respect, patience, and grace we have to do it.

There actually was a movie set here, 1994's *Chungking Express,* directed by Wong Kar Wai, an anthology about Indian drug smugglers, Chinese cops, and short-order cooks. "The place was always a mystery to me," says Kar Wai, who grew up in the Tsim Sha Tsui area of Kowloon, in the shadow of the Mansion. "The people living in and living on it seemed very different from those I encountered. You can't help but have fantasies about what was actually happening inside. Of course, as a child, I was prohibited by my parents from visiting the place."

No one seems to remember the building's architect, and the Hong Kong Land Development Corporation has no record of the original design. Perhaps the architect would prefer to remain anonymous, for among the structure's foibles is that all public space, and plenty of private apartments as well, receive no natural lighting. According to Valerie Portefaix, a Hong Kong architect and coauthor of *Mapping HK,* it would be geometrically impossible to create a darker building. Day and night blur within the Mansion; neon streetlights serve as stark illumination for the dim halls and stairwells.

Yet the five-building complex, dubbed a "Mansion" by its optimistic developer in 1961, was intended as spacious, affordable housing for the new, monied, urban classes of the then bustling British colony. In a promotional sketch from the early '60s, the city-block-sized development appears as a glittering monument to Hong Kong's capitalist potential: sturdy, white towers with generous plazas on the first three floors dwarf every other building in the neighborhood. English army officers and Chinese actresses once inhabited the tony flats along Nathan Road, just around the corner from The Peninsula, one of the most expensive hotels in the world. Ironically, the generous (for Hong Kong) square footage of the flats may have been one reason the Mansion began its slouching descent. In the late '60s, Indians and other Commonwealth citizens moved into the apartments, and a few decided to subdivide the 1,100 square foot units into guest houses to maximize occupancy and revenue.

At the time, Hong Kong was emerging as the back end of the hippie travel circuit that ran from Istanbul straight through Asia. Western travelers, depleted by Indian heat and Afghani hash, bivouacked at the Mansion to replenish, refit, maybe visit a dentist or tailor, and buy an air ticket before moving on. Gradually, merchants opened up offering each and every one of these services, as well as a few more illicit trades that the predominantly male clientele might support.

"When I arrived here in 1967, it was a sort of backpackers' place, illegal Indian restaurants, brothels, and nightclubs," says Arthur Hacker, author of *The Hong Kong Visitor's Book*. "Whatever you wanted: drugs, to see a naughty show, a blue movie, there were always the usual heroin and hashish." By the 1970s, the English and Chinese families had moved on. The original landlord, fed up with what was becoming an increasingly chaotic piece of real estate, sold off shares in the building to the new owners, who continued to subdivide, jury-rig, and partition so that the current floor plan bears no resemblance to whatever the developers had envisioned.

Today, the building is strikingly out of place on a street of posh Bally and Versace boutiques; it sits on arguably some of the most valuable real estate in the world. However, with over nine hundred owners holding shares of the building, the ownership structure is so confused that purchasing and developing the property is virtually impossible.

The ratty, exhaust-colored façade of the building features a thousand air conditioners leaking metallic water, a hundred windows punched seemingly at random through the ferro-concrete, and a dozen rickety balconies piled with offal and empty crates. Reminders of past tenants can be made out in fading painted signs: CHAK MAI IVORY FACTORY, FREEZINHOT BOTTLE COMPANY, and YUM-YUM FILTERS, among others. Over the years, tenants and owners have laid hundreds of miles of questionable wiring and run a few million gallons of water through improvised PVC and bamboo piping. The Hong Kong Department of Water and Power has made efforts over the years to regulate the mess, but a quick trip up any of the stairwells reveals tangled wiring and dense shrubs of telephone and DSL line, all mashed into corners and sometimes sparking ominously amid thick, sedimentary layers of trash. Fire is a scourge of the Mansion. The worst fire occurred in 1989, when eleven people died in a blaze on the lower floors.

The police sweep the Mansion from time to time, seeking to flush out those who have overstayed visas, as well as to crack down on drug dealing. One-girl brothels, called *yat lou yat fung* in Cantonese, are legal in Hong Kong. Besides this legal loophole, the Mansion's layout makes it difficult for the police to bust hookers or drug dealers. Only two creaking elevators serve each building, which forces police to climb the stairs. As most of the unsavory elements of the building operate out of the higher floors, by the time officers have huffed and puffed their way to the seventeenth floor, the perpetrators and hustlers, alerted by cell phones and pagers, are long gone down interior stairwells.

Talk to locals and residents and they'll tell you about the stabbings and heroin trade, the padlocks they pile onto their doors to protect themselves from crime.

So why do thousands of Western tourists, some of whom could afford better lodging, still shack up at the Mansion?

Like Bangkok's Khao San Road or Jakarta's Jalan Jaksa, Chungking has become a legendary jumping-off point, the same seedy rooms used to plot a thousand getaways, and not just for a holiday but for a whole new life. These tiny rooms represent a nadir of sorts. Most of those passing through Chungking Mansion are very far from home and at the end of a run of horrendous bad luck. You don't show up at the Mansion on a winning streak. There are approximately eighty guest houses and microhotels in the Mansion, and if you're here in one of the five-by-ten cubicles, chances are you weren't a Brahmin back home in Boston or Bengal. The Indians, Pakistanis, Russians, Bangladeshis, or Nigerians — none of them were born into their indigenous privileged classes, and so they've struck out, hopeful of prosperity in this hustling, little "autonomous zone." And because these tiny rooms are a last resort, they become a sort of landing zone. In the swelter and squalor — threadbare mattresses you hope aren't bug infested, a toilet, no seat — your mind hatches subtle schemes to improve your lot, plans to get out and up from here.

We never did try that snake's blood injection. But after some goading from the Leftenant-General, we bought a bag of dubious-looking grey matter that he assured us were magic mushrooms. On a bright afternoon, we brewed some mushroom chai on a borrowed hot plate and drank a hideous-tasting tea that did little more than put us to sleep for about twenty hours. When we woke up, we hurriedly checked our wallets, passports, and plane tickets, and finding everything intact, packed up and took the elevator downstairs. While we were waiting to hail a cab to the airport, we ran into the Leftenant-General one more time. He told us we were leaving one day too early. He had a line on some Ecstasy.

"It'll be even better than those mushrooms," he assured us.

"How long have you been at the Mansion?" I asked.

He shrugged. "Eight months."

We caught a taxi and then our discount flight to Bangkok. We'd bought the tickets at a Chungking Mansion travel agent. And we'd gotten a great deal.

Dark Passage

FROM *National Geographic*

"I CAN SMELL THE SEA FROM HERE," says the prisoner. That seems a wild improbability coming from a man in a soundproof cell in northern Malaysia, several miles as the gull flies from the closest salt water. All I can smell in this humid, whitewashed prison is the faint tang of ammonia used to clean the floors.

It is hard to know what to believe of the prisoner's claims. At times he has declared his innocence and then later confessed to being a willing criminal. He mentions he has three children, later the number is four. His passport lists his name as Johan Ariffin, but Malaysian authorities doubt that's his real name. His age is noted as forty-four (streaks of gray in his black hair make that plausible) and his residence as Batam, an Indonesian island just south of Singapore. Men like him often come from Batam, a guard says.

Though his jailers remain unsure who he is, they know exactly what he is: *lanun* (pronounced la-noon). When asked for a direct English equivalent, an interpreter explains that there is none, that it is a word freighted with many layers of culture and history. The short, imperfect answer is: The prisoner is a pirate.

He earned that epithet when Malaysia's marine police captured him and nine accomplices after they hijacked the *Nepline Delima*, a tanker carrying seven thousand tons of diesel fuel worth $3 million, in the Strait of Malacca. It was one of several attacks reported during 2005 in the 550-mile channel separating the Indonesian island of Sumatra from the Malay Peninsula, Singapore perched at its southern tip.

For centuries, this sliver of ocean has captivated seamen, offering the most direct route between India and China, along with a bounty of resources, including spices, rubber, mahogany, and tin. But it is a watery kingdom unto itself, harboring hundreds of rivers that feed into the channel, miles of swampy shoreline, and a vast constellation of tiny islands, reefs, and shoals. Its early inhabitants learned to lead amphibian lives, building their villages over water and devising specialized boats for fishing, trading, and warfare. Some made their living as pirates, preying on foreign vessels that dared to ply their waters. Armadas of these skilled sea raiders in light, maneuverable craft regularly plundered passing ships and retreated upriver to fortified villages. Their raids yielded troves of gold, gems, gunpowder, opium, and slaves, which they used to build powerful sultanates that dominated much of the Sumatran and Malaysian coastlines.

Sailors chronicled the horrors they faced in the strait and nearby waters. One nineteenth-century episode involved the capture of British Captain James Ross. Believing his ship held a stash of silver coins, *lanun* forced him to watch as his young son was lashed to an anchor and drowned. Then they cut off Ross's fingers joint by joint.

European colonizers and their navies brought the sultanates under control in the late 1800s, but the *lanun* were never eradicated. The twenty-first-century inheritors of their tradition continue to hunt these waters, mainly in three incarnations: gangs that board vessels to rob the crews; multinational syndicates that steal entire ships; and guerrilla groups that kidnap seamen for ransom.

Modern *lanun* have no shortage of targets. Each year, according to Lloyd's of London, some seventy thousand merchant vessels carrying a fifth of all seaborne trade and a third of the world's crude oil shipments transit this critical choke point in the global economy. The strait's geography makes it nearly unsecurable. It passes between Malaysia and Indonesia, known for thorny relations, further complicating the security picture. Some 250 miles wide at its northern mouth, the strait funnels down to about 10 miles across near its southern end and is dotted with hundreds of uninhabited mangrove islands, offering endless hideouts to all manner of criminals.

Since 2002, the International Maritime Bureau (IMB) has recorded 258 pirate attacks in the Malacca Strait and surrounding waters, including more than two hundred sailors held hostage and eight killed. The insurance arm of Lloyd's classified the strait as a war zone in June 2005. Malaysia, Singapore, and Indonesia responded by bolstering security in their respective waters, and Lloyd's suspended the rating in August 2006.

But counting pirate attacks is murky business. Noel Choong, head of the IMB's Piracy Reporting Centre, estimates that half of all pirate attacks go unreported. "In some cases the ship's owners dissuade the captain from reporting an attack," he says. "They don't want bad publicity or the ship to be delayed by an investigation." As a result, no one knows for sure how many pirates remain active in the Malacca Strait.

Ocean Predator

Which brings us back to Ariffin, who is serving a seven-year prison sentence. A lawyer hired by the Indonesian consulate has been his only visitor. The closest the guards let me get to him is the other side of a scratched, bulletproof window looking onto an interview cell. When the guards bring him in, he isn't the imposing figure I'd envisioned. He stands barely five feet tall, and his open collar reveals a faded heart tattooed on his sagging chest. He looks more like a weary pickpocket than a pirate, confused that a foreigner has requested to see him.

He and my interpreter pick up telephones on either side of the window. I explain that I have read about his case. That I have traveled from the other side of the world to hear his story; to ask him why he became a *lanun*; to hear how it is possible for a handful of men to hijack a ship as large as the *Nepline Delima*.

Ariffin sits silently, the telephone pressed to his ear, his eyes shifting between the interpreter and me, his shirt damp with sweat. "The lawyer took all my money," he says finally. "I have no soap. I haven't brushed my teeth since I got here."

I offer to leave some toiletries for him with the guards. His demeanor brightens, and slowly he begins his story, or at least one version of it.

The plot was hatched in a Batam coffee shop, Ariffin says, when a Malaysian shipping executive approached an Indonesian sailor named Lukman and inquired whether he could organize a crew to hijack the tanker. Ariffin, who went to sea in his teens and rose through the maritime ranks to become a mechanic, had served with Lukman on a few crews. Lately both of them had struggled to find work, and Lukman asked if he wanted in on the heist. It would be an easy job, he promised, because a member of the tanker's crew was in on the plan.

As a young crewman, Ariffin says he was once on a ship attacked by pirates. They waved parangs (machete-like knives), threatened to kill everyone, and took cash and food. He smiles wryly at the irony. "It is very hard for Indonesian seamen. We all need money."

He told Lukman he was in. "All we had to do was board the tanker, tie up the crew, and sail to open sea," Ariffin says. They would meet a tanker coming from Thailand, transfer the fuel, and abandon the *Nepline Delima*. Lukman promised Ariffin $10,000 for manning the tanker's engines.

The plan began smoothly. Posing as tourists, Ariffin, Lukman, and two other seamen from Batam pretended to snap photos as they rode a ferry up the strait to the Malaysian port of Pinang. There they met six other men Lukman had recruited from Aceh, Sumatra's northernmost province. "They weren't seamen," said Ariffin. "We needed their muscles."

At a nearby beach, they stole a fiberglass speedboat, painted it blue, and loaded it with gasoline, water and food, two cell phones, a GPS, and five freshly sharpened parangs. In addition, each man brought a ski mask, a change of clothes, some cash, and a passport. After midnight, they slipped into the strait. Meanwhile, the turncoat crew member was sending text messages from the tanker, updating the ship's position, course, and speed. Most important, Ariffin said, "he told us when he would man the watch."

A few hours later, the pirates, wearing ski masks and wielding parangs, commanded the *Nepline Delima*'s bridge. The tanker's distress signal had been disabled, and sixteen of its seventeen crew lay bound and blindfolded in a locked cabin, some of them bleeding. The pirates set a new course for the Thai tanker on the open sea. By the next evening the gang would be on their way back to what Batam pirates call "happy happy," a blur of hedonism, ranging from extravagant amounts of crystal meth and Ecstasy to marathon sessions with prostitutes. Or, if Ariffin is to be believed, home to his family.

The problem was the seventeenth crewman. Soon after the pirates had boarded the tanker, Ariffin, guarding the speedboat, heard one of the sailors yell: *"Lanun!"* Bedlam erupted on the ship's decks as the pirates tried to round up the frightened crew. Lukman and two others were on the bridge. They switched on the public address system and started beating the captain until his shouts for the crew to surrender blared over the ship's loudspeakers. "Please, they are killing me," he cried. Sixteen crewmen eventually gave up. Each was asked his name, then bound and blindfolded. "We had a copy of the ship's manifest," said Ariffin, "we knew one was missing."

Meanwhile, the sea had picked up. Ariffin tied the speedboat to the tanker's railing and scrambled aboard to find the engine room. It was there, an hour later, that he got a frantic call from Lukman on the bridge. The missing crewman had escaped in their speedboat, stranding them on the tanker. Ariffin ran the *Nepline Delima*'s engines at full throttle trying to reach international waters, but even at top speed the tanker could make only about twelve miles an hour. Within a few hours the Malaysian marine police had cut off their escape. Ariffin went up on the deck and lit a cigarette. "There was nothing to do," he said. "Allah had his hand on that sailor."

A guard signals that our time is up. I hurriedly tell Ariffin about my plans to visit Batam. The guard puts his hand on Ariffin's shoulder. The prisoner squeezes the phone. For the first time, I notice his muscular forearms. He speaks quickly before the guard leads him away.

"He said go to the coffee shop behind the Harmoni Hotel," says the interpreter. "Tell the seamen there that John Palembang said hello. And don't forget about the toothbrush."

Cinderella's Dark Sister

"You want girls?" the cab driver asked on our way to Nagoya, one of Batam Island's largest towns. "Drugs?" He caught my eye in the rearview mirror. "I can get for you. Everything. No problem."

If Singapore, just seven miles to the north with its glittering skyline and robust economy, is Southeast Asia's Cinderella, Batam is her dark sister. The two are located across from each other where the Malacca Strait feeds into the smaller Singapore Strait, and a ceaseless parade of ships, more than a thousand a week, passes between them. Most do business in Singapore, home to one of the world's preeminent free ports and expanding financial and technology sectors.

In the 1980s Indonesia tried to mimic Singapore's success and began to transform Batam, one of the Riau islands off Sumatra's eastern coast, from a malaria-ridden fishing outpost into a tariff-free zone for entrepreneurs. Developers carved golf courses out of jungles and built casinos to lure tourists from Malaysia and Singapore. Investors backed factories and strip malls, office parks and apartment blocks. Indonesians flocked to boomtown Batam to find work. The island became a hub for maritime brokers, who hired sailors for shipping companies.

Batam, however, lacked Singapore's strict rule of law. Patronage and corruption took hold, and the island quickly became a haven for an exotic assortment of gangsters, smugglers, prostitutes, and pirates. Illegally harvested timber, embezzled diesel fuel, stolen cars, drugs, weapons, and poached animals moved through its ports. Droves of Singaporean men ferried over on weekends to visit the growing number of brothels filled with impoverished girls. Meanwhile, some of the maritime brokers quietly engaged in their own side business: recruiting pirates for Asian crime syndicates. In 1997 the boom went bust when the Asian financial crisis hit. The investment money evaporated from Batam, leaving the island littered with abandoned construction sites. Unemployment rose, driving more people to the black economy. Though in the past couple of years investors had begun returning, the island still harbored a large class of residents who could only be described as desperate.

I asked the cab driver about the coffee shop behind the Harmoni Hotel. It's in Jodoh, he said, referring to Nagoya's seediest precinct. "Many murders there. Better you call me and I bring girls to you."

Phantom Swiftlets

The first sounds one hears during a morning walk through Jodoh's narrow avenues are the whistles of swiftlets. Even the vendors hawking fruit, secondhand clothing, and used appliances smuggled from Singapore can't compete with the ebullient birdsong. It is one of

Jodoh's many deceptions: the mating calls are taped and broadcast over loudspeakers to attract real swiftlets to build nests in the empty top floors of numerous buildings. The nests are harvested and each sold for hundreds of dollars to restaurants for bird's nest soup.

Another deception is the "coffee shop," a euphemism for the gambling dens where seamen meet brokers, trade gossip, drink beer, and bet a numbers game. However, in the year since Johan Ariffin, née John Palembang, has been in prison, much had changed in Batam. Most notably, Indonesia's new police chief has cracked down on gambling on the island, much to the detriment of the tourist trade, which relied on the stream of Singaporeans who filled Batam's resorts. When I arrived at the coffee shop behind the Harmoni, its windows were blacked and the front door was chained. This might have dimmed my hopes for finding John Palembang's friends had it not been for Jhonny Batam. I'd been given his name — one of his names — by someone he trusted. He was described as a gentleman of opportunity. A ship captain by trade, he had piloted vessels for both legitimate companies and less scrupulous entities. He was said to know every ship in port and every coffee shop deal in Batam. If anyone knew John Palembang, it would be Jhonny Batam.

At first, contacting him was like chasing one of Jodoh's phantom swiftlets. Calls to his cell phone went unanswered until finally one morning he phoned to say he was stranded on Bangka Island, south of the Malacca Strait. Some "business" had gone badly, and he was broke. I agreed to wire him $80 for a plane ticket back to Batam.

As agreed, Jhonny Batam appeared the next day on a backstreet near a row of butcher shops. Animal blood ran in the gutters beneath the stifling odors of fresh meat. Jhonny, a handsome, bearish man in his fifties, wore an immaculate white sports shirt and pressed slacks, his wavy black hair perfectly coiffed. A fake gold Rolex dangled around his wrist, and he might have passed as a golf pro if not for the tattoos inscribed on his knuckles.

In a nearby restaurant, he said he knew John Palembang, whom he called a low-level seaman. The coffee shop grapevine had laughed at news of the *Nepline Delima* fiasco. "Amateurs," Jhonny scoffed. He began to describe his own career, how he had piloted tugboats and a ferry before taking the helm of a small cargo vessel. In time, he built a network of friends among sailors and harbor workers. Along the way he took side jobs, smuggling untaxed garlic, cigarettes, electronics, and drugs. In the 1980s, he relocated to Hong Kong to work for Chinese crime syndicates. There his repertoire broadened to include making large cargoes "disappear."

He estimated that 75 percent of heisted cargoes were inside jobs involving the ship's crew, often the captain. "That's why most are not reported," he said, explaining that shipping companies often write off these losses rather than suffer bad press and risk losing their insurance.

It works like this, he said. A ship broker would call him and say there's a customer who needs diesel fuel. "I know a crewman on a tanker," Jhonny says. "I call his hand phone and ask him if he is happy. If he says yes, no problem. But if he says no, I tell him I make him happy, and then we make a plan." But the crewman won't work legitimately again, I said. He laughed. "Seamen have lots of names. Some have three or four passports. No problem."

Over two weeks, I interviewed several of Jhonny's former crewmen spread among the Riau Archipelago and a captain who knew him in Hong Kong. All corroborated what Jhonny told me. One sailor said he trusted Jhonny because "he never lies. He always pays what he says he will pay. Sometimes the legal ships don't do that."

In my hotel room, we laid a map of the Malacca Strait on the bed. Jhonny's thick fingers traced the coastlines with practiced familiarity. He pointed to places with obscured shoals and noted currents and unmapped islands. "This area," he drew his finger around Batam and Singapore, "too many patrols now." He moved his finger to a spot south of the strait, "now the best place for shopping is here."

"Shopping," Batam argot for the lowest level of piracy, is roughly equivalent to robbing a liquor store. Even the smallest cargo ships and tankers carry sizable amounts of cash, used to buy supplies in port and to pay the crew. Often these ships are older and have less security than newer, larger ships. Sometimes, Jhonny says, the captains are running their own scams, conserving fuel by going slow, then selling the excess to passing ships and pocketing the cash. He explained that shopping trips are carried out by teams of "jumping squirrels," pirates who use wooden boats called *pancungs*, rigged with powerful engines, to stalk the ships at night and climb up the sides and rob the crew. I tell him I would like to meet a jumping squirrel. "It's possible," he said, and dialed a number.

Bulletproof Jumping Squirrels

It was dark when a slender young man with bleached highlights in his short dark hair and a small silver hoop in his left ear knocked on the door. He looked stunned to be greeted by a foreigner and grinned nervously at Jhonny, his smile marked by the black, ragged edge of a rotted front tooth. "Is this dangerous?" he asked.

Jhonny introduced him as Beach Boy. With his bronze skin, athletic physique, and large waterproof watch, he looked the part. Just ten months out of an Indonesian prison, Beach Boy had served two years for his role in hijacking a barge carrying more than a million dollars' worth of crude palm oil. After making off with the cargo, his gang scattered. But Beach Boy's accomplices betrayed him to the police. Once in custody, he says he was interrogated, beaten, and shot in the leg. He rolled up his left pant leg to reveal a fist-size scar on his calf. "The bullet is still in there," he said. Yet the most painful consequence of his prison term, he said, was the loss of his family. His wife wrote him in prison that she had left him for another man.

I asked Beach Boy why he had become a pirate. "I can't get work," he said. Jhonny explained that Indonesian sailors often lacked the maritime certifications required to work on commercial ships. For years, young men like Beach Boy relied on older seamen to teach them the trade and then obtained counterfeit credentials to avoid the expensive training needed to become legally licensed seamen. But in recent years the international shipping community had clamped down on such practices, leaving many experienced Batam sailors unemployed.

I pressed him on how his team was able to board ships undetected. "We use magic," he said. "We cast a spell to make the crew stay asleep. We can be invisible, bulletproof." He pointed to his head. "It's a power that you learn." Then how did you get shot, I asked. "They fired twice," he said. "I resisted the first bullet but wasn't strong enough for the second."

Later that night at an outdoor café, Jhonny and I loitered over a few beers, and he revealed that he believed in mathematics, not magic. He borrowed a pen and on a napkin demonstrated how he could reduce my telephone number, or any seven-digit figure, to the number eight using a series of equations. "It looks like magic," he said. "But it is mathematics." Numbers, he said, always had fascinated him. As a boy he'd memorized several of these numeric parlor tricks and later taught himself algebra and geometry. At sea he'd come to trust numbers far more than superstitions. They told him how far he traveled, when to turn, how much fuel his ship needed, how hard the wind blew. Numbers were predictable, accountable, reliable — qualities that were hard to come by in Jhonny's world.

He continued to doodle on the napkin and asked if I'd heard of the golden mean, which he described as a ratio discovered by Greek mathematicians that represents perfect balance. Riau seamen had their own golden mean, he said, which measured the tipping point between working within the bounds of the law versus working illegally. As long as this Malaccan version of the golden mean favored robbing ships, there would be pirates in the strait.

Pirate Training

A few days later, Jhonny, Beach Boy, and I caught a cab to the port. Beach Boy had arranged to show me how a team of jumping squirrels boarded a ship. He said there was an uninhabited island not far from Batam where he occasionally trained.

At the end of a sun-bleached jetty, two muscular young men, "Muhammad" and "Hakim," waited for us in a wooden *pancung*. Beach Boy explained that these boats were ideal because their weight and shape let them cut through a ship's wake, unlike fiberglass boats, which were much lighter and would bounce in rough water.

We sat in the boat, two by two, and I ended up next to Muhammad. His round cheeks and perfect teeth gave him a boyish appearance, but weeks before he had completed a two-year prison term for his role in a shopping trip. "Are you ready to learn how to steal a ship?" he asked.

With the sun beating on our shoulders, Hakim steered out of the harbor and made for a dense forest that appeared to be floating on top of the water, one of the strait's innumerable mangrove islands. It seemed an impenetrable mass of gnarled roots and tangled limbs,

but Hakim found a little cut and piloted the boat into the labyrinth. It was cool inside the mangroves, and we slipped in and out
of deep shadows following the watery path until it opened on a
cloister of stilt houses. *"Assalamu alaikum,"* Hakim called out. No
answer. He cut the engine. Beach Boy grabbed a limb and held the
boat steady as Hakim drew a parang, its curved blade glistening
with oil used to keep it razor sharp. With quick, latent blows Hakim
chopped out a two-foot section of a root and tossed it into the
pancung.

We navigated out of the mangroves and headed for a small island
about a mile away. Once ashore, Beach Boy disappeared into its
dense jungle. The rest of us remained on the beach, which had a
broad view of the shipping channel. Nine vessels chugged through
the strait, including a liquefied natural gas tanker that towered
over the others like a skyscraper. The Singapore skyline loomed beyond. "A few years ago this was a favorite place to begin an attack.
Now there are too many patrols," said Muhammad, flashing his
perfect teeth, "but there are other places." I asked him why he'd
gotten into piracy. "Partly for the money," he said, "but it is fun, an
adventure, like James Bond."

Beach Boy emerged from the jungle with a twenty-foot-long bamboo stalk. He stripped the shoots off the bamboo, while Hakim
used the parang to hew the mangrove root into a footlong spike.
When they finished, Hakim lashed the spike at an angle to the end
of the bamboo. "This is how we climb onto the ship," Beach Boy
said, motioning to a nearby tree as if it were the side of a ship. "The
tekong [driver] maneuvers the *pancung* right up to the stern," he
said, lifting the pole and hooking the spike onto an upper branch.

In one fluid motion he grabbed the pole with both hands and
pulled himself upward, lifting his legs, then clasping the bamboo
with his feet and driving his body upward inchworm fashion. In seconds he reached the top and then slid down the pole. "This is how
five jumping squirrels can all board a ship in less than a minute."
He handed me the pole. "Now you try."

I kicked off my shoes and copied the technique. The bamboo's
natural joints offered a good grip, even when wet, and its stiffness
made it easier to climb than a rope. To reach the decks of taller
ships, Beach Boy said they would lash two or three bamboos together. I reached the top and slid down. "You could be a pirate,"
Muhammad said. The others laughed. I started to put on my shoes

when I felt a powerful grip on my shoulder and a cold blade of a parang on the back of my neck. "Then you grab the first sailor you see," Muhammad barked in my ear, "tell me where the money is." My heart skipped a beat before I realized he was just demonstrating the next step in an attack. "And the sailor will follow you like a water buffalo."

Back in the *pancung*, we headed for Batam, but as we approached the harbor, Hakim veered toward one of the hulking cargo ships anchored just outside. Crewmen were hanging wash on the railing. Beach Boy waved, and the sailors lazily waved back. Hakim maneuvered the *pancung* to the ship's stern and drew up beside the rudder. "This is the hole," Muhammad said, his voice echoing off the steel hull. "The crew can't see us here." I looked up and saw that the curving hull shielded the *pancung* from the deck. "When the ship is moving, the water is very rough here." He pointed to a spot on the surface over the ship's massive propeller. "The *tekong* has to hold the *pancung* steady while we raise the bamboo and climb up. That's why the *tekong* always gets the biggest share of the money."

"But you have to board the ship, subdue the crew, find the money, and not get killed," I said. "That's easy," he said. "Are you ready to try?"

Happy Happy

Back in Batam, Jhonny and Beach Boy offered to show me where pirates would go to get "happy happy." Jhonny and others told me that after major heists pirates would often jet off to luxury hotels in Jakarta and blow big wads of cash on unimaginable indulgences, including a strip club where you could eat sushi off the bellies of the dancers. But after a shopping trip, Batam pirates might celebrate at one of the local karaoke bars. "We will go to Die Nasty," said Jhonny. Beach Boy nodded.

Late that night, the three of us walked through Jodoh's dark streets, where beckoning young women in low-cut blouses vamped under lighted signs advertising karaoke. We arrived at our destination, which turned out to be a club called Dynasty. The dank room smelled of clove cigarettes and was dimly lit with orange bulbs that cast a lurid glow. A waitress escorted us to a table and brought over beers. Beach Boy scanned the menu of songs that customers could request to sing. Along the far wall, a row of young women sat beneath a line of spotlights. Each wore a round badge with a number. They giggled coquettishly, competing to make eye contact with us. "Karaoke hostesses," Jhonny explained. He went over to the women and made his way down the line, smiling and chatting. Finally he returned with a young woman who settled between Jhonny and me.

"What your name?" the woman asked in heavily accented English, patting my thigh. I told her and mentioned that I was here just for the karaoke. "Yes," she said, "everyone come to Die Nasty for karaoke."

Beach Boy selected his songs, and the waitress came over with the microphone. The music began and the lyrics to Led Zeppelin's "Stairway to Heaven" were projected onto a large screen. "There's a lady who's sure all that glitters is gold, and she's buying a stairway to heaven." Sitting in the dark, holding the microphone close to his mouth, Beach Boy seemed transformed. He closed his eyes and crooned in a pleasing tenor. "Ooh, it makes me wonder."

The girl next to me leaned close. I could smell her perfume mingled with the alcohol on her breath. "Please can you help me? I am ugliest girl at Die Nasty. I have no customer in two week." She said she had to pay the owner of the club each month for room and board and to reimburse the cost of her travel to Batam from her village in eastern Java. I slipped her a little cash.

Jhonny finally took the microphone. By this time there were a few empty bottles in front of him, and his mood was effervescent, joking with the karaoke hostesses, teasing the waitress, buying drinks. He sang an old Rod Stewart song, "Sailing," but halfway through I noticed he wasn't following the English lyrics. He seemed to be singing in Indonesian and making up the words as he went. Everyone was laughing until the chorus came back, and he returned to the lyrics on the screen. He waved his arms, motioning us all to join in, and soon everyone at the Die Nasty was in Jhonny Batam's thrall.

The Seventeenth Crewman

One sailor who was never charmed by a pirate was Mohamed Hamid. He was the crewman who escaped from the *Nepline Delima* and led the police back to rescue the crew. I went to visit him at his home in Malaysia, far from the Malacca Strait. The experience had pushed him to abandon a promising career as a sailor at age twenty-eight. He asked me not to reveal his village because he fears retribution.

We sat on mats on the porch of his father's stilt house, and he recounted what he called the most frightening night of his life. He heard the captain's pleas over the loudspeakers and was on his way to the bridge to surrender when one of the pirates suddenly put a knife to his throat. "I thought this is my death," he said, but instinct took over and he hit the pirate with an elbow, jumped down three flights of stairs, and scurried under some pipes on the main deck. He lay there reciting Muslim prayers, trying to compose himself, when he saw the rope tied to the railing leading to the pirates' speedboat.

He described his escape as almost comical. He caught his foot on the railing and fell into the speedboat. Then it took several agonizing minutes to cut the thick rope with a dull pocketknife. Afterward he lay sweating in the bottom of the boat as it drifted from the tanker into total darkness. Feeling his way to the stern, he traced the wires from the motor to the ignition switch. Clouds obscured the stars that would have guided him to land; rain began to fall. In the distance he could still hear the cries of his captain over the tanker's loudspeakers as the pirates beat him. "I prayed to Allah, 'You brought me this far, please show me the way.'" He cranked the engine and hoped he was headed toward help.

Less than twenty-four hours later, Hamid was hailed as a hero. He had reached the Malaysian island of Langkawi and had been able to guide the marine police back to the *Nepline Delima*. After a tense standoff, all ten pirates surrendered.

Eventually nine of them received jail sentences. One pleaded not guilty and is still awaiting trial. The shipping executive and the alleged conspirator on the *Nepline Delima* were arrested. Both say they are innocent. Their trials are pending. Hamid was stunned to learn of the charges against his fellow crewman. "It was like finding out the devil is your brother."

Two Months Later

I was back in the United States at a wedding reception when my phone vibrated with a text message from Jhonny Batam: "Got job as master on motor tanker . . . Jhon." Guests were climbing on stage to sing with the band, and for a moment I was back at the Die Nasty watching Jhonny and Beach Boy sing karaoke. No pirate attacks had been reported in the Malacca Strait since I left. Indonesia and Malaysia had called on foreign governments to help fund their patrols. Without more resources, it is unclear how long the cash-strapped Indonesian navy will maintain its current level of vigilance.

As for the fate of this tanker, maybe, I told myself, Jhonny had embarked on a new path, thankful for legal work, loyally serving his new employer. But if there were more money to be made working another angle, I could hear him say, one must be true to the pirate's golden mean. After all, Jhonny Batam is a gentleman of opportunity.

PETER HESSLER

Wheels of Fortune

FROM *The New Yorker*

THE FIRST ACCIDENT wasn't my fault. I had rented a Volkswagen Jetta and driven to my weekend home in Sancha, a village north of Beijing. I parked at the end of the road, where the pavement widens into an empty lot. It's impossible to drive within Sancha; like virtually all Chinese villages, it was built before anybody had cars, and homes are linked by narrow footpaths.

About an hour after I arrived, my neighbor asked me to move the car, because the villagers were about to mix cement in the lot. That day, Leslie, my wife, and I were both on our computers, trying to do some writing.

"I can move it if you want," my neighbor said. His name is Wei Ziqi, and he had recently completed a driving course and received his license. It was his proudest achievement — he was one of the first in the village to learn to drive. I handed him the keys and sat back down at my computer. Half an hour later, he returned and stood in the doorway silently. I asked if everything was all right.

"There's a problem with the car," he said slowly. He was smiling, but it was a tight Chinese grin of embarrassment, the kind of expression that makes your pulse quicken.

"What kind of problem?" I said.

"I think you should come see it."

In the lot, a couple of villagers were staring at the car; they were grinning, too. The front bumper had been knocked completely off. It lay on the road, leaving the Jetta's grille gaping, like a child who's lost three teeth and can't stop smiling. Why did everybody look so goddamn happy?

"I forgot about the front end," Wei Ziqi said.

"What do you mean?" I asked.

"I'm not used to driving something with a front end," he said. "During my course, we only drove Liberation trucks. They were flat in front."

I had parked the Jetta parallel to a wall, and he had backed up and turned the wheel sharply, not realizing that the front end would swing in the opposite direction. I knelt down and inspected the bumper — it was hopelessly bent.

He got some wire and tied the bumper to the front end. He offered repeatedly to pay for it, but I told him not to worry; I'd deal with the rental company. The next day, I set off to return the car.

Driving is something that I take very seriously. When I turned sixteen, I was told that handling an automobile is a privilege and a responsibility, and I still get nervous thinking about the day that my mother drove me to the Wilkes Boulevard United Methodist Church, in Columbia, Missouri, to take my first driving exam. The state's Division of Motor Vehicles rented office space in the building, and the exam began and ended in the church parking lot. In mid-Missouri, it was widely known that when it came to judging sixteen-year-old males the D.M.V. was even tougher than the Methodists. They failed boys for not checking the blind spot, for running yellow lights, for tiny adjustments on parallel parking. There were rumors that any boy who was visibly confident would flunk — if you believed that you were predestined for a license, then the folks at the Wilkes Boulevard United Methodist Church would prove otherwise. I took the test in my family's Dodge Caravan, and afterward the examiner gave me a stern speech. It began with the statement "You're lucky we don't professionally evaluate you," and ended with "I hope I don't see you in the hospital someday." Between these remarks, the man acknowledged that I had passed by the barest of margins, and that was all that mattered. There was no purgatory at the D.M.V. You either failed or you passed, and success meant that, as long as you avoided trouble and kept up the paperwork, you'd never have to take another driving exam in the state of Missouri.

After moving to Beijing, I was surprised that my Missouri license had some currency in the People's Republic. The country was in the early stages of an auto boom; Beijing alone now registers almost a thousand new drivers every day. All Chinese applicants are required to have a medical checkup, take a written exam, complete a technical course, and then pass two driving tests. But the process has been pared down for any foreigner who already has certification from his home country. These days, a driver from overseas takes only a written exam, but in 2001, when I applied, I had to pass a special foreigner's road test. The examiner was in his midforties, and he wore white cotton driving gloves with tobacco stains on the fingers. He lit up a Red Pagoda Mountain cigarette as soon as I got in the car. It was a Volkswagen Santana, the nation's most popular passenger vehicle at the time.

"Start the car," the man said, and I turned the key. "Drive forward," he said.

We were north of the city, in a neighborhood that had been cleared of all traffic — no cars, no bikes, no pedestrians. It was the most peaceful street I'd ever seen in the capital, and I wish I could have savored it. But after fifty yards the examiner spoke again. "Pull over," he said. "Turn off the car."

The Santana fell silent; the man filled out forms, his pen moving efficiently. He had barely burned through the tip of his Red Pagoda Mountain. "Is that all?" I said.

"That's it," the man said. He asked me where I had learned Chinese, and we chatted for a while. One of the last things he said to me was "You're a very good driver."

That summer, I began renting cars from a company in southeastern Beijing. The car rental industry was a new one; five years earlier, almost nobody in the capital would have thought of renting an automobile for a weekend trip. But now my local company had a fleet of about fifty vehicles, mostly Chinese-made Jettas and Santanas. Usually, I rented a Jetta, which cost $25 per day and involved an enormous amount of paperwork. The most elaborate part of the process was a survey of the car's exterior, led by an employee, who recorded dents and scratches on a diagram. This inspection often took a while — the Jetta is a small automobile, but Beijing traffic made the most of the limited canvas. After documenting the damage, the employee turned the key in the ignition and showed me the gas gauge. Sometimes it was half full; sometimes there was a quarter tank. Sometimes he studied it and announced, "Three-eighths." It was my responsibility to return the car with exactly the same amount of fuel. One day, I decided to make a contribution to the fledgling industry.

"You should rent cars with a full tank, and then require the customer to bring it back full," I said. "That's how rental companies do it in America."

"That would never work here," said the employee who usually handled my rental, whom I'll call Mr. Liu. He was a big man with thinning hair that flopped loosely over a wide forehead; he always seemed to be in a good mood. He sat with two other men in the front office, where they smoked cigarettes as if it were a competition. The room was so full of smoke that I could hardly read the company evaluation sign that hung on the wall:

> CUSTOMER SATISFACTION RATING: 90%
> EFFICIENCY RATING: 97%
> APPROPRIATE SERVICE DICTION RATING: 98%
> SERVICE ATTITUDE RATING: 99%

"That might work in America, but it wouldn't work here," Mr. Liu continued. "People in China would return the car empty."

"Then you charge them a lot extra to refill it," I said. "They'll learn."

"You don't understand Chinese people!" Mr. Liu said, laughing, and the other men nodded. As a foreigner, I often heard that statement, and it had a way of ending discussion. The Chinese people had invented the compass, silk, paper, gunpowder, the seismoscope; they had sailed to Africa in the fifteenth century; they had built the Great Wall; in the past decade they had expanded their economy at a rate never before seen in the developing world. They could return a rental car with exactly three-eighths of a tank of gas, but filling it was apparently beyond the realm of possibility. Finally, I dropped the subject. There was no way to argue with somebody as friendly as Mr. Liu.

He seemed especially cheerful when I returned the Jetta with the ruined bumper. In the past, I had brought back cars with new dents; this was inevitable in a city with more than two million cars, most of them handled by rookies. But I had never done any serious damage, and Mr. Liu's eyes grew wide when he saw the Jetta. "Waah!" he said. "How did you do that?"

"I didn't." I described Wei Ziqi's lack of experience with hooded cars, and Mr. Liu looked confused; the more I expanded on this topic, the blanker his expression became. At last, I abandoned the front end — I offered to pay for the bumper.

"Mei wenti!" Mr. Liu said, smiling. "No problem! We have insurance! You just need to write an accident report. Do you have your chop?"

I told Mr. Liu that my chop — an official stamp registered to one's work unit, in my case *The New Yorker* — was at home.

"No problem! Just bring it next time." He opened a drawer and pulled out a stack of papers; each was blank except for a red stamp. Mr. Liu rifled through the pile, selected one, and laid it in front of me. The chop read, "U.S.-China Tractor Association."

"What's this?" I said.

"It doesn't matter," he said. "They had an accident, but they didn't have their chop, so they used somebody else's. Then they brought this page to replace it. Now you can write your report on their page, and next time bring a piece of paper with your chop, so the next person can use it. Understand?"

I didn't — he had to explain this arrangement three times. It dawned on me that the wrecked bumper, which had never been my fault, and in a sense wasn't Wei Ziqi's fault, either, because of the unexpected front end, would now be blamed on the U.S.-China Tractor Association. "But you shouldn't say it happened in the countryside," Mr. Liu said. "That's too complicated. Just say you had an accident in our parking lot."

He wrote out a sample report and Leslie copied it, because her written Chinese was much better than mine. I signed my name across the tractor chop. The next time I rented a car, Mr. Liu told me that the insurance had covered everything. He never hassled me about bringing in the paper with my chop, and I decided to leave it at that — I was an old customer, as Mr. Liu liked to say.

When you live in China as a foreigner, there are two critical moments of recognition. The first occurs immediately upon arrival, when you are confronted with your own ignorance. Language, customs, history — all of it has to be learned, and the task seems insurmountable. Then, just as you begin to catch on, you realize that everybody else feels pretty much the same way. The place changes too fast; nobody in China has the luxury of being confident in his knowledge. Who shows a peasant how to find a factory job? How does a former Maoist learn to start a business? Who has the slightest clue how to run a car rental agency? Everything is figured out on the fly; the people are masters of improvisation. This second moment of recognition is even more frightening than the first. Awareness of your own ignorance is a lonely feeling, but there's little consolation in sharing it with 1.3 billion neighbors.

On the road, it's particularly horrifying. China still doesn't have many drivers — there are only twenty-eight automobiles per every thousand people, which is about the same rate that the United States had in 1915. But a 2004 World Health Organization report found that China, while having only 3 percent of the world's vehicles, accounted for 21 percent of its traffic fatalities. Last year, 89,000 people died in accidents. It's a nation of new drivers, and the transition has been so rapid that many road patterns come directly from pedestrian life — people drive the way they walk. They like to move in packs, and they tailgate whenever possible. They rarely use turn signals. If they miss an exit on a highway, they simply pull onto the shoulder, shift into reverse, and get it right the second time. After years of long queues, Chinese people have learned to be ruthless about cutting in line, an instinct that is disastrous in traffic jams. Toll booths are hazardous for the same reason. Drivers rarely check their rearview mirrors, perhaps because they never use such an instrument when they travel on foot or by bicycle. Windshield wipers are considered a distraction, and so are headlights.

In fact, the use of headlights was banned in Beijing until the mid-eighties, when Chinese officials began going overseas in increasing numbers. These trips were encouraged by governments in Europe and the United States, in the hope that glimpses of democracy would encourage China's leaders to rethink their policies. In 1983, Chen Xitong, the mayor of Beijing, made one such visit to New York. During his meetings with Mayor Ed Koch, Chen made a crucial observation: Manhattan drivers turn on their lights at night. When Chen returned to China, he decreed that Beijing motorists do the same. It's unclear what political conclusions Chen drew from his encounters with American democracy — the man ended up in prison for corruption — but at least he did his part for traffic safety. Nevertheless, there's enough debate about headlight use to merit a question on the written driving exam:

278. During the evening, a driver should
    (a) turn on the brights.
    (b) turn on the normal lights.
    (c) turn off the lights.

Recently, I picked up a study booklet for the exam. It consisted of 429 multiple-choice questions and 256 true-false queries, any of which might appear on the test. Often, these questions successfully captured the spirit of the road ("True or False: In a taxi, it's fine to carry a small amount of explosive material"), but I wasn't convinced that they helped people learn to drive correctly. After carefully studying the booklet, though, I realized that it was descriptive rather than prescriptive. It didn't teach people how to drive; it taught you how people drove:

77. When overtaking another car, a driver should pass
    (a) on the left.
    (b) on the right.
    (c) wherever, depending on the situation.

354. If you are driving toward a big puddle and there are pedestrians next to the water, you should
    (a) accelerate.
    (b) slow down and make sure that the water does not splash them.
    (c) continue at the same speed straight through the puddle.

80. If, while preparing to pass a car, you notice that it is turning left, making a U-turn, or passing another vehicle, you should
    (a) pass on the right.
    (b) not pass.
    (c) honk, accelerate, and pass on the left.

Lots of answers involved honking. In Chinese automobiles, the horn is essentially neurological — it channels the driver's reflexes. People honk constantly, and at first all horns sound the same, but over time you learn to distinguish variations and interpret them correctly. In this sense, honking is as complicated as the language. Spoken Chinese is tonal, which means that a single syllable can have different meanings depending on whether it is flat, rising, falling and rising, or falling sharply. Similarly, a Chinese horn is capable of at least ten distinct meanings. A solid *hoooooonnnnnk* is intended to attract attention. A double sound — *hoooonnnnnk, hoooonnnnnk* — indicates irritation. There's a particularly long *hoooooooooonnnnnnnnnnnk* that means the driver is stuck in traffic, has exhausted curb-sneaking options, and would like everybody else on the road to disappear. A responding *hoooooooooooooooonnnnnnnnnnnnnnnnnk* proves that they aren't going anywhere. There's a stuttering, staggering *honk honk hnk hnk hnk hnk hnk hnk* that represents pure panic. There's the afterthought honk — the one that rookie drivers make if they are too slow to hit the button before a situation resolves itself. And there's a short, simple honk that says, "My hands are still on the wheel, and this horn continues to serve as an extension of my nervous system." Other honks can be found on the exam:

353. When passing an elderly person or a child, you should
     (a) slow down and make sure you pass safely.
     (b) continue at the same speed.
     (c) honk the horn to tell them to watch out.

269. When you enter a tunnel, you should
     (a) honk and accelerate.
     (b) slow down and turn on your lights.
     (c) honk and maintain speed.

355. When driving through a residential area, you should
     (a) honk like normal.
     (b) honk more than normal, in order to alert residents.
     (c) avoid honking, in order to avoid disturbing residents.

The second accident wasn't my fault, either. I was driving in the countryside, and a dog darted out from behind a house and lunged at my Jetta. This is a common problem; dogs, like everybody else in China, aren't quite accustomed to having automobiles around. I swerved, but it was too late: the dog thudded against the front of the car. When Leslie and I returned the Jetta, the three men were smoking cigarettes beside the company evaluation sign. None of the numbers had changed in the year and a half since my last accident — "Appropriate Service Diction Rating" was holding steady at 98 percent. Mr. Liu inspected the Jetta and noted cheerfully that the plastic cover for the right signal light had been smashed. He asked what I had hit.

"A dog," I said.

"*Gou mei wenti?*" he said. "The dog didn't have a problem, did it?"

"The dog had a problem," I said. "It died."

Mr. Liu's smile got bigger. "Did you eat it?"

I couldn't tell if Mr. Liu was joking — he was a dog owner himself, and I had seen him playing with his pet in the office. "It wasn't that kind of dog," I said. "It was one of those tiny little dogs."

"Well, sometimes if a driver hits a big dog he just throws it in the trunk, takes it home, and cooks it," he said. He charged us $12 for a new signal light cover — it was too minor for the insurance, and there was no need to call in the U.S.-China Tractor Association.

Every Chinese applicant for a license must enroll in a certified course, at his own expense, and he must spend at least fifty-eight hours in training. This suggests a high degree of standardization, but much depends on the instructor, who is called a *jiaolian,* or "coach." Often, coaches have developed their own theories and regimens, like the martial arts masters of old. Wei Ziqi's coach disdained front-end vehicles, and he also forced his students to begin every maneuver in second gear. It was more challenging, he said; first gear would only make them lazy. Another woman I know had a coach who forbade the use of turn signals, because they distracted other drivers. When Leslie decided to learn to use a stick shift, she hired a private coach in Beijing. On the first lesson, the man introduced himself, sat in the passenger seat, and adjusted the rearview mirror so that it faced him.

"How am I going to see what's behind me?" Leslie asked.

"I'll tell you what's behind you," the coach said. He was like the martial arts guru who blindfolds his pupil: trust is the first step toward mastery.

Recently, I went to observe some courses at the Public Safety Driving School in the southeastern city of Lishui. Local car ownership was still low — only twenty households out of every thousand had bought a car within the past six months. But that was twice the previous year's rate, and the city's factory economy was in the middle of a boom. The driving school was busy, and classes moved through three stages: the parking range, the driving range, and the road.

One afternoon, I watched six students embark on their first day. An instructor called Coach Tang began by raising the hood of a red Santana. He pointed out the engine, the radiator, the battery. He showed them how to unscrew the gas cap. The door was next — the students practiced opening and closing it. Then he identified the panel instruments and the pedals. The students circled the Santana warily, fiddling with parts, like the blind men and the elephant. Finally, after an hour, they were allowed to enter the vehicle. Each of them sat in the driver's seat, where they shifted repeatedly from first to fifth gear, with the engine off. Watching this made me wince, and after a while I said to Coach Tang, "Isn't that bad for the car?"

"No," he said. "It's fine."

"I think it might be bad if the motor's off," I said.

"It's completely fine," Coach Tang said. "We do it all the time." In China, instructors of any type are traditionally respected without question, and I decided to keep my mouth shut. But it wasn't always easy. For the next step, the students learned to use the clutch by setting the parking brake, starting the engine, shifting into first gear, and then releasing the clutch while adding gas. The motor whined against the force of the brake; the torque dipped the front end up and down. By the end of the day, you could have fried an egg on the Santana's hood, and my palms began to sweat every time another driver gunned the engine.

Nobody was allowed to operate the vehicle until the second day of class. There were four men and two women, and all of them were younger than forty. Each had paid more than $300 for the course — a lot of money in a city where the monthly minimum wage was roughly $65. Only one person came from a household that currently owned an automobile. The others told me that someday they might buy one, and the university students — there were four of them — believed that a driver's license would look good on a résumé. "It's something you should be able to do, like swimming," a student named Wang Yanheng told me. "In the future, so many people in China are going to have cars." He was a senior, majoring in information technology. The one person from a home with automobiles (three) was a nineteen-year-old sociology major whose father owned a plastics factory. When I asked what the factory produced, the woman ran a finger along the rubber lining of the Santana's window. "This is one of the things we make," she said.

The students spent ten days on the parking range, and during that time they performed exactly three movements: a ninety-degree turn into a parking spot, the same maneuver in reverse, and parallel parking. Every day, for as many as six hours, they practiced these turns over and over. Like any good martial arts master, Coach Tang was strict. "You must have forgotten your brain today!" he yelled, when a student brushed against a pole. "Don't hold the gearshift loosely like that!" he shouted at another. "If you do, your father will curse you!" Sometimes he slapped a student's hand.

The next step was the driving range, where the skill set became more demanding. Drivers were required to stop within twenty-five centimeters of a painted line, and they guided the car through an obstacle course of tight turns. The final skill was the "single-plank bridge" — a concrete riser, a foot high and only slightly wider than a tire. Students had to aim the car perfectly, so that two wheels perched atop the riser — first the left tires, then the right. If a single wheel slipped, they failed the exam. The students spent most of their ten days practicing the single-plank bridge, and I asked a coach why it was so important. "Because it's very difficult," he said.

"Right, I understand that," I said. "But when is it useful on the road?"

"Well, if you're crossing a bridge with a hole, and there's only one place where the tires can go, then it's important to be able to do this."

The Chinese have fantastic driving imaginations — the written exam was full of situations like this. They seemed ridiculously unlikely, but the level of detail was such that I suspected it must have happened to somebody, somewhere: .

279. If your car breaks down atop the tracks of a railroad crossing, you should
    (a) abandon it there.
    (b) find some way to move it immediately.
    (c) leave it there temporarily until you can get somebody to repair it.

The course ended with a week and a half on the road, and I accompanied another class on its final day. With the coach in the passenger seat, students took turns driving along a two-lane rural road. There were certain movements they had to perform: shift to fifth, downshift to first, make a U-turn, stop at the imitation traffic light. They had been instructed to honk whenever they pulled out, or made a turn, or encountered anything in the road. They honked at cars, tractors, and donkey carts. They honked at every single pedestrian. Sometimes they passed another car from the driving school, and then both vehicles would honk happily, as if greeting an old friend. At noon, the class had lunch at a local restaurant, where everybody drank beer, including the coach, and then they continued driving. One student told me that a day earlier they got so drunk that they had to cancel the afternoon class.

Throughout the course, there had been no variables, no emphasis on responding to situations. Instead, students learned and rehearsed a small number of set pieces, which they would later combine and apply to actual city driving. It reminded me of how Chinese schoolchildren learn to write: they begin with specific strokes, copying them over and over, and then they combine these into characters, which are also written repeatedly. In China, repetition is the cornerstone of education, and virtually every new skill is approached in this manner. It's one reason that the Chinese have been far more successful at building assembly-line factories than at innovation.

It also explains many of the problems with driving in China. On the final day of class, a student begged me to let him drive my rental car back to the road range, for more practice. In a moment of extremely poor judgment, I agreed, and those turned out to be the most terrifying seven miles I had ever experienced in China. Twice I had to yell to keep him from passing on blind turns; another time, I grabbed the wheel to prevent him from veering into a car. He never checked the rearview mirror; he honked at everything that moved. The absolute lack of turn signals was the least of our problems. He came within inches of hitting a parked tractor, and he almost nailed a cement wall. When we finally made it to the range, I could have fallen on my knees and kissed the single-plank bridge.

Foreigners in Beijing often said to me, "I can't believe you're driving in this country." To which I responded, "I can't believe you get into cabs and buses driven by graduates of Chinese driving courses." On the road, everybody was lost — *une génération perdue* — but it felt better to be the one behind the wheel.

I had nothing to do with the third accident. I couldn't even drive — I had broken my left kneecap, and the Jetta that we had rented was standard transmission. Despite having served as a blindfolded acolyte of a local driving master, Leslie still didn't feel comfortable behind the wheel, and one afternoon she asked me to accompany her on some errands. I sat in the back, my broken leg propped up, giving advice every time she stalled. ("More gas!") It was snowing; traffic was miserable; we spent two hours hustling in and out of shops. After the last stop, Leslie turned the key and the Jetta lurched straight ahead into a brick wall.

I said, "Use the clutch."

There had been a distinct crunching sound, but we didn't check the car; by now, we were desperate to get home. Near the Lama Temple, as we waited to make the last left turn of the day, we were hit by another car. The driver backed into our side and then pulled away. There wasn't time to fumble with my crutches, so I hopped out on my good leg. Fortunately, traffic was backed up, and I caught him in about seven hops. I pounded on the window. "You hit my car!"

The driver looked up, surprised: a one-legged foreigner, hopping mad and smacking the glass. He stepped out and apologized, saying that he hadn't felt the impact. Together, we inspected the Jetta — fresh dent above the left rear wheel. The man said, "I'll give you a hundred." That was about thirteen dollars.

In China, after a minor accident people usually settle the matter on the street, in cash. This routine has become a standard part of life — once, I saw two small children playing a game in which they repeatedly rammed their bikes and shouted, *"Pei qian! Pei qian!"* — "Compensate! Compensate!"

Leslie used her cell phone to call the rental company. Mr. Liu didn't sound the least bit surprised to hear that we'd had another accident. All he said was "Ask for two hundred."

"That's too much," the other driver said. "This is really minor."

"It's not our decision."

"Well, then, we'll have to call the police," he said, but it was clear that he didn't want to do this. A dozen bystanders had gathered around the cars, which were parked in the middle of the snowy street. With Chinese accidents, the crowd is more like a jury than an audience, and a middle-aged woman bent over to inspect the dent. She stood up and announced, "A hundred is enough."

"What do you have to do with it?" Leslie snapped. "You can't even drive!"

That must have been correct, because the woman shut up. But the driver refused to pay two hundred. "Should we accept one-fifty?" Leslie asked me, in English. Lao-tzu said it best: A man standing on crutches in the snow will not bargain long over a dent to a crappy Jetta rental. Later that day, Leslie returned the car and the one-fifty in cash. Mr. Liu noticed that another light cover had been broken when she hit the brick wall. He said, happily, "What did you kill this time?" When I hit the dog, the same cover was $12; this time, he asked for only $3. It must have been a special price because we did so well at the Lama Temple.

The fourth accident was entirely my fault. It was my last day in China, my last Jetta — the next morning I had a one-way ticket to Honolulu. On my way to return the car, I got stuck in a terrible traffic jam, and wailing horns filled the air — these were the honks that mean, "Let me out of here!" In front, a taxi driver saw an opening and lurched ahead; I lurched after him; he stopped short; I didn't.

We got out. I took a look and winced: dents on both sides. "A hundred," I said.

"Are you kidding?" the man yelled. "This is at least two hundred!"

Suddenly, I felt extremely tired. Ten years in China, six years of driving, more honks than the Tower of Babel — "Let me out of here!" The man jabbered angrily, talking about how long it takes to fix a dented bumper, but I couldn't think of any response. "A hundred," I said again.

A crowd gathered, and the cabbie began to play to the jury — it was a bad dent; he worked long days; repairs took time. A tiny old woman stepped forward and touched his arm. "Take the money," she said softly. The cabbie looked down at her — she couldn't have been more than five feet tall — and fell silent. He didn't say a word when I handed him the bill.

In the rental-company lot, Mr. Liu ran a finger along the dent. "No problem!" he said.

"Look, I'm happy to pay for it," I said.

"You're an old customer," he said. "Forget it." We shook hands and I left him at the front desk, smoking a cigarette beneath the eternal sign:

CUSTOMER SATISFACTION RATING: 90%
EFFICIENCY RATING: 97%
APPROPRIATE SERVICE DICTION RATING: 98%
SERVICE ATTITUDE RATING: 99%.

MELIK KAYLAN

Georgia in the Time of Misha

FROM *Travel + Leisure*

ON A WARM NIGHT IN TBILISI, where the glossy air has bas-reliefed everything (and everyone) into a kind of celebrity pop-up, I find myself living a glamour moment among the newly minted café society of Georgia. It's a Studio 54 photograph of sorts, but taken in a country wedged roughly between Chechnya and Iran. And so the scene feels at once familiar and strange: men etched in designer poses, fine-boned models having too much fun, that feeling of being at precisely the right place at the right time — all punctuated by the blank stares of VIPs ignoring VIPs. Very Warhol. Perfectly déjà vu. We're on a veranda looking down at the tree-lined Mtkvari River winding through the capital's archaic elegance. It's the after-party of a fashion show, and the peculiar assortment of people illustrates Georgia's ancient role as a merging point of cultures along the Silk Road.

Just inside the red cordon, elbow against the wall, stands Georgian soccer star and Dolce & Gabbana model Kakha Kaladze, who plays in Italy for superclub A.C. Milan. Nearby sits Natalia Kancheli, a sometime aide to Georgia's young president, Mikheil "Misha" Saakashvili, and daughter of composer Giya Kancheli. You have seen her kind in first-class lounges en route to London, Paris, Tokyo — heartbreakers in dark sunglasses, mysterious in the world and very much of it. Two tables away sits the burly son of the late Saparmurat Niyazov, in his time the world's most bizarre leader-for-life after Kim Jong Il of North Korea. Until last year, Niyazov Sr. ruled the former Soviet republic of Turkmenistan. Largely impoverished, the country has massive natural gas deposits, which served mostly to pay for giant banners and statues of Niyazov, including a notorious forty-foot gold-plated one that revolves to salute the sun all day. What is it like to be his son? Not too cheerful, apparently. "I visited your capital, Ashgabat, back in the nineties," I say, "and I enjoyed it immensely." He eyes me ironically. "You were surely drunk," he says, smiling, and turns to gaze at his vodka. He probably thinks he's said too much already. Just beyond him is a slender, soft-spoken young Tbilisian with a smooth-shaved head who deploys the Georgian investments of an oil-rich Kazakh corporation, part of a flow of wealth that represents the ancient Silk Road common market coming back to life, Kazakhstan being the new oil powerhouse of Central Asia.

Money, fun, and exuberance are suddenly flowing through Tbilisi from all directions. In the few short years since January 2004, when the nonviolent Rose Revolution brought President Saakashvili to power at age thirty-six, the country has experienced a historically unprecedented forward surge. After centuries of confinement under Persian, Ottoman, Czarist, and Soviet rulers — and a decade during which two provinces, with Russian incitement, seceded from the country — Georgia has come into its own. Little more than five years ago, citizens routinely tapped into public telephone and electricity cables for service; no one paid taxes; everyone took bribes. A million Georgians (out of a total population of 4.5 million) emigrated abroad. For a while, all over the post-Soviet geosphere the word *Georgian* was an adjective denoting mafia shenanigans.

It has all changed with bewildering speed. The police don't take bribes, the mafia has fled, new roads are being paved. There are more Georgians returning than leaving; new office buildings, hotels, and airports are going up; and even the vile Soviet-era concrete apartment blocks have been repainted in bright colors. If you want to know what "efflorescence" looks like, this is it. Georgia and Tbilisi are going through a bona fide "era," the Era of Misha (as Georgians call their president), which may seem fairly routine to us (after all, we have the Clinton era, the Bush era) except that Georgians couldn't have their own era until the Soviets left, and they only had chaos in the aftermath of that. In short, Georgia is poised to reclaim its own chosen destiny, after having it hijacked by one neighbor or another for more than five hundred years.

*

Georgia's capital strikes the newcomer as improbably beautiful, a postcard-perfect lost kingdom set inside high hills surmounted by ancient forts and rock-steady fifteen-hundred-year-old Byzantine churches. Downtown Tbilisi unfurls along Rustaveli Avenue, lined with neoclassical theaters and palaces that house state offices, and dips down to the ancient quarter, the *maidan,* a Turco-Farsi word meaning "central square." There the scene turns sepia: a synagogue looks out on the striated brown-brick cupolas of the *hammam.* Its entrance is a peaked portal glittering with turquoise tiles, like something out of Isfahan. (The word *tbilisi* means "warm place.") In the small *maidan,* low two-story wooden houses nestle together, with flower-strewn balconies one can almost stretch up to touch. All is human-scale, harmonious, and seasoned by age. The river flows just behind, then Tbilisi rises up again, on bluffs fronted by more wooden villas.

This was always the most far-flung Christian capital on the map, the last outpost of the West as it merged into the exotic. But it gives off an unsettling familiarity. One has seen its like before somewhere; the world knew this aesthetic well at some point. It took me a while to realize that there's an arc of such cities with precisely such a fusion of layers . . . early Christian, then Ottoman, then Czarist-Hapsburg, with a last glimmering of art nouveau (elegant curved steel balconies and gates snaked by flower-stem patterns). They run from Belgrade through Sofia and Bucharest and on to Tbilisi in the Caucasus. One remembers them from antique postcards, yellowing magazines, even from Tintin stories — always framed in rugged mountains and threaded by a robust river, and always graced by a sleepy Islamic street with a donkey cart. They flowered before and after World War I, jewels of the *ancien régime* for a brief moment before Nazism and Communism buried them from sight — along with their old bewhiskered royals in chesty poses, ornamental military uniforms, faux-Parisian streetlights, and sleek cavalry horses.

I stumbled onto a bit of the hidden residue of Tbilisi's prewar heyday through Gogla, whom I met at a café atop the bluffs across the river. A fluent English speaker in his early thirties, Gogla attended school in the United States and now works for a multinational construction company, building hotels in the capital. Hearing English chatter, he table-hopped over to me. Everyone knows everyone here, and pretty soon he offered to show me around town.

I said I wanted to see some of Tbilisi's lovely, mysterious houses. "You should just go and introduce yourself. Georgians love Americans," he said. "Come, let's try it." We drove across the river to an elegant half-lit street with two towering houses, one with a chateau-like roof hidden by trees. We walked up its grand staircase, and from the third-floor landing we glimpsed an exquisitely gilded ceiling behind the leaded windows. We knocked on several doors until one opened. Gogla chatted away, and soon we found ourselves in a teak-paneled, high-ceilinged room of great dignity, once a library.

The building dated from 1914, the year the Great War started. The Soviets took Tbilisi a decade later in a notoriously bloody campaign of repression. Like so many large houses that belonged to the bourgeoisie, this one was soon seized by the state. It was shared out between twenty-two families, which is how it remains today. We asked about the room with the gilt ceiling — it had been the ballroom. An old woman lived there alone, her bed in the middle of the parquet floor. The house exhaled a thwarted affluence everywhere we turned, a hidden narrative that perhaps stood for the wider experience of Tbilisi and Georgia as a whole — or perhaps the flowing Georgian wine had overenhanced our senses, as our hosts, a seven-member family, came in and out, gently offering to top up our glasses, delighted at the impromptu visit.

Most people would acknowledge that the Soviet years added very little of aesthetic value in buildings or monuments to any country. But Tbilisi developed a unique ministyle of its own — well, maybe not so mini. One might call it the Bond-villain aesthetic of retro-futurism, first conceived in the 1960s and periodically refreshed only in Tbilisi. Here and there defiant, freestanding architectural follies soar up mysteriously from the encircling hills. The cloud-topped TV Tower, on the highest hill, looks like an abandoned Soyuz rocket and lights up in sparks at night. Right beside it, the once-neglected aerial-tram pavilion, now being renovated, espouses the international *Casino Royale* vernacular. Swivel your head a few degrees and another peak shows an emerging airport terminal-style fantasy adorned with a helipad and arcing glass façade. It's being built for an oligarch. Then, way below, a mile or two downriver, you see a vertical bunker occupied by a different oligarch. The overall effect of these preposterous forms is both grand and quaint — and entirely glamorous, suggesting a city with splendid, eccentric dreams.

The XX Century hotel sits plumb in the middle of an area called Sololaki, a decaying warren of mostly wooden villas from the late 1800s with enclosed gardens. It honeycombs up from the town center until it hits the sheer bluff. The hotel — two stories of cinderblock and brick — aims for a kind of ironic Soviet-era chic, and succeeds rather well. Thick cloth wires thread up from old-style clunky switches. Bulky ceiling fans whir away. Industrial carpeting spreads out underfoot. When I stayed there, Zaza Tsitsishvili, the architect, apparently a descendant of the old Georgian royal family, had just finished it. He said to me, "We all lived in the last century, and now it's history. But we feel nostalgic and familiar in it. That's how I wanted to make the hotel." The exhilarating view encompasses Persian-style bosky courtyards and distant cliffs where myriad Byzantine churches seem to float on air.

One night, I decided to explore Sololaki and quickly got lost in the dark, narrow streets. Honeysuckle blossoms and overhanging mulberry trees brushed my face. I could watch people eating and drinking *en famille* in bright indoor bulb-light. Around 11 P.M., I crested a hill and stumbled on a bricked-up Byzantine church atop a rubble-strewn miniplateau. A forgotten spot; the city twinkled below. This, I realized, encapsulates Tbilisi's charm — the city seems, still, so undiscovered, even by the locals. You can make it your own and craft a personal, improvised chain of unheralded experiences. Which is not to say that Tbilisi lacks conventional commercial entertainment — but even in those places, as with Rome or Florence, ancient stones in shadows murmur of their history while you eat or dance. Sidewalk bars and cafés aplenty have opened in the last couple of years, especially on Chavchavadze Street, alongside the boutiques and galleries near the town center. In Tbilisi, life can turn happily picaresque at any moment.

In the morning, I went antiquing along the elegantly fin-de-siècle Marjanishvili Street, across the river. The area itself glimmers with belle époque touches on theater façades and storefronts. Inside the shops, among the objets d'art, I felt again the presence of Tbilisi's last flush of European classicism: bronze statuettes, impressionist mountain views, old photographs, aristocratic swords and uniforms. I looked at lampshades and small chandeliers, numerous and beautifully shaped, thanks to Tbilisi's art nouveau heritage. For between $200 and $300 you can get a really fine sculpted lamp. I also sought out nineteenth-century shooting paraphernalia: Georgia once thrived as a center of haute hunting culture, always conducted in grand style at far-flung mountain lodges and pavilions, with fabulous outfits and antiquated weapons. I saw lots of lovely inlaid nineteenth-century rifles and flintlocks — all very expensive. So I went to a cheaper locale: the Dry River Bridge weekend flea market, which stretches along the river through a little park and down some steps into a proper bazaar full of jewelry, silver cutlery, Soviet medals, and, yes, old guns — which are mostly fakes. Walking in the nearby park, I spotted a wolfskin and a bearskin negligently tacked up to a tree, and almost bought those instead. But I balked at the prospect, uncertain of the ethical (and hygienic) issues involved.

Some days before I leave, I get a call from President Saakashvili's people, responding to my request for an interview. He wants to take me along on a visit to the Black Sea resort of Batumi, the capital of the Autonomous Republic of Adjara, on the Turkish border. Adjara was one of the secessionist provinces, a black hole of corruption and warlordism, and was backed by Russia until two years ago, when Saakashvili simply people-powered his way in after various military face-offs. The despot of ten years (1994–2004), Aslan Abashidze, fled to Russia. One might call him the paradigm of a warlord, a wondrous magical-realist character who closed all the parks in Batumi and imposed a multiyear evening curfew because he loathed the sight of people having fun. This in a town that before Georgia's independence was the Soviet Union's tourist hub along its Black Sea Riviera. Abashidze allowed all the roads to crumble, except one — the one his son would drive on to give his ten Ferraris a periodic workout. The province had one export, Jeep-mounted machine guns, and earned much of its revenue from the Russian military base and the oil terminal that serviced Black Sea tankers. Batumi achieved renown as a seaside jewel beginning in 1900, when oil began to flow from the Baku oilfields in Azerbaijan and went out to the world by ship. The Rothschilds and Nobels who made millions from the pre-Communist Baku bubble chose nearby Batumi as their elegant fun-in-the-sun way station.

I'm not told how we will get to Batumi, which is a seven-hour drive away. The chauffeur steers between potholes on a road leading to a seedy military facility on the outskirts of Tbilisi. I'm rushed to a large, bug-eyed helicopter of Soviet vintage, the kind with spidery, drooping rotor blades. Then the president charges in, followed by his numerous bodyguards. We soar up past the Tbilisi Sea, the reservoir where Tbilisians go to shake off the summer heat. We're escorted by an identical chopper, two shadows flashing on hills below. Within fifteen minutes we see the serried white caps of the Great Caucasus mountain range. That way lies Chechnya. Georgia of ancient memory undulates below, wild and myth-strewn from Prometheus to the Amazons. Suddenly, we're over a beach, landing near an Oriental-roofed dacha patrolled by guards. I've barely settled in the semicomplete local governor's residence when I hear a shout: "Hurry up, they're waiting for you." I run out and down to the beach where Saakashvili is standing dripping next to two Jet Skis. "Go ahead," he says, "try it out." Off we go along the coast, choppers and launches trailing, little dots of people waving from the beaches.

Saakashvili, in his idiosyncratic Georgian way, is serious about fun. He builds amusement park rides, colorful fountain shows, and the like all over the country: "I want to brighten things up," he says. "Georgia was the main tourist destination for the entire Soviet sphere. People are coming back and bringing others. They know that more democracy and private enterprise equals more hope and affluence and, yes, more fun."

Like Tbilisi, Batumi is a place awakening from the spell of history. Brutish Soviet apartment blocks crumble around exquisite belle époque *quartiers*. Subtropical in climate, the shoreline rises at times into cliffs topped by swaying bamboo forests and tea and nutmeg farms. The Turks ruled here until the mid-nineteenth century; neoclassical minipalaces line the waterfront. During the day, the governor walks us through the Old Town — still being rebuilt after Abashidze. Saakashvili takes me on a drive along the coast: "Those are all new hotels," he says. "Here is the new Chinese restaurant and the new Dutch restaurant." He points to a multicolored pagoda and a large white windmill nearby. Later, on a lovely Black Sea evening, we all dine atop a faux wooden galleon in dry dock. A crimson sun melts away, and the water turns steely soft. The table groans with dishes, very Georgian both in amount and content. I spot the two standards of the national cuisine: *khinkali* and *khachapuri,* big meat dumplings and a kind of pizza, comfort foods nonpareil, surrounded by a spread of tomatoes, cheese, spring onions, and radishes.

In Tbilisi, on my last night, I am invited to dinner at the house of the minister for privatization, Kakha Bendukhidze. We eat at a long wooden table, with his beautiful wife, Natasha, on their flagstoned back porch. Natasha found a painting in town that day entitled *Bendukhidze at Table,* showing our host — a large man — tucking into a table-length fish. President Saakashvili suddenly appears with an Italian restaurateur in tow. He just flew to St. Petersburg today to meet Putin for a specially arranged rapprochement. Instead, it turned into one more sour incident in an ongoing saga of hostility. Putin kept Saakashvili waiting for four hours, then met him for a mere fifteen minutes. Gifts were exchanged. They barely said hello. So, in disgust, Saakashvili and his retinue went to the best restaurant in town. "It was so good that I realized we had to have one just like it here," he says. The restaurateur, chuckling, says, "He told me I had to see Tbilisi — he hijacked me on his jet."

Saakashvili asks about my stay. I find myself, in one of those surreal, comic moments that Georgia inspires, describing the wolf- and bearskins I saw at the flea market but had failed to purchase. "I have a Siberian bearskin," Saakashvili says. "Would you like it?" *Well* . . . I say, and so it is that an enormous Russian bearskin appears in my hotel room — a gift originally given to Saakashvili (I'm told by an aide) by the Kremlin, and emblematic of Russian power. I understand why Saakashvili might not want it. As for me, I can hardly refuse this mad, outsize, Georgian gesture of affection — to be explained across multiple security barriers in myriad time zones, "You see, the president of Georgia gave it to me . . ." Don't tell Mr. Putin I have his bear.

JOHN LANCASTER

Next Stop, Squalor

FROM *Smithsonian*

THE DHARAVI SQUATTER SETTLEMENT in Mumbai is often described as the biggest slum in Asia. It sits between two rail lines in the northern part of the city, on a creek that once sustained a thriving fishery. The creek is now a sump of sewage and industrial waste, and the air above Dharavi is foul.

By one estimate, the slum is home to ten thousand small factories, almost all of them illegal and unregulated. The factories provide sustenance of a sort to the million or so people who are thought to live in Dharavi, which at 432 acres is barely half the size of New York City's Central Park. There is no discernible garbage pickup, and only one toilet for every 1,440 people. It is a vision of urban hell.

It is also one of India's newest tourist attractions. Since January of last year, a young British entrepreneur, Christopher Way, and his Indian business partner, Krishna Poojari, have been selling walking tours of Dharavi as if it were Jerusalem's walled city or the byways of Dickens's London. There seems to be a market for this sort of thing: almost every day during the recent December holidays, small groups of foreign travelers, accompanied by Poojari or another guide, tramped through Dharavi's fetid alleys in a stoic quest for . . . What? Enlightenment? Authenticity? The three-hour excursions are slated for mention in a forthcoming *Lonely Planet* guide, and they cost about $6.75 a head — more if you want to go to Dharavi by air-conditioned car.

Poverty tourism — sometimes known as "poorism" — did not originate in Mumbai (formerly Bombay). For years, tour operators have been escorting foreign visitors through Rio de Janeiro's infamous favelas, with their drug gangs and ocean views, and the vast townships outside Cape Town and Johannesburg, where tourists are invited to mix with South Africans at one of the illicit beer halls known as shebeens. A nonprofit group in New Delhi charges tourists for guided walks through the railway station, to raise money for the street children who haunt its platforms.

But the Dharavi tours have been especially controversial. In a lengthy report last September, the Indian English-language *Times Now* television channel attacked them as an exercise in voyeurism and a sleazy bid to "cash in on the 'poor-India' image." That report was followed by a panel discussion in which the moderator all but accused Poojari of crimes against humanity. "If you were living in Dharavi, in that slum, would you like a foreign tourist coming and walking all over you?" he sputtered. "This kind of slum tourism, it is a clear invasion of somebody's privacy . . . You are treating humans like animals." A tourism official on the panel called the tour operators "parasites [who] need to be investigated and put behind bars," and a state lawmaker has threatened to shut them down.

The critics, it seemed, had claimed the moral high ground. But could they hold it?

One sunny morning this past December, I met Christopher Way at Leopold's Café, a popular backpackers' hangout in Mumbai's bustling Colaba district. At thirty-one, he is boyish and bespectacled, with a thatch of tousled brown hair and a thoughtful, unassuming manner. Over glasses of freshly squeezed mango juice, he told me that he grew up near Birmingham, England, and after graduation from Birmingham University, set off on a path to become a chartered accountant. But Way was afflicted with chronic wanderlust. In 2002, he visited Mumbai and liked the city so much that he stayed five months, volunteering as an English teacher and cricket coach in a local elementary school. He subsequently took an extended holiday in Rio, where he signed up for one of the favela tours. Although frustrated by the guide's lack of knowledge about the shantytown, Way says he found the experience fascinating. It occurred to him that he might be able to do something similar in Mumbai.

As many as half of that city's 18 million or so residents live in squatter settlements, so there was no shortage of potential venues. But Dharavi, as the largest and most established of Mumbai's slums, was the obvious choice. Way's idea was to showcase the settlement's economic underpinnings in a way that would challenge stereotypes about the poor. "We're trying to dispel the myth that people there sit around doing nothing, that they're criminals," he said after we had walked across the street to his office, a grubby, windowless space barely big enough for his desk and laptop computer. "We show it for what it is — a place where people are working hard, struggling to make a living, and doing it in an honest way."

To smooth things out with local bureaucrats and Dharavi residents, Way needed an Indian partner, and he found one in Poojari, now twenty-six, a farmer's son who had migrated to Mumbai as an unaccompanied twelve-year-old and put himself through night school by working in an office cafeteria. The two men formed a company, Reality Tours & Travel, and bought a pair of air-conditioned SUVs. Way bankrolled the venture with income from rental properties he owns in England. Besides the Dharavi tours — which can be combined with visits to Mumbai's red-light district and Dhobi Ghat, a vast open-air laundry — the company offers sightseeing of a more conventional nature, along with hotel bookings and airport transportation. Way has pledged that once the company starts making a profit, it will donate 80 percent of its slum-tour earnings to a charitable group that works in Dharavi. "I didn't want to make money from the slum tours," he says. "It wouldn't have felt right."

Except on its website (realitytoursandtravel.com) and a sign on a lamppost near Leopold's Café — SEE DHARAVI (THE BIGGEST SLUM IN ASIA) — the company does not advertise the slum excursions. But as word has spread over the Internet and by other means, business has grown steadily, drawing visitors from around the world.

Late one morning I met Poojari at the Churchgate railway station, where we hopped on a dilapidated commuter train for the twenty-five-minute ride to Dharavi. Waiting for us there was tourist Jeff Ellingson, a twenty-nine-year-old technology professional from Seattle. Before we got started, Poojari explained that the company has a no-photography policy, to keep the tours from becoming too intrusive. (For the same reason, each group is limited to five people.) Then we took a pedestrian bridge over the railroad tracks.

Dharavi stretched before us like a vast junkyard, a hodgepodge of brick and concrete tenements roofed with corrugated metal sheets that gleamed dully in the sunshine. Poojari gave us a moment to take it all in. "We'll show you the positive side of a slum," he declared.

In the face of such squalor, his words seemed jarring. But Dharavi's industriousness is well documented. Its businesses manufacture a variety of products — plastics, pottery, blue jeans, leather goods — and generate an estimated $665 million in annual revenue. In other words, Dharavi is not just a slum, it is also a node on the global economy.

Dharavi's industries are arranged geographically, like medieval guilds, and the first alley we visited belonged to recyclers. In one small "godown" (as warehouses are known on the subcontinent), men were disassembling old computer keyboards. In another, men smeared from head to toe in blue ink stripped the casings from used ballpoint pens so they could be melted down and recycled. A few doors down, workers used heavy chains to knock the residue from steel drums that had once contained polyester resin. Poojari told us that some of Dharavi's empty plastic bottles come from as far away as the United Kingdom. "People from a rich family, when they drink from a plastic bottle, they don't know what happens to it afterwards," he said. "Here, you see."

Few of the recyclers wore gloves or other protective gear, despite exposure to solvents and other chemicals that caused my eyes and throat to burn after just a few minutes. The working conditions were typical of Dharavi's unregulated businesses. Some of the worst were in the foundries. From the door of one dark, unventilated space, I watched a heavyset worker dressed in a sarong ladle molten steel into a belt-buckle mold that he held between his feet. His *bare* feet. After cracking open the mold to reveal the glowing red buckle in its bed of sand, he glanced up, and for a moment our eyes met. His face was wooden, expressionless. I mumbled thanks and moved on.

Not for the first time on the tour, I felt like an interloper, and I wondered how the slum workers and their families felt about white-skinned strangers who showed up to gawk from the threshold. For Dharavi was undeniably grim. As we neared its center, the alleys narrowed and cantilevered balconies closed out the sun, casting everything in a permanent gloom. Children played next to gutters that flowed with human waste, and hollow-eyed men bent nearly double under the weight of burlap-covered loads. But if the people of Dharavi resented us, they kept it to themselves. Some even seemed happy to take part in our education. "Here, everybody is working," a man said genially, and in perfect English, as we paused outside the yogurt-cup recycling operation where he sat sipping tea with the owner.

The welcoming reception probably had something to do with the tour operators, who have cultivated good relations with the slum workers as well as local police. There are, moreover, certain rules. From the door of a one-room garment factory, I spotted a boy who looked to be no more than eight sitting with other workers at a long table, where he was embroidering fabric with fine gold thread. I nudged my guide: "Ask him how old he is." Poojari shook his head no. Pointed questions were not part of his compact with the slum dwellers.

As it happens, Ellingson and I did not see many child laborers in Dharavi, perhaps because of laws limiting employment of children under fourteen or, more likely — as Way suggested later — because they were sequestered out of view. We did see several schools, however, and plenty of kids in uniforms. "By plane you are coming?" one boy asked in English, before declaring, with evident pride, "I'm studying in eighth standard."

Blighted though it was, Dharavi had the feeling of an established community. Signs in Hindi advertised the services of doctors and dentists. An outdoor barber administered a shave with a folding razor. A laundryman stood against an alley wall, pressing clothes with an ancient-looking iron. At a small factory where recycled plastic was melted down and turned into tiny pellets for use by toymakers, the owner, who was in his late twenties, told us that his father had started the business three decades ago. Like many of the slum dwellers, the factory owner was a Muslim, although Dharavi is nothing if not diverse. Its residents come from all over India, and many have lived there for a generation or more. Poojari said that one of the slum neighborhoods is dominated by the descendants of potters from Gujarat state who settled in Dharavi in 1933. When we visited the potters' district in the early afternoon, we were puzzled to find few signs of life, other than smoking kilns and an old man napping on a rope cot. It turned out that most of the potters and their families had taken the afternoon off to attend a wedding.

Ellingson drew a comparison with Palestinian communities he had toured in the West Bank. They were "a lot wealthier, but it's like society has broken down," he said, adding that in Dharavi, "it feels like something is functioning." I had to agree.

For one thing, almost no one asked for money, or even tried to sell me anything. Only once was I approached for a handout, by an elderly woman. That was a big change from Colaba, the main tourist district, where it is difficult to walk more than a few steps without being accosted by a beggar — usually a young woman with an infant on her hip — or a peddler hawking laminated maps. Perhaps people in Dharavi were simply too busy. And some of them clearly had rupees in their pockets. Besides the food stalls and handcarts piled high with okra and squash, there were video parlors showing Bollywood hits, several bars, and on one thoroughfare, a spiffy-looking electronics store plastered with Sony decals.

"They're happy to be here," Poojari said as we paused outside a small factory where women were stitching blue jeans. "They don't want to move out of Dharavi." I don't know about "happy," but on the latter point, Poojari was probably correct.

Because of its prime location — on rail lines near the heart of one of the world's most crowded cities — Dharavi sits on valuable real estate, and its residents are not about to give up their stake. The slum is the focus of a looming showdown with municipal authorities and developers who want to turn it into office towers, luxury apartments, and shopping centers. Families that can prove they have lived in Dharavi since 1995 would be entitled to a free apartment in the same area, but the new dwellings would be so small — just 225 square feet — that many prefer to stay where they are. Nor is it clear what would happen to the thousands of businesses that provide Dharavi residents with jobs.

We finished the tour on the side of a busy four-lane road, where the festive sounds of a Hindu wedding ceremony — apparently the one the potters had gone to — spilled from a gaudy tent. We paused to peek inside, and I spotted the groom sitting awkwardly beneath an enormous gold turban. No one gave us a second glance, and I had to wonder about the motives of those in the Indian media and elsewhere who claimed on behalf of the Dharavi residents to be offended by the tours. Surely their ire could have been better targeted at the municipal authorities who had failed to provide the community with basic sanitation. I wondered whether the critics weren't simply embarrassed by the slum's glaring poverty — an image at odds with the country's efforts to rebrand itself as a big software park. In any case, it seemed to me that the purpose of the tour was not to generate pity, but understanding. That's not to say that it made me an expert — I was only there a few hours, after all. Were the people I saw in Dharavi the victims of globalization, or its beneficiaries? I still don't know. But at least the question had been raised in my mind.

EMILY MALONEY

Mr. Tingler

FROM *TheSmartSet.com*

ONCE, IN BRAZIL, I ended up eating dinner in a section of Salvador called Pelourinho, which my *Lonely Planet* said was the old slave-auctioning and whipping site, but that was now filled with charming, overpriced tourist restaurants. I was with a Japanese girl I had met in Rio. She swore like a Yakuza member, but she read her guidebook diligently. I was alone as usual, and she allowed me to follow along as she took the right buses to the beach and showed up at the bank to change money during business hours. In exchange for my freeloading she occasionally demanded we must eat some of the "must eat" dishes in some of the "must eat" restaurants pictured on the shiny pages of her Japanese guidebook. Monika, a Canadian who was model gorgeous and fluent in her parents' Portugal-style Portuguese, but had trouble walking on all the cobblestone in flip-flops, ate with us. Yoko deliberately ordered us dishes from Africa with okra and shrimp and peppers, and we sat outside in the warm night (where slaves used to be whipped) listening to drumbeats in the distance and talking about how unforgiving the Brazilian bathing suits were.

I walked back to the hostel to take a shower. When I got back to my room from the bathroom, I heard police sirens outside. I leaned out the heavy, framed colonial window with a swimmer's towel to my hair. An Israeli on the guys' floor below me looked up. "You should come down here," he said, gesturing from my floor to his with a lit cigarette.

So I came down without shoes to lean out the hallway window and try to see the police. He offered me a Marlboro from a box with a photo of a premature baby hooked up to machines on it. He had another box that illustrated impotence with a woman in a king-size bed looking away from a man with his head in his hands. A third box featured a photograph of black charred lungs. They must have been meant to deter kids and illiterate adults from smoking, but although I don't normally smoke, I took and started to smoke a cigarette from the low-birth-weight-baby box for the novelty of it.

It felt good. I told the Israeli that I sort of liked violence, which is the sort of asinine thing only someone who has never been the victim of violence or has never been forced to victimize others can say. What I meant was that I find memorable those times that are so confusing and intense that you are forced to be totally conscious of the present moment. So I followed up by saying, "I mean I don't like it, but at the same time I like it. You know?" He agreed as we looked down the street and saw some riot police marching on the cobblestone. He told me his name, which was unpronounceable and hard to remember. I tried to say it a couple of times, but then gave up. I told him my name was Emily, and he said he knew that name from *Beverly Hills, 90210*. I forgave him for having seen that much *90210*. He said, "Maybe, Emily, you would not like violence so much if you came from somewhere with more of it." I agreed with him, and he explained how there were some fun times in the Israeli army, but mostly it was a waste of time.

I soon heard Monika stumbling up the steps in her flip-flops, a loud posse of youth hostel guests trailing behind her. Yoko's favorite swearword, *makatsuku*, floated up to us several times before they reached our floor. When Monika and Yoko did reach the second floor, they said they didn't know what was going on outside with the police and they both raised their eyebrows with interest about the Israeli. I shook my head no, we were just two people sharing a conversation about violence and an entire pack of cigarettes decorated tastefully with a photo of an underweight baby.

Once they passed, the Israeli told me that after he got out of the army, he spent a year in Maryland selling massage devices called Mr. Tinglers from a cart in the mall, and that's how he was able to save up enough money for this trip to South America. "Wait," he said, and ran to his room. When he came back he was carrying the Mr. Tingler contraption, which was a little wooden knob with wires coming out of it. I laughed at the amount of space this must be taking up in his luggage, but he told me to stop laughing and turn around and close my eyes. So I did. As he let Mr. Tingler's wires come down over my skull, he spun me around and kissed me.

Being hit on is about as common for me as being caught up in street violence, and it felt similarly thrilling and overwhelming. He pulled me into the hostel bathroom and we made out against the tiled wall. Every moment with him made me feel suddenly conscious and clear-headed. Then he pulled away from me for a moment. It hit me I was making out in a hostel bathroom with someone whose name I couldn't pronounce who had seduced me with a Mr. Tingler. My breath smelled like Marlboros. I felt dumb, so I told him I should go back to my bunk, and he was cool about it.

When I went downstairs for breakfast in the morning, Mr. Tingler and I nodded to each other and smiled. His table was full of Israelis speaking Hebrew, and Monika and Yoko had saved a seat for me. The TV was turned to CNN, which was focused on violence somewhere. I could not tell where. The experts in their suits and hairsprayed hair presented the conflict as if conflict was inevitable. They agreed it was happening now and could be prevented, but at the same time at the conclusion of the piece they smiled politely and signed off as if the violence was also occurring in a land so distant it might as well be the past.

BRYAN MEALER

The River Is a Road

FROM *Harper's Magazine*

JUST AFTER DAWN in early October I stood on the banks of Kinshasa's commercial port and stared into a wall of rippling heat that danced on the water. Enormous cranes loomed like giant headless chickens near the water's edge, and beyond them sat the triple-decker tugboat that would take me up the Congo River.

The captain of the *Ma'ungano* was a stout Frenchman named Albert-Henri Buisine, an old soldier who'd been raised in Congo and had spent two decades in the service of Mobutu Sese Seko, the dictator whom he once considered his closest friend, a genius he thought the world was cruel to dismiss. The captain's office was decorated with maps of the region's many rivers, all eight thousand miles of which snaked and splintered across weathered charts on the walls. Sitting behind his desk, the captain explained how the war had closed the rivers and tributaries, isolating millions of Congolese. Soldiers had killed and raped in the villages, so the people had escaped to the capital, leaving behind a way of life they'd nurtured since the proud days of the African kingdoms. Many had walked hundreds of miles through the jungle, leaving their dead along the trail. "And you should see them all now," the captain said. "Starving in the slums while still dreaming of the forest."

The 1996–2003 conflicts had sucked in six African armies, and more than four million people had died, most of them from starvation and sickness as villagers fled through jungles to escape the gunfire and pillage. The fighting still flared in spurts along the eastern borders near Rwanda and Uganda, but most of Congo was now at peace. In July the country had even held presidential elections, the first since independence from Belgium in 1960.

The end of conflict was good news for the river and the forest, the captain said, because things were finally beginning to heal. Peace and elections had given people a sense of confidence, and for the first time in a century a dream of prosperity was taking hold among the Congolese. Boat captains were braving the river, people were returning home, and money was changing hands. As for the captain, he'd be pushing 2,600 tons of freight on two barges all the way to Kisangani, which is where I wanted to go.

For three years I had covered the bloody aftershocks of the conflict, as a freelancer and as the Kinshasa correspondent for the Associated Press. I came to Congo looking for war and I found it, spending every waking minute engrossed in its senseless death. In the end, all the blood had gotten to me, and I left Congo and the AP. But now, with peace taking hold, I was beginning to feel some hope for this damaged country. If a revival was happening along the river, I wanted to see it.

I had already spent three days combing the ports, sucking in the dust and exhaust and having no luck finding a ride, discovering I'd just missed one boat going upriver or that another wasn't leaving for weeks. Now, sitting across from Buisine, I was so relieved that I started to gush, explaining how anxious I was to finally pierce the interior and be with the people, see how they really lived. "Live instead of die!" I said, regrettably.

"*Bon,*" the captain said, smiling, and walked around the desk. "But tell me something. Will you prefer local or European cuisine? It's important I give the chef plenty of notice."

The Congo River, like the rainforest it penetrates, is the second largest in the world; only the Amazon carries a greater volume of water. It stretches three thousand miles from the country's southern highlands and hooks like a scythe over the equator before emptying into the Atlantic at a rate of more than one million cubic feet of water per second. The sheer force of that union has created grooves in the ocean floor almost a mile deep.

The 1,077-mile trip upriver from Kinshasa to Kisangani is one of the world's great journeys. It was along this legendary stretch of water that Arab slave ships once sailed with human cargo bound for the Middle East; here that Henry Morton Stanley battled cannibal tribes and staked the first flags for colonial Belgium, which ruled the country for almost eight decades, killing and torturing tens of

millions of Congolese for the ivory and rubber in their forests. And
it was on this journey in 1890 that a colonial station agent named
Joseph Conrad witnessed so much death that he was inspired to
write *Heart of Darkness,* a description the country has yet to live
down.

I was traveling with Riccardo Gangale, a photographer based in
Kigali, Rwanda, one of a freewheeling fraternity of Italian photog-
raphers who usually made their way through bloody Central Africa
on motorcycles. I'd also hired a fixer in Kinshasa to help with trans-
lations. Severin Mpiana was an electrical engineer with a university
degree, but since unemployment was nearly absolute, he was now
working with foreign journalists. Severin came from a solidly mid-
dle-class family, a rarity in Congo. His father was a banker who'd
put five children through college. Severin had never traveled the
interior of his own country, so the trip was as much an adventure
for him as it was for me.

Our plan was to ride with Buisine as far as Mbandaka, about five
days upriver, then jump to the public barges that cruised the waters
carrying hundreds of traders on their decks. We had heard that the
barges were crowded and filthy, that some boats were marooned on
sandbars for weeks and others sank from overcrowding or colli-
sions in the night. Sanitary conditions were dire, with most barges
having only one toilet for hundreds of people. It was a demoraliz-
ing and often deadly way to trade and travel, but the resilient Congolese sucked it up and endured. And so would we.

With the *Ma'ungano* leaving the next day, we set to work preparing for our journey. We spent a sweltering afternoon in Kinshasa's
central market, purchasing the necessary gear: a durable orange
tarp for slapdash shelters; nylon rope; foam mattresses; pots and
pans; plastic cups and buckets; pills for pain, malaria, and worms;
and dozens of cans of sardines, beans, and corned beef hash. For
days, Riccardo and I had dedicated ourselves to a rigorous Get Fat
Diet, gorging on steaks, doughnuts, and lots of cold beer, trying to
gain weight we'd inevitably lose through sweat and diarrhea. I also
brought along the *Traveler's Guide to the Belgian Congo,* an old tour
book published in Brussels in 1951, back when the colony was the
dazzling gem in darkest Africa. For seventy-five years, the colonial
masters had ruled the Congolese with barbarism and oppression.
But they'd also built sleek European cities connected by gorgeous

highways, luxury trains, and river steamers. How quickly all of that
had vanished in the years since independence. The forest had attacked the empire as if it were a gaping wound, leaving only ugly
scars.

The *Ma'ungano* was one of the last vestiges of the colonial era,
and it was only fitting to begin my journey along its decks. My experience in Congo had always been looking down, from United Nations choppers and armored personnel carriers and balcony apartments shielded by guards and razor wire, from the Land Rovers we
used to escape the misery and smell of disease when it all became
too much. I knew there'd come a time on this journey when turning back wasn't an option, and it was only then that I'd find what I
wanted to know.

That evening we stayed aboard the *Ma'ungano* drinking cans of
Castle beer on the decks, content with our good fortune. Not only
did we have a personal chef; we also had a private cabin equipped
with soft beds, a hot shower, and an air conditioner more efficient
than most I'd owned in the States. I went to bed wired with antici-
pation and awoke to the rumble of engines in the pink 5 A.M. haze.
Running outside, I saw the river bubbling under the rudders; it was
the color of clean motor oil. Seconds later we were moving, but so
slowly that landmarks stayed in view for hours. By late afternoon,
we could still see Kinshasa. I passed the next several days in regi-
mental fashion, waking up before light to climb atop the wheelhouse and watch the sunrise, kicking away the thousands of silver-
winged moths that had perished in the searchlights the night before. A large breakfast of omelets, bread, and avocado was served
on the terrace, and afterward I would jump down to the barges and
hang with the crewmen.

One morning Severin and I walked to the tip of the first barge to
take in the view. The two barges stretched the length of a football
field and were fully loaded, the rounded humps of freight covered
in brightly colored tarps. We tiptoed delicately over the ropes and
tie-downs that crisscrossed our path, and squeezed around two Chinese passenger vans bound for a customs station deep in the trees.
Once we reached the end of the barge, the ever-present sound of
the engines faded, leaving only the bright splash of water against
the slow-moving steel. In front of us the river stretched five miles
across. Patches of puffy green hyacinth floated past, along with co-

lossal islands of grassy earth ripped from the shore by the fierce current. The best seat in the house, I thought, and I wasn't the only one. One of the crewmen already occupied a chair at the edge of the barge. He was fast asleep, with one hand tucked lazily down his pants.

His name was Kalu, and for the past two years he'd worked as a loader and deckhand, traveling the river with Buisine about five times a year. His true field of expertise was botany, which he'd studied as a forestry student in Kisangani. It was also at university that he'd sung lead vocals in a band that played the dark and sweaty nightclubs of the city.

"My friend and I played all the time. We loved to sing," Kalu said. "I wrote songs about everything: love, disappointment, the slave trade."

Singing was Kalu's passion, but the pressures of a career and a family forced him to abandon the dream. He felt the muse slipping away, so he often spent time on the bow of the boat, waiting for inspiration to strike.

"Maybe the view will make me want to write a song," he said, sighing. And after two minutes of absolute silence, he sat up with a jolt of revelation and calmly proclaimed, "The Congo River is a road. And I am only a witness on this road."

One of his old band mates, Papi, was also working for Buisine aboard the *Ma'ungano*. Although they saw each other every day on the river, they never reminisced about old times, and Kalu told me he hadn't even sung a note in two years. But this was just a rough patch, a thirty-two-year-old man going through one of life's transitions.

"My music is still in my blood," he said, pausing to gather his thoughts off the soft river sheen. "Maybe it's not over. I figure all I need to do is record two songs, really big songs, and then my voice will become immortal."

A golden voice could do wonders to balance the weight of life along the river. The dark legends still hung like bad fruit from the trees. Beyond these riverbanks were the red-rubber graveyards where Belgium's King Leopold built his rubber kingdom and helped fuel the Industrial Revolution. For decades, thousands of tons of rubber and ivory were carted out of the jungles on the backs of Congolese slaves; it was a horrific era of murder and insanity that emptied the country of half its population. The places we now passed — Kwamouth, Bolobo, Lukolela — were the hunting grounds of the colonial Force Publique, where villages were once torched for failing to meet quotas, where children were butchered, their tiny hands severed and delivered to headquarters.

When one of the crewmen told me they still hauled raw rubber on the barges, I launched into a long speech about the atrocities that had taken place along these *very banks* — the amputations, the village raids, the heads on pikes. I guess I was hoping for some kernel of survivor wisdom in return, something we could all lean on in times of struggle. But when Severin finished translating, the crew stared at me like I'd just asked how to buy a MetroCard.

"No," the guy said, looking at his friends for reactions. "We don't know about this stuff. You might want to ask the old people."

Walking back, Severin shook his head and gasped. "So many people here, they have no idea of their own history."

Perhaps the span of two cruel wars had been enough history for the crewmen to endure. But to Buisine, history was everything, and it all came together right here. "To understand Congo," he'd say, "you must first understand the river."

During the afternoons, when the heat drove us indoors, the captain would stand at the wheel and mix the bad lessons with the good. His eyes would focus on the channel and he'd explain the things he knew, like how the water silvered at dusk and hid the sandbars, or how the bank appeared dangerously close in the cool morning air. He'd point out whirlpools roiling in the deep spots, crocodiles camouflaged in the mud, or, along a wooded island, a tree whose leaves cured hemorrhoids. After the rains, we trained our eyes upriver and watched ghost ships hover over the water. Low pressure from the storm can play tricks on your eyes, the captain explained, and through a pair of binoculars the boats returned to earth as the rust-eaten barges they really were.

At other times Buisine would point to the distant bank, where a brick building stood shrouded in vines and decay, a remnant of colonial days, and tell the story of the hospital or timber mill the locals had permitted the forest to reclaim. He told me how during the grand days of the colony, rivermen pushed more than two hundred million tons of product a year up and down the Congo. Now, he says, they're lucky if they move even two million. And because there were more and bigger boats, the river was dredged then, and a well-trained captain was easy to find. There were signs posted along the banks indicating sandbars and snags, depth and direction of tributaries; signs telling the rivermen they weren't alone on the black water at night. The captain would wax sentimental about these years before the collapse, when he was young and the country made sense, and during these reveries his eyes never left the river.

He'd been there from the beginning and had watched the dominoes fall one by one. He'd grown up in the eastern town of Bukavu, where his family owned a quarry and cinchona plantation on Lake Kivu. He later served in the French navy and, once discharged, returned to Bukavu looking for quick money and adventure, organizing gorilla tours in nearby Kahuzi-Biega National Park and leading tourists up the smoldering Nyiragongo volcano in the Virunga Mountains.

But the government seized the family's plantation in the mid-1970s, during Mobutu's nationalist land-grab campaign known as "Zairianization." Buisine's uncle walked into his office one morning and found an African sitting in his chair, a midlevel government official from Kinshasa who'd never picked up a shovel. Cinchona (the natural source of quinine) requires meticulous pruning and cultivation, but the new owner rushed the harvest, and the entire crop died. "People whose families had worked there a century committed suicide right then," said Buisine. Years later, Buisine was working at Kinshasa's Palace of the People when he received a phone call one morning at 5 A.M. It was President Mobutu, screaming over the line: "Buisine! From now on you work for me." Mobutu had been impressed by the Frenchman's military background and family history in Congo. Buisine took the job. "Despite everything that had happened," he explained, "when the president calls, you can't say no."

Buisine served as Mobutu's personal superintendent for sixteen years, organizing the dictator's daily schedule, security, and logistics. He was chained to Mobutu's shadow at all times, even living four straight years aboard the lavish presidential yacht, the *Kamanyola,* as it drifted aimlessly down the Congo River. Sometimes, when the Big Man's mood was right, Buisine would mention his family's land. "He'd tell me, 'We'll fix that, we'll fix that. *C'est pas grave,*'" Buisine remembers. "Other times he'd say, 'Look at everything Europe lost during the world wars, and it's doing fine now. Don't make such an issue of this Zairianization.'"

And while Mobutu siphoned off billions in public funds to build palaces, like the one deep in the jungle equipped with a runway for Concorde jets, and to fly in masseuses direct from China, the country rapidly fell apart. Civil servants went unpaid for years, soldiers mutinied and looted the cities clean, inflation soared, water and electricity disappeared, and the average Congolese suffered on $120 a year. Mobutu's era of kleptocracy and neglect finally ended when rebels marched into Kinshasa in early 1997 and installed Laurent Kabila as president. The Big Man fled to Morocco and later died, and Buisine was taken from his home and arrested. He spent nine months in prison, then retreated, upon his release, to the relative quiet of Kinshasa. There, he waited out the war as it ravaged everything Mobutu hadn't already destroyed.

Buisine now led the simple life of a river rat, making his run six or seven times a year. Each trip was spent in the company of his commander, Abraham Bukasa, a tall, slender man with salt-and-pepper hair, whose own military career had also been destroyed by the Big Man's many whims. In 1978, gendarmes threw the young navy sergeant into an underground prison on suspicion of aiding a failed coup. Many of his friends were executed or died from abuse.

Bound by military experience and their own place in Congo's tragic history, the two friends now spent their days on the river. "The river was created by God," said the commander. "It won't change. Only men change."

When United Nations peacekeepers arrived in 2001 to help maintain a cease-fire, Buisine volunteered to help pilot the first UN boats upriver to assess the damage; in recent years, as river traffic slowly increased, he has helped the UN draft the first modern navigational maps of the Congo River. Many of the earth's navigable bodies of water have been mapped using satellite images, which can be downloaded into onboard computer systems or sold as disks. The images are reflected in the printed charts used by most captains, to update new construction of levees or bridges, and to account for bank erosion and shifts in sandbars. In Congo, maps like these were just another bit of the modern world that had passed by the jungle.

Buisine picked up a thick, spineless book of weather-beaten pages and slapped it down on a nearby stool. It was a set of hand-drawn charts issued by the old Belgian-run river authority, meticulously drafted in black and white, and last updated in 1936. "This is all we have in Congo," he said.

Buisine told me that the UN recently provided him with military satellite images of the river that he runs through a global-positioning program. On a large monitor inside the wheelhouse, a red icon of a boat chugged up the bend. Buisine updated the digital map with each trip, recording changes in current speeds, shifts in sandbars, and average depth in the rainy and dry seasons. Village names and coordinates appeared in pop-up windows, along with tribal affiliations and logistical data in the event of UN intervention. The information will someday combine to form a massive database of the river, which Buisine hopes will be available to the public. Each morning I ducked into the wheelhouse to check the progress of the tiny red boat, and each morning the jungle squeezed in a little closer. Outside, the uniform brick settlements of the old colony disappeared and gave way to moldering huts set high above the river on stilts of bamboo. Smoke from breakfast fires crept through their porous roofs, giving the huts the appearance of giant animals steaming in the mist.

But the solitude of the forest was alleviated by the traders who lived there and flocked to the *Ma'ungano* day and night as she passed. They'd strike out from shore in long dugout canoes filled with fish and vegetables, four or five people in each one, stabbing the current with hand-carved paddles the shape of raindrops. We'd watch them from a kilometer out, standing upright as they pumped their arms in perfect unison to make the interception. The river traders supplied the crew with their meals, and it was also how we supplemented ours. We'd buy huge, ten-pound tilapia and give them to the cook, along with spinach, roasted peanuts, green onions, plantains, papaya, and exotic white apples. I bought wild honey so fresh that bees still clung to the arm of the old man who poured it. And we bought mangoes to store in the ship's deep freeze, taking them out on hot afternoons and peeling them with pocketknives. It was like eating ice cream.

In my old guidebook, the local "natives" were dressed in rows of beads and colorful loincloths, their bodies covered with sprawling mutilation tattoos, their lips and ears adorned with brass hooks and trinkets. It was as if nothing had changed since the days of the old monarchies, when the mighty Kongo and Bakuba kingdoms, with their sophisticated systems of law and governance, held sway in this region, back when kings sat on thrones inlaid with ivory. Back before they were discovered. The photos in the guidebook were likely posed, snapped by one of the pith-helmeted agents who also appeared in those pages. Even under the colonial thumb, the Congolese looked proud and dignified. But finding that spirit now was like looking for warrior braves on the Great Plains of North America. The people standing along the riverbank were destitute. No ornamentation here, just rotten secondhand rags that barely hid their nakedness. Bloated children would rush out of thatched huts and wave when they saw white faces. Their mothers often stood behind them, rubbing their stomachs and begging for money. The farther we went, the worse off they appeared. And every time I saw them I felt a little more lost. The point of no return was near, and I began to wonder when the little red boat on the captain's screen would disappear altogether.

Buisine joined me on the deck one afternoon as I watched the villagers along the banks. The war really leveled these people, I offered. He shrugged. "They had nothing even before the war," he said. "They have no education, and their diet is nothing but fish and alcohol from the cradle to the grave. Nothing has changed for hundreds of years. I mean, they still make fires by rubbing sticks together."

I sometimes teased Severin about moving out to the "country" and settling down, living the simple life with the river people, but the joke would fall flat. "To think we had one of the greatest civilizations in Africa," he said once, shaking his head. "But now . . ." Severin had grown up around some of the world's nastiest poverty just outside his door in Kinshasa, and I think he was hoping, like me, to find something better in the vast, green interior. "Now these people can't even read, only count," he'd say, echoing Buisine. "No school, no prospects for the future. What will become of their children?"

One afternoon, Buisine explained an elaborate plan he'd been pondering for years, a plan to turn the Congo River into a national park for tourists. I laughed at first, since anything related to tourism in Congo struck me as an impossible dream. But he was serious. "I used to speak with Mobutu about this for hours," he said. "Mobutu was very passionate about the land and environment." The plan was to transform the river into a massive nature preserve that stretched from Kisangani to the Atlantic. The vast chain of hundreds of river islands would be stocked with wild game, which would be imported from South Africa, where private game parks were becoming wildly overpopulated. Instead of killing the animals, Buisine said, the businessmen who owned the reserves were eager to partner with people in Congo, where many of the animals have been decimated by war. "All the islands on this river represent the ecosystems of Central Africa," said Buisine. "You have primary and secondary forests, swamps, savannah — everything."

There would be antelope and zebras, leopards and lions, elephants and hyenas. All the villagers living along the river would be appointed game wardens and rangers in order to maintain the park and guard the animals from poachers. Tourists would spend days cruising the park by riverboat, stopping at rustic lodges along the way to camp, barbecue, and sip cocktails. Villagers would visit the boats during the day for "cultural lessons," teaching tourists how to fish, weave casting nets, or carve the masks this section of Congo was famous for.

"It would be the greatest, most unique national park in all the world," Buisine mused. "And every person who lives on this river would be part of its glory." He explained how he'd been pitching the plan for the past decade, first to Mobutu, then to various environmental groups. Everyone agreed it was a good idea, but nothing was ever done. The South African business partners were already lined up. The plan would cost billions to implement, but it was necessary if the river were to maintain its virgin ecosystem before democracy and peace brought development and ruin. "The Congo River is the great lungs of the world," he said. "We must preserve and maintain this living thing. It's the only good thing we have left."

Upriver in Ngombe, the *Ma'ungano* was intercepted by two motorboats carrying men with guns. Several muscled men with AK-47s and aviator sunglasses jumped aboard and ran toward the captain's room. I was sitting on the terrace when they charged past. At first I thought we were being hijacked by pirates or robbed by the army, but they turned out to be soldiers loyal to Jean-Pierre Bemba, a popular rebel leader who had once controlled this region during the war. Bemba's troops had officially joined the army in order to share in the new government, and Bemba himself had become vice president. In the recent elections, Bemba had run for president and narrowly lost in the first round to Joseph Kabila, who came to power in 2001 after his father, Laurent Kabila, was assassinated. Just weeks after the vote, Bemba's men battled the presidential guard in the streets of Kinshasa and trapped me in the Grand Hotel. The two men would face off again in a runoff election on October 29, which Riccardo and I planned to cover somewhere upriver.

The soldiers told Buisine they had a prisoner they were transporting to Mbandaka. They needed a ride, a free ride. Buisine cringed and agreed, and one of the soldiers signaled for the prisoner to come aboard. He was barefoot and dressed in fatigues, his arms flexi-cuffed behind his back. His face was swollen and red from a heavy beating. The soldiers pushed him into a metal shed on the barge and sat guard out front, eating bananas and tossing the peels into the river. With guns now aboard the *Ma'ungano,* the mood quickly darkened throughout the boat, and everyone became tense and agitated. No matter how far you ran, I thought, the war would always find you.

There was a major dressed in a crisp uniform aboard the prisoner's barge, and after instructing his men, he walked into the captain's room, where Buisine sat at the wheel. Buisine smiled and greeted him warmly. The major had once been a Mobutu bodyguard during the heyday of pink champagne and Concorde flights. When Laurent Kabila's rebels stormed the interior of the country in 1997 to oust Mobutu, the major's position was overrun, and he was forced to join the rebels or be killed. He joined the rebels, and when Kabila's men took Kinshasa, he attacked his former troops. He later deserted and joined Bemba's thriving rebel army in the jungles in their fight against Laurent Kabila. Despite being in the national army, the major still considered himself a rebel officer.

Buisine hadn't seen him for years, and for the next few hours the two dinosaurs did some catching up. Have you seen so-and-so? No, he's dead. What about so-and-so? Dead, too. And so-and-so? He's in

Europe, couldn't find a place in the new government. They talked about the upcoming runoff, how a Kabila victory could spell disaster for those sympathizing with Bemba. The major's men were scared. "Do yourself a favor," Buisine told the major. "Keep a low profile. In six months, this whole place could be fucked."

Buisine instructed the cook to prepare a meal and a bed for the major, and once the captain was alone, I asked him if the army had a satellite phone in Ngombe. It was just a small fishing village and there was no cellular coverage. No, he said, I don't think they have a sat phone.

"Then how did they know you were coming?" I asked.

"The neighboring village told them," he said. "With drums."

We reached Mbandaka, exactly seven hundred kilometers up the river from where we began, on the seventh day. There was no electricity in the town, and already dozens of oil lamps flickered on shore in advance of the rapid darkness. As we pulled into port, we saw what appeared to be a floating refugee camp with hundreds piled aboard, living under tents made from humanitarian flour sacks. Plumes of smoke from charcoal stoves shrouded the steel deck, and somewhere a radio blared a wobbly tune as its batteries slowly died. Men danced drunk in the shadows and toddlers rolled naked in the coal dust. She was called the *Ndobo,* and her barges pointed upriver, toward Kisangani. We immediately knew: *That's our boat.*

Riccardo, Severin, and I leaned over the rail when the *Ma'ungano* touched its barge against the *Ndobo* to tie up. And when the crowds of people camped below saw our white faces, they roared and chanted, *"Mundele! Mundele! You've arrived!"*

Severin sighed. "These people are waiting for us," he said, his face pinched and worried. I asked him what *Ndobo* meant in Lingala. "The hook," he answered, and walked back into his room.

The boat would travel to Ndobo, its namesake town located 550 kilometers upriver. It was operated by a Lebanese timber company that was logging thousands of square kilometers of forest between Ndobo and Kisangani. The *Ndobo* had come from Kinshasa with passengers loaded on its three barges and, upon reaching its destination, would return to the capital loaded with timber bound for Europe. A few hundred more passengers were expected to board that day, and they'd already started arriving. The fare was $10.

We needed to stake out a prime location on the barge, so the next morning we hurried down the market road, looking for a vendor who specialized in the long wooden poles used for barge shelters. Mbandaka is a river city, and everything bought, sold, and traded in the market somehow caters to the ships that drift by. I'd heard stories about Mbandaka, none of them very good. It was grim, hopeless stuff: boat sinkings, mutinies, cholera. The city floats on the map like some lost outpost severed from the world and rendered completely insane by the silence. Mbandaka is the last exit before things turn wild for good. Once you pass Mbandaka, you have to go all the way.

Mbandaka straddles the equator at the junction of the Congo and Ruki rivers, and was founded by Stanley in 1883 as one of the colony's first stations. Formerly called Coquilhatville, the city was a thriving port during the days of rubber and ivory, with hundreds of Europeans living in white stone villas shaded by groves of coconut palms. The old steamers bound for Kisangani (then Stanleyville) would stop at the equator station, giving passengers time to visit the botanical gardens in Eala, which featured more than four thousand species of local flora. But, like everything else, the city slowly collapsed when the Belgians pulled up stakes after independence.

When Rwandan-backed rebels invaded Congo in late 1996, their goal was to exterminate the Hutu extremists who'd orchestrated Rwanda's genocide and then escaped into the Congolese mountains. Thousands of innocent Hutu also feared retribution and mixed into the mass exodus across the border. Many headed west into the dense jungle as rebels pursued them. For seven months they were chased through the forest, many dying from malaria, cholera, and starvation, until they reached the Congo River near Mbandaka. The river was too swift and wide to cross over to neighboring Congo-Brazzaville, where they'd hoped to find asylum. Many tried to swim and disappeared in the current. The rest simply collapsed along the banks and awaited their fate. When rebels arrived soon after, missionaries working nearby stood helpless as hundreds were shot and hacked to death with machetes and bayonets. The bodies were flung into the river. Residents downstream in Kinshasa say the bloated corpses floated past for days.

I found no memorials for the dead in Mbandaka, but their ghosts seemed to riot on the streets to agitate the living. As we walked in search of materials for our shelter, crowds along the market road soon pressed all around. Several plump, red-cheeked women pushed their way to the front. They held smoked monkey carcasses, hogtied with bellies cut open and fangs exposed in a horrific death mask. A small crocodile was flung at our feet, its jaws bound with vines, its eyes like dark, smoky windows. Children ran forward to beat it with sticks; others taunted the beast with stones. *"Mundele! Mundele!"* they shouted. The croc thrashed wildly, beating its powerful tail against the mud in a final stand against the enemy. It was then snatched away and tossed into the grass, where a group of the reptiles were dying slowly in the sun.

We found the long wooden poles we needed at the far end of the market and carried them back to the barge. We claimed a small empty space nearest the tug and set to work building our house. The wooden poles were lashed together with nylon rope to form a reinforced A-frame, which we secured to railway ties along the barge. Our roof was constructed from the orange tarp and woven grass mats we'd bought in the market. Inside, there was barely room for the three of us to sit, much less sleep. We celebrated that night with cold beer and steaks at the only good restaurant in town. The dim fluorescent lights of the Metropole drew swarms of insects so large they cast slow-moving shadows across the empty tables. A dance floor was situated in the middle of the outdoor patio, where a fat woman waltzed with a man too drunk to keep time. The slow *soukous* ballads played from an old cassette deck that ebbed and flowed with surges in the generator and sometimes blew static so loud patrons shielded their heads as if they were under attack.

The waitress sat drinking at a dark corner table with a large white man who spoke fluent Lingala — a Belgian, I guessed — dressed in a starched oxford shirt with several empty bottles in front of him. His skin was the color of ash, with pasty liver spots creeping up his neck and cheeks. There was something already dead about him, the way his face moved in and out of the shadow but never really took shape; watching him was like staring at a scarecrow from a fast-moving car. Like the town, he seemed to float in some restless space, cut off long ago and unable to find his way back. He put the chill on me. I ordered a beer and shifted my chair, keeping my back to the colonial ghost in the corner.

The next morning, around four hundred people crowded the barges of the *Ndobo* as we pulled out of port and said goodbye to

Mbandaka and the luxury of the *Ma'ungano*. Our proud little shelter offered a wide-open view of the left bank, but as the hours slowly passed, the sunlight and precious silence disappeared, never to return. Plastic sheeting and threadbare tarps were pulled from heaping bundles, poles materialized from nowhere, pots and pans rattled on the deck, and radios thundered to life. In a very short time, a small village had risen up around us. These were the river traders, the men and women who move Congo's economy like a great army of ants. Every journey was a roll of the dice, a chance to double down or wash up in the backwater. But they took the risk because life in the city was far less forgiving. Traveling the river was the good life.

"*Mundele,*" my neighbor yelled. "Put away your notebook and come drink some wine!" It was 11 A.M., an hour after leaving port, and the party aboard the *Ndobo* was in full throttle. Our neighbors to the right, Lucy and Toni, were pouring milky palm wine into plastic mugs. A new camp began every four feet, and every four feet a different radio blasted its buoyant rumba. The sun radiated through the orange tarp like a heat lamp, sucking at our energy. Small chores, such as filtering water or washing dishes, stole our breath and left us wilted. I finally put away my notebook and just focused on not passing out.

The three barges were so crowded that corridors soon formed through the floating village. One walkway barreled past our tent, and most people stopped to stare at the two *mundele* who had come aboard. "*Bonjour,*" we'd offer, like freaks in a cage, until the people laughed and sauntered off.

The barges were like giant floating supermarkets, and one could buy almost anything in the great bazaar that spread itself along the steel deck. Walking through the narrow corridors you found essential items like lye soap in blue and pink blocks, Angola brand toothbrushes sold in packs of six, safety razors, plastic mirrors, lead spoons, needle and thread, travel-size bags of raw sugar, beads and necklaces, women's panties with LOVE embroidered on the crotch, rubber sandals, nylon fishing nets, Betasol lotion, and Tiger Head batteries that lasted exactly four hours.

On the barge you could find quinine and chloroquine for malaria, hydration salts for diarrhea, and pills for intestinal worms and pain. There were nurses and midwives, witch doctors and preachers, and a man for just about every trade. Our neighbor Lucy sold the secondhand clothing worn by almost everyone on the barge and along the river: the ubiquitous American T-shirts donated to charities and dumped on the African market. Everywhere you looked was a strange remnant of home; the old grandmother who advertised a strip club in Kentucky or the stoic fisherman whose shirt read I'M THE BIG SISTER.

Lucy was from Kinshasa, and she had pretty green eyes and short dreadlocks woven with decorative blue thread. She'd traded along the river for the past decade, through war and peace and all the trouble in between. During the war, when the river was closed, she was forced to walk hundreds of miles through the jungle north of Kinshasa. Soldiers and rebels prowled the narrow trails. Friends were raped by soldiers in front of their children, and everyone was taxed and robbed for the "war effort." Lucy had already lost everything twice to storms and thieves. "When you lose your stuff, there's nothing for you," she said. "They don't sell insurance on the river." With every trip, Lucy would sink her savings into merchandise in Kinshasa and hope to double her profits along the river. Everything else on the barge was also a hustle, including the plastic chairs she rented to us for a dollar a day and the small money she made each morning selling cups of coffee boiled with ginger root. Other traders supplemented their income by selling fried beignets smeared with homemade peanut butter or bowls of fresh catfish soup.

I could tell that the river traders made an impression on Severin, who had warmed up to our neighbors considerably. Their brassy resilience and resourcefulness impressed him, and he now counted many friends on the barge, joking and debating politics and religion. He later discovered that Lucy even lived on his street in Kinshasa and was friends with his mother.

"They are loud and uneducated, but the river people are teaching me many things," he said one night. "How to make money from nothing and survive. In many ways, their life is better than in Kinshasa. Notice they eat five meals a day! Only the rich can eat like this in the city."

I began spending time with an army lieutenant named Pierre Kitebo, who was traveling back to Kisangani. He had been lost in the great labyrinth of war and faraway deployment and had not seen his family in eight years. The army had finally granted him a leave, so he set out to find his family, carrying only an old photo of his wife to keep him warm and a vague idea of where they lived. He'd spent three weeks on another barge from Kisangani to Basankusu, where he finally found his family in a small hut deep in the jungle. When Pierre had left eight years before, his youngest daughter, Benedite, was still in her mother's womb. She didn't recognize the tall, beaming man in army fatigues when he walked out of the trees.

"They all ran out and hugged me," he said. "They were happy to see their daddy."

He now sat in a cramped, ragged lean-to, surrounded by his wife, two sons, and daughter, who were finally going home to Kisangani, where he trained soldiers in an army camp. He pulled the little girl close to his chest and kissed her head. "They were naked when I found them," he said. "But there will be no more suffering now."

Here, I thought, I was beginning to see signs of recovery. I'd also found it in people like Lucy and Solange, another neighbor, who'd already doubled her $400 investment. I saw the recovery in men like Jean Kalokula, whose last river journey had been with a convoy of pirogues during the war. They'd traveled at night to avoid checkpoints and slept in the jungles during the day, until malaria finally killed most of his party. He'd buried their bodies on the lonely middle islands and limped back to Kinshasa to wait out the war. He was now traveling the river again for the first time since then, a man who was proud to be going back to work. In all of these people, a sense of dignity had been restored.

But after a few days on the barge, having found the story I thought I'd come for, something started to change. All the romance I'd imposed on the river and its people began to fade. Their all-night drinking now grated on my nerves, and the endless heat only fueled the slow crawl of madness. It would be days, maybe even weeks, before we reached Kisangani. The river owned me now.

Sometimes I'd sit in my tent for hours, stoned on the humidity, watching the molecules behind my eyes ignite like tiny starbursts, when an evil stench would smack me awake. One afternoon I swore someone's head was on fire. The heat made the smell stick in the back of my throat. I followed a pale cloud of smoke to where a woman sat flipping a giant dead monkey over a charcoal stove, scorching the fur and scraping the char with a broad machete. Its innards were still intact and boiling out of its mouth. The next morning, while rolling up my mattress, I discovered tiny pea-shaped objects writhing beneath my bed. *Maggots,* I thought, the word like a blinking banner across my mind. *Maggots* on *my pillow. Maggots* on *my pillow.* I kicked the maggots away with my boots and went in search of breakfast. That same afternoon, while eating a stick of beef jerky, I looked down to find a matted wad of pubic hair resting on my arm. I shrugged, blew it back into the wind, and finished my jerky.

The dirt and stench, the pigs and chickens that ran wild and defecated where people ate, the mountains of ripe bushmeat in every camp — these annoyances we learned to handle. But as the days stretched on, the imposing isolation of the river fed tiny fears and anxieties until they festered into their own little nightmares. It finally peaked a few nights later as I sat on the tie post by the water's edge. I'd sat there watching the sun crash behind the jungle, illuminating the soft mist that crept along the water. And now in the darkness I was enjoying the first cool breezes of the day, and for some reason the radios didn't seem so loud. For the first time in days, I was even feeling a bit hopeful again. As I sat there, I actually wrote in my notebook, "Watching the river moving past — this is what keeps the spirit strong when you get low. This is when I love this place the most."

Suddenly the engines faded and I felt the barge veer to the bank, where it eventually stopped. Not only did we stop; I watched the tugboat *Ndobo* disengage from the barges, turn around, and disappear downriver, stranding us on the riverbank in jet black darkness. The taillights vanishing in the night seemed to be sucking my breath after them. And when they were gone, I panicked.

Riccardo was standing nearby, aiming his flashlight into the black vacuum of the jungle's edge. He smiled. "What do you call it?" he said. "The white man's grave? Well, man, they've left us in the white man's grave." I walked back to our tent, where Severin had just returned from his nightly rounds. "It's the captain's son," he said. "He was burned very badly. They had to find a hospital."

"The nearest hospital is two days away," I said. I looked for panic in his eyes but found none, not even the slightest hint of irritation.

He was maddeningly calm. "No one seems to care." He shrugged. "This is their life."

It was true. Instead of panicking, the Congolese only amped up the party. The saucy rumba now roared behind an arsenal of fresh batteries, and jugs of palm wine sloshed from camp to camp. Stranded on a remote stretch of river in the middle of the jungle, they reacted by dancing as if it were their last night on earth.

I shined my light down the barge and saw several men pissing in the river. This was normal; there was only one toilet for all four hundred people, so the guys usually did their minor business over the side. But now, near the bank, the current was stagnant, and just a few feet downstream, half a dozen women were scooping up the same water and drinking it. "We've gotta get off this boat," I gasped. "We've gotta get off this boat or we'll all die of cholera."

The year before, a barge had been hit with cholera on the same remote stretch east of Mbandaka. By the time the passengers reached the next town, dozens were dead on the deck. Yes, I thought, it would happen just like that, here and now. I watched the cholera move like a phantom across the barge, sliding its finger across the throats of little children, before sliding into me. The black wall of jungle pulsed all around, and I could feel it swallowing me like a dying star.

A little later, Riccardo returned with a handful of whiskey packets that were sold all over the barge. And after a few of those, I began to feel better. I still desperately wanted to get off, and I could tell that Riccardo agreed, if only for the sake of forward progress. We decided our only prayer was flagging down a passing boat, but we hadn't seen one in nearly two days. "What about Buisine?" I said. "He can't be more than twelve hours behind." That was it, we decided, Buisine would save us! We began to fantasize about the *Ma'ungano* rumbling past and sending its dugout to the rescue. "So long, suckers!" we'd yell, using our boots to beat away the doomed crowds who would try to tag along, to weasel in on our air-conditioning and hot showers. All night I lay awake listening for the sound of diesel engines passing by.

The *Ndobo* finally returned the next afternoon. It had traveled three kilometers downriver to Mankanza, where there was a small clinic. The three-year-old son of the *Ndobo*'s captain had tipped a pot of boiling oil over his body, but the doctor in Mankanza could do little for his burns. There was no medicine, so Riccardo and I treated the boy with ointment from our medical kits until we reached Ndobo three days later.

I was glad to leave the barge, and watched impassively as the traders picked apart our shelter down to the very last rope. They could have it. We hitched a ride with the timber company car to Bumba, where we were planning to cover the runoff election. And since the *Ndobo* was turning back around for Kinshasa, Bumba was where we hoped to find a motorized pirogue to Kisangani. We'd now traveled 1,337 kilometers in fifteen days.

Like Mbandaka, Bumba is an old Belgian trading port that crumbled long ago. Here the Congo stretches twelve miles across at its widest point, though this imperial view was blocked by chains of wooded islands that seemed to throttle the great river and suck the living air from the town. There were two bars for killing the time, and the beer was cool and plentiful, but no restaurants or cafés. We took our meals in the Hotel Mozulua, where the heat and mosquitoes kept us awake at night and pushed us to press forward.

The runoff election was the most significant step toward peace and stability in the country's history. But we'd become so impatient to keep moving that it became little more than a distraction. The vote was no mystery either. For much of the war, Bumba and the surrounding region had been occupied by Bemba's rebel force, who'd raped and murdered and lived by the gun. Yet despite these crimes, almost everyone supported Bemba for president. Bemba's tribe hailed from the forest, and it was said that President Joseph Kabila wasn't even Congolese, that his roots were in Tanzania. To them, it explained why the president had auctioned off much of the country's mineral wealth to foreigners. And with no reliable source of news in the jungle, rumor trumped all.

The morning polls went smoothly enough, and Riccardo and I toured the various stations and interviewed voters. I found myself having the same conversations I'd had during every other African election I'd covered.

"What kinds of changes will you demand from the winner?"

Silence. "Hmmm."

"So you're demanding peace, electricity, and better schools for your kids?"

"Oh, yes, yes . . . peace. Peace and schools."

We'd just hired bike taxis back to the hotel when everything went strange. The once crowded streets suddenly were empty, void of dogs and children and women ferrying to the market. Looking around, I saw people staring out windows and sheepishly standing in doorways — both bad signs. A government lorry rumbled past loaded with soldiers brandishing their readied guns. And when we turned a corner toward the hotel, my heart sank to my shoes.

A mob of about a hundred young men was rumbling down the dusty roadway carrying machetes, sticks, and rocks. Earlier that morning, a Kabila supporter had been caught stuffing a ballot box in one of the stations. The mob had burned the ballots and set fire to several buildings. They now rioted through the narrow streets, spewing venom against Kabila and thieving foreigners. When they saw us, it was like we'd stepped right into their trap. *"Ay, étranger!"* they shouted, and quickened their pace. Riccardo raced toward them with cameras held high. And whereas I would usually follow, this time I froze.

As a reporter in Congo, I'd endured my share of drunken soldiers and guns, but it was mobs that terrified me the most. All it took was one rock in the face to draw first blood and the rioters would pounce like wolves. I'd been through some bad times in Togo and Somalia and in Kinshasa, but that morning in Bumba, I suddenly felt my luck had run its course. A voice, diamond-sharp in my mind, told me to turn back immediately. There were no lives left. If I stayed, only bad things would happen.

"Allez! Allez!" I screamed at my driver, a small boy whose body had gone rigid. "Severin, tell this kid to go!"

We turned onto a deserted backstreet and moved parallel with the angry crowd, struggling for speed on the sandy roads. Some of the mob caught up and held rocks to our heads, leering and shouting threats. But we finally found our intersection and soon were safe within the high walls of the Hotel Mozulua.

Later that afternoon, soldiers charged the mob with bullets and tear gas. Three people were killed and dozens were beaten and arrested. One of those killed was a fifteen-year-old boy, gunned down in the street. His uncle found us at the hotel that night. "He was only throwing rocks," the man said. "And they shot him in the head. His brains aren't even there anymore." Of the hundreds of towns and villages in Congo where people voted that day, Bumba was the only one to erupt in violence. Overall, the election was hailed as a landmark success, a victory for peace after a decade of blood. But standing in the dark courtyard of the Mozulua, listening to another man plan another funeral, it sounded the same to me.

In the end, there were no boats to take us to Kisangani, so we hired a convoy of bicycles and continued east into the boiling sun. Our journey led us off the river and far into the jungle, beyond any guidebook or map. The war had ended, but peaceful revival had done little for the crowds of children who lined the forest track, their stomachs bloated from hunger, their mothers begging us to save them, begging us to do something. There was nothing I could do, nothing except pedal faster, leaving behind the naive ideas I'd clung to along the road.

PANKAJ MISHRA

The Train to Tibet

FROM *The New Yorker*

ON AN EVENING in late December, amid the chaos of Beijing West Railway Station, I stood in line for a train that looked little different from any of the other long-distance services shuffling into the vast Chinese hinterland. And yet the train I was about to board, the new Chinese service from Beijing to Lhasa, in Tibet, runs on the highest railroad in the world. Traversing a region known for earthquakes, low temperatures, and low atmospheric pressure, the railroad, which cost $4.2 billion to build, is an extraordinary feat of modern engineering — perhaps even, as the former Chinese premier Zhu Rongji has claimed, "an unprecedented project in the history of mankind." In two days, the train brings you to a region that thwarted some of the boldest travelers and explorers of the past.

The route's prospect encourages the laziest kind of armchair fantasy — of great expanses of the "roof of the world" rolling into view with silky black yaks grazing in the grasslands and prayer flags fluttering from gold-topped temples. The train is meant only partly for seekers of Tibet's romance, however. Beijing claims that the railroad between Golmud, in Qinghai Province, and Lhasa, which began operation on July 1 last year, will help speed up the modernization of the country's second-largest region, one of the remotest and least developed. Many critics, meanwhile, have denounced the railroad as a means for the Chinese authorities to strengthen their hold on Tibet, further settling the region with China's ethnic majority, the Han Chinese, and eroding indigenous Tibetan culture. Tibet, which is almost as big as Texas, California, and New York

State combined, also holds vast reserves of copper, iron, lead, zinc, and other minerals vital to China's economic growth.

In the long, disorderly line for the train, there were hardly any foreign tourists. I noticed several Chinese officials cutting ahead, dressed in Western suits and trailed by armed soldiers. Polite uniformed coach attendants stood rigidly at attention outside the pine green cars, but no one asked to see my expensively acquired permit for travel in Tibet.

Once aboard, I found my "soft sleeper" cabin, the ticket for which had cost about twelve hundred yuan, or some hundred and sixty dollars. Containing four bunk beds, it seemed very cramped. The introduction of luxury rolling stock is scheduled for the end of this year; the cars will feature private suites measuring a hundred square feet, and tickets will cost a thousand dollars a day. Meanwhile, it seemed that any impulse to luxury, or even basic comfort, had been squeezed out of my compartment. Flat-panel televisions, headphones, and a solitary white plastic rose in a narrow glass vase only highlighted its bleak functionalism. The ceiling was very low, and the space between the lower berths was barely wide enough for one person to stand up in, let alone four passengers struggling with severe altitude sickness.

To my relief, no one showed up to share my cabin. Indeed, despite subsidized fares and Chinese claims that 450,000 people took the train in its first two and a half months of operation, the train seemed far from full. I changed into my nightclothes, and hurried to the toilet at the end of the railcar; squat-style, it did not promise to stay clean for long. Back in the compartment, an attendant brought a thermos of hot water and then a rubber tube wrapped in a plastic packet. Wordlessly, he showed me how to attach it to the oxygen valve above my berth. The extra oxygen was a necessary precaution — the air in the mountains of Tibet contains 35–40 percent less oxygen than at sea level — but made the compartment look like a mobile clinic.

As the train slid away from Beijing, a P.A. system came to life. After a long speech in Chinese, a deep voice with a strange American accent unctuously intoned, "Dear passengers," and began to relay impressive statistics about the 700-mile railroad extension from Qinghai to Tibet: laid by a hundred thousand workers over five years, it traverses 340 miles of permafrost, often at altitudes between thirteen and sixteen thousand feet. Chinese pride in the railroad is intense, as I knew from a three-hour documentary that had been broadcast on the state-run CCTV channel in 2006. It had detailed the history of successive efforts by Chinese leaders to build the railway, and the struggles and sacrifices of construction workers, and had also asserted China's commitment to bringing "modern civilization" to Tibet, which it described as "a once remote and backward place." It claimed that Tibetans had been "yearning for decades" for the rail link to Lhasa, and showed Tibetans singing, in Mandarin, of their love for the Chinese motherland.

Such propaganda notwithstanding, the greatest rail construction ventures in history, in the American West and the Siberian East, do not come close to matching the technical achievement of the railroad to the Tibet Autonomous Region (as the land previously ruled by the Dalai Lama has been officially called since 1965). Laying rail tracks across Tibet's permafrost is especially risky, because the surface is prone to melt as temperatures rise. Chinese engineers faced this challenge with innovative cooling strategies. They elevated tracks; they put in a network of pipes to circulate liquid nitrogen and cold air beneath the rails in order to keep them frozen throughout the year; they installed metal sunshades in south-facing locations to deflect warmth from the sun. Although the carriages of the train looked old to me, they had UV-resistant coatings and an eco-friendly wastewater-storage system, and their underbellies were enclosed to protect wiring from snowstorms and sandstorms. A complex mechanism drew in outside air and released nitrogen and other gases while pumping oxygen-enriched air through the train.

I went to sleep early and woke up when it was still dark outside. For hours afterward, I lay in bed, waiting for light to nibble at the edges of the curtains. The light, when it came, was gray and dirty. Thick mist lay outside, through which the sun appeared as a sickly yellow blur. The view from the window, divided cleanly by the white plastic rose, did not improve as the day leaked away. Mist, smog, and dust stifled the passing scenery; the only color lay in sheets of blue plastic covering vegetable fields beside the tracks. Once, a station sign proclaimed a resonant place-name: XI'AN. We were in the antique heartland of China, watered by the Yellow River. Occasionally, the train, moving swiftly and smoothly, appeared to be in a gorge; we seemed to be traveling through Gansu, which has some of the roughest landscape in China.

In the dining room, as plain as an office canteen, the officials I had seen cutting in line on the platform were having a noisy meal, voices raised and chopsticks fluttering in the air. Their guards stood at a respectful distance while a pretty Chinese waitress hovered around them.

Fantasizing about this trip, I had often seen myself in the dining car, eating spicy tofu and drinking green tea, as the train to Lhasa ambled to its highest point, Tanggula Pass. But when the waitress finally delivered to me the tattered English version of the menu, it turned out to be resolutely unglamorous, with "vegetable stock" but no spicy tofu. I settled for fried eggplant and rice.

Back in my compartment after lunch, I called — on my British cell phone, which miraculously worked — a Tibetan exile in Dharamsala, the Dalai Lama's hometown in India. My friend had escaped recently, after living for some years near the railroad in Qinghai. He seemed both surprised and pleased to hear from someone traveling through his old haunts. He told me to compare the number of Tibetan passengers and workers on the train with the number of Chinese. He said, "No one will talk to you, but just go and count the number of Tibetans."

I had seen some Tibetans, recognizable by their full faces and burning-red cheeks, on the platform in Beijing the day before. They had seemed as anxious as everyone else to get on the train. In the morning, there had been four young Tibetans — in knockoff Nikes and identical raffish suede jackets — in the dining car. The pretty waitress, who had been ingratiating with the officials, was brusque with them, placing a single menu on their table without a glance in their direction, and then ignoring their attempts to get her attention.

I had been tempted to approach them. But I knew from an earlier visit to Tibet, in 2004, that Tibetans seen talking to foreigners, especially journalists, could invite unwelcome attention from the apparently numerous spies, informers, and plainclothes policemen. Were Tibetans on the train being monitored? I couldn't tell. But the Tibetan in Dharamsala was categorical about the train's purpose: it was meant to help Han Chinese move to Tibet to take advantage of the benefits and concessions offered by the Chinese government; it was also meant to take mineral resources out of the region.

Shortly before boarding the train, I had heard a fierce version of this argument from a Tibetan poet and essayist named Woeser. Many young Tibetan exiles in India and the West regard Woeser as a heroine, the first major secular voice within China to speak out against Chinese rule over Tibet. In the bleak grayness of December Beijing, at the hotel where I had arranged to meet her, she struck a defiantly ethnic note, wearing a gold-and-red Tibetan jacket with a side opening, suede boots, and orange-streaked silver earrings. I had expected to meet someone bearing the visible strain of state oppression, but Woeser seemed unbowed. Curiosity animated her broad oval face, making her look much younger than her forty years, and she smiled quickly between bursts of fervent speech.

"The train is a colonial imposition," she said, and she quoted Edward Said's description of imperialism as "geographical violence." She told me that Chinese rule over Tibet had grown much more repressive in the previous two years. She added, "Han Chinese already dominated Lhasa, and since the train arrived in July the city has changed even faster." Her vehement tone made me look around nervously for likely eavesdroppers.

In the struggle over Tibet, Woeser is an anomalous figure. Nothing in her background inclined her toward dissidence. Her half-Tibetan father had been a teenage soldier in China's People's Liberation Army (P.L.A.), which "peacefully liberated" Tibet in 1951, establishing Communist rule over a mostly Buddhist population and eventually forcing its leader, the Dalai Lama, to flee. (Soon after, China strengthened its hold on Tibet with a new road from Golmud to Lhasa, along much the same route as the one now taken by the railroad.) Born in 1966, Woeser was, as she writes in one of her poems, "raised under the bugle of the P.L.A." in Tibet. She was ten when Mao Zedong died, in 1976, and she burst into tears when she heard the news.

Woeser's first language is Chinese — she still doesn't read or write Tibetan — and as a young poet, she told me, she had no interest in politics until she read, in the late 1980s, a Chinese translation of a book about Tibetan refugees by John Avedon (son of

Richard Avedon). Through the '90s, she worked in a government job in Lhasa, as the editor of the magazine *Tibetan Literature.* It was not until 2000, when she met her partner, Wang Lixiong — an expert on Tibet, though he is Han Chinese — that she began to write critically about Chinese rule over Tibet. In 2003, the Chinese authorities moved against her. They banned her most popular book, *Notes on Tibet,* ostensibly for praising the Dalai Lama. She lost her job and was forbidden to leave the region. Ordered to receive "re-education" by visiting construction sites of the railroad in order to write articles praising the project, she managed to leave Tibet. She now lives with Wang Lixiong and his mother in a Beijing suburb.

A recently translated volume of Woeser's and Wang Lixiong's writings, *Unlocking Tibet,* offers a forthright statement about the Chinese challenge to Tibetan culture and identity. Last year, Tibet's economy grew even faster than China's rate of 10.7 percent, helped by subsidies from Beijing — which, in recent years, have constituted more than half of local government revenue — and more than a million tourists each year. These days, Lhasa resembles a Chinese provincial city on the make. Crowds of people, mostly Han Chinese, swarm thoroughfares lined by shopping malls, new glass-and-steel office buildings, and massage parlors and hair salons, which are often fronts for brothels. In *Unlocking Tibet,* Woeser naturally deplores these changes. She also criticizes the manner in which the Chinese government has restored many Buddhist monasteries and temples that had been destroyed during Mao's Cultural Revolution. The Tibetans who flock to these temples seem to enjoy considerable religious freedom, but Woeser, in an essay on the Potala Palace, accuses the Chinese of turning the Dalai Lama's former residence in Lhasa into a mine of "unlimited commercial opportunities."

It was hard not to feel that Woeser, awakening late to Tibet's plight, was trying to make amends, through her ardent denunciations of the Chinese regime, for the long years when she was a member of the Tibetan elite, unthinkingly loyal to its Chinese overlords. I was struck by the similarity of her situation to that of a young Tibetan monk she describes in one of her essays: taken by Chinese authorities to a human rights conference in Europe, the politically innocent man is thrown into confusion and sorrow by an angry crowd of Tibetan exiles accusing him of being a "Communist lama."

Woeser's outspokenness about Tibet also disconcerted me because I had found it impossible to meet Tibetans in China willing to speak to me, even off the record. Recent reports by human rights organizations assert that Buddhist monks in Tibet are still forced to denounce the Dalai Lama, and Tibetans are prohibited from possessing pictures of him. Woeser seems especially vulnerable. In 1999, Wang Lixiong was detained and interrogated by security officials in Muslim-dominated Xinjiang for more than a month. A policeman, Woeser told me, permanently monitors their apartment.

I asked Woeser if she wanted me to keep some of her remarks off the record. No longer smiling, she spoke rapidly to the interpreter, and then stared expectantly at me as I listened to the translation.

"I don't care," she said.

Woeser's emphatic rejection of the railroad made me uneasy — in part because I have loved trains since childhood. My father worked for Indian Railways, and I grew up in sleepy provincial towns, close to railway yards, where the days resonated with the melancholy sighs of loitering steam engines and the contemptuous shudder of express trains speeding to the distant cities of Delhi, Madras, and Bombay. Every morning, slow mail trains delivered early editions of newspapers that had been printed the night before in their metropolitan bases. I often walked to the railway station to meet them. On the platform, where bundles of newspapers and magazines thrown by invisible hands landed with a dusty thud, I watched with awe as the soot-blackened engineers went off duty. There were rumors about their alcoholism and violent domestic habits, but on these mornings they always seemed to be returning home from heroic expeditions.

By the 1970s, steam was giving way to diesel and coaches were being designed in a modern functional style. But you could still find first-class railcars embodying colonial luxury. I traveled on them with my family on long journeys two or three times a year. As we sat in teak-paneled compartments with glass windows, inset mirrors, and embossed-leather seats, the sensation of movement infused eating, sleeping, and reading with a new sensuousness. The unremittingly dark nights, the stationmaster holding an oil lantern on a deserted platform, acquired a fresh mystery; there was great drama in the figures of peasants working in the flat fields under vast skies, and also in the small-town bazaars, whose garish shop signs managed to stoke longing as keenly as the familiar cries of hawkers that erupted at every stop.

Like much else in India, the railways seemed as though they had always been there. In fact, they were introduced in 1851, by the British, part of a worldwide surge in rail construction during the nineteenth century, which gave governments and businesses freer access to markets and resources in the remotest parts of Europe, America, Asia, and Africa. Indian nationalists accused the British of using railways to plunder their most valuable colonial possession. Mohandas Gandhi, whose political awakening began when he was expelled from a first-class rail compartment in South Africa because of his skin color, condemned railways as carriers of disease and disrupters of self-sufficient rural economies. But Gandhi's political heirs did not share his suspicion of Western-style modernization and development. Railways continued to expand in post-independence India, binding far-flung towns and villages into the fourth-biggest rail network in the world. In the film *Pather Panchali,* the first in Satyajit Ray's Apu Trilogy, the symbolically charged arrival of the train in the Bengal countryside heralds the displacement of a rural family.

In tradition-bound China, railways initially incited similar anxieties. Mandarins of China's last imperial dynasty purchased the few miles of rail track that had been laid by European traders near Shanghai and tore them up. But the nation-builders of Republican China quickly recognized the political uses of the railways. As early as the 1900s, when China had no real authority over Tibet, Sun Yat-sen, the founder of modern China, had outlined a plan to connect Lhasa to the Chinese rail system. However, civil war and the Japanese invasion insured that at the time of the Communist takeover, in 1949, China had only a few thousand miles of track, mostly in the north and northeast of the country.

Since then, the Chinese rail network has expanded dramatically and become one of the largest in the world. Reaching Golmud, in Qinghai, in 1984 and Kashgar, in Xinjiang, in 1999, it has economically integrated these remote provinces, making them available for large-scale resettlement by Han Chinese immigrants, and strengthening Beijing's political control.

The link from Golmud to Lhasa, across the almost impassable

Kunlun Mountains, which form a natural boundary at the north of the Tibetan plateau, has been the most ambitious of China's rail ventures. In 1889, visiting a country deeply humiliated by Western powers, Rudyard Kipling had wondered, "What will happen when China really wakes up, runs a line from Shanghai to Lhasa . . . and controls her own gun-factories and arsenals?" China has now woken up.

Later in the afternoon, when I walked through the train, the Tibetans seemed fewer and more subdued. Most were in the cheapest, "hard seats" carriage, tickets for which cost around fifty dollars. Built with scant regard for the human form, the hard seats encouraged a bolt-upright posture for forty-seven hours. The Tibetans had already slumped into a miasma of cigarette smoke and a faint smell of yak butter.

Many of the Chinese were grouped in the "hard sleeper" compartments, tickets for which cost around a hundred dollars. Empty instant-noodle cups lay on the floor, the P.A. system was turned up high, and people shouted into cell phones. It was hard to spot potential immigrants among them. Was it the young rake with quasi-punk hair and Lenovo laptop, or the middle-aged man with the *People's Daily* open on a battered leather briefcase? In one cabin, six teenage girls sprawled on narrow bunks, bored faces turned toward the door. There were more of them in the next cabin — two neat rows of equally listless expressions.

With the world outside obscured, a mood of lethargy and irresponsibility seemed to be spreading through the train. In the dining car, the guards, who had been stiffly solemn before their Chinese bosses, were flirting with the waitress. The coach attendants huddled in another corner of the car, smoking.

The commentary droned on: "Dear passengers, tea is a common drink among Tibetan people." I listened for a while, hoping for something like the story I had heard on the CCTV documentary of construction workers on the railroad stopping to let migrating antelope pass. But the P.A. system dealt mostly in bombast. Such-and-such a bridge or tunnel was a "masterpiece" in the history of rail construction; the railroad was to help develop Tibet in a "scientific, harmonious way."

Neither modern science nor harmony seemed to have played

much part in the development of the industrial city of Lanzhou, whose outskirts began to drift past the window in the afternoon — an assemblage of rusting machinery, slag heaps, and landfills; of chimneys and brick kilns belching thick smoke; of concrete tenements whose broken windowpanes were held together with cellophane and old newspapers. Western modes of mass production seemed to have re-created in China the squalor of nineteenth-century British coal and mill towns.

China's urbanization — arguably the most expansive and swiftest in history — has already exacted a steep environmental price from Tibet, whose rapidly melting glaciers feed the biggest rivers in Asia. The Marxist faith in the human ability to use technology to conquer nature means that there is no restraint in China on the Faustian fantasy of gigantic public projects, as demonstrated by the Three Gorges Dam, on the Yangtze River, which has already displaced 1.4 million people. When speaking of the railroad to Tibet, the Chinese sound like the true inheritors of the old European zeal for science and industry, as assured as colonial officials of another era were of their superiority over apparently benighted natives.

The railroad's frailty had become apparent in the weeks following its opening. Chinese engineers, however ingenious, had not fully reckoned with global warming, which was raising temperatures faster than expected, and the foundations of the rail line had already begun sinking into the permafrost by the end of July. Thawing could cause tracks to bend and slump, and bridges to crack. In late August, a dining car derailed 250 miles north of Lhasa, with no apparent effect on the train's oxygen-supply system. I tried not to think about the journey's likely perils as I drifted off to sleep for the second night on the train.

While I slept, Qinghai, a barren, inhospitable land settled by Chinese political prisoners in the 1950s and '60s, passed in the night. The train steadily gained altitude. When I awoke, just after we passed Golmud, the air felt thin, although oxygen was now pumping hard into the compartment. Groggily, I opened the curtains and then sat dazzled before a startlingly white landscape — its forbidding aspect tempered and endowed with heartening intimacy by the unearthly radiance of Tibetan light.

All through that morning, the train twisted and climbed through the Kunlun Range, between mountains with needle-sharp peaks and sunny slopes. Occasionally, the mountains retreated, and then treeless valleys opened alongside the tracks, scored by streams of a glittering chalky white. The artificial rose in my compartment now appeared translucent.

The train clattered past empty railway stations and huts with corrugated-tin roofing; they looked like temporary dwellings for construction and maintenance workers. The highway to Lhasa ran alongside us, empty except for an occasional military convoy.

The P.A. system announced the Tanggula Pass, the highest point of our journey. At 16,640 feet, a thousand feet higher than Mont Blanc, the pass is higher than the altitude at which light aircraft fly. I had a mental image of the pass based on visits to other high passes in Tibet: the snowcapped mountains arrayed imperiously against the blue sky, supervising subsidiary ranges that stretched in rich layers below them. But I couldn't tell when we passed Tanggula. None of the cairns or prayer flags that frame views of Tibetan passes appeared. The railway seemed to have forgone some of the dramatic vistas offered by the road. It ascended gently to the Tibetan plateau, without any of the hairpin turns and loops of the kind that trains negotiate in the Himalayas.

The snow on the hills thinned, exposing wind-abraded rock. The ground showed through, brown and stony, and then we were in flat grassland with soft brown hills at the edge, their peaks sugared with snow and resembling the conical caps of Tibetan Buddhist sects.

Once, a herd of antelope skipped beside the tracks. Looking for more of them, I saw black nomad tents on a distant hillside. Yaks with white stripes on their backs appeared in the dank yellow grass. The train whizzed past empty stations; on the rare occasion that we stopped, there were hardly any Tibetans to be seen. This seemed the strangest aspect of a rail service designed to benefit local people: their meager presence outside as well as inside the train.

I read and napped for a while, and then took another walk through the train. I had a slight headache, and my swollen bag of dried apricots popped easily and spilled its contents on the floor. But the altitude was having a deeper effect on many people on the train. The guards I had seen carousing in the dining car looked drained, barely able to focus their eyes on the flat-screen television. In the chair car almost no one sat upright. The hard sleeper, too, was a mess of slumped bodies. A faint smell of vomit lingered in the air. Remarkably clean so far, the toilet in my carriage had begun to overflow.

Outside, a few walled settlements in the Tibetan style began to appear — fortresslike houses with sloping walls; red, blue, and green prayer flags at the turrets; and flat roofs, often topped incongruously with the red flag bearing Communist stars. A few miles out of Nagqu, the biggest Tibetan town north of Lhasa, the sun began to set. Long blue shadows crept down from the stony slopes of mountains even as the lingering light set their snow-flecked peaks ablaze.

On the highway, two leather-clad and goggled motorcyclists appeared, zooming through the jagged shadows on the tarmac, shrinking into the distance until they disappeared entirely. We passed a wide lake, the waves at its shore frozen into odd sculptural forms suggesting entrapment and desolation. As the train straightened after a long curving tunnel near Lhasa, a nomad emerged from his tent on a hillside. Fantastically dressed in fur hat, sheepskin coat, high boots, and silver buckles, he stopped and gazed at us — interlopers in his world — with what could have been either fear or disdain.

It was dark when the train, moving swiftly through Lhasa's outskirts, pulled into the great vault of the city's new railway station. The announcements on the P.A. system bounced off the building's high ceiling, wide platforms, and pedestrian tunnels, and dissolved into meaningless echoes. In the neon-lit concrete wilderness outside, the straggly crowd of tired passengers appeared diminished. The parking lot was several hundred meters away from the main building, and the P.L.A. soldiers with machine guns and the checkpoint on the road leading to the city were reminders of Chinese fears about security in Tibet.

On my first morning in Lhasa, I saw the Chinese-built quarter of the city — a grid of long roads lined by supermarkets, restaurants, bars, and night clubs — through Woeser's eyes. The old quarter — centered on Jokhang, the holiest Tibetan temple — long reduced to an oasis in the hectically and garishly expanding city, seemed to have shrunk since my previous visit. But it hadn't lost the atmosphere of a medieval market-cum-pilgrim town: skullcapped and thinly whiskered Muslims from Kazakhstan displayed mosaics of nuts and dried fruit; open-fronted shops sold dried yak meat and blocks of yak cheese; and antique stores sold prayer wheels, semiprecious stones, daggers, and saddles. Mingling with the merchants and the hawkers were the pilgrims, chanting and spinning prayer wheels as they circumambulated the gold-roofed Jokhang. A mysterious euphoria seemed to drive the dusty prostrators in their frayed gloves and knee pads, and the tiny aged matriarch in greasy robes tapping her forehead to the faded silk scarves hanging from the holiest chapel inside the Potala Palace.

In the encroaching Chinese city, new, hybrid identities for Tibet were on offer. The three white arches of the railway bridge over the Kyichu River were apparently designed to evoke *khatags,* the silk scarves that are a traditional Tibetan token of reverence. The railway station itself, a colossal structure with sloping walls of white and oxblood red, seemed to compete, in both size and detail, with the red and white of the Potala Palace, which looms above Lhasa on a large outcrop to the north of the city. Such selective borrowings reflect the fact that, in recent years, Tibet and Tibetan Buddhism have inspired a cultlike devotion among newly affluent Han Chinese. A stylish Chinese poet I met in Beijing last year blew perfect smoke rings as she lamented the immaturity of China's urban culture, and professed profound interest in Tibet. *Kekexili* (*Mountain Patrol*), a popular Chinese film released in 2004, perfectly encapsulated this new Chinese romance, presenting the Tibetans as a proud, earthy, and honest frontier people. There are shops in almost every major Chinese city selling what a signboard in downtown Shanghai describes as BUDDHISM ACCESSORIES: Tibetan prayer wheels, bells, and incense.

In my hotel, the Brahmaputra Grand, glass cases displayed antique guns, swords, armor, metal utensils, Tibetan masks, and statues, while the mostly Chinese staff, dressed in colorful Tibetan costume, greeted guests with an exaggerated bow and a heavily accented *"Tashi delek."* The hotel, which opened two days before the train to Lhasa's maiden journey, billed itself as Tibet's "first five-star hotel" and a "unique museum hotel." In the marble lobby, whose wall decorations, Buddhist statues, winding staircase, and gold-plated mandala created an overwhelming impression of gaudiness, a wide-screen television replayed endlessly an interview with the hotel's owner, a soldier turned businessman from Sichuan. According to a glossy magazine placed in every room, the owner understood "the law of development of objective reality" and was someone who "spends all energy throughout his life in inheriting and flourishing Tibetan culture."

Despite the awkward translation, the words betrayed a kind of truth. From the beginning of market reforms in China, Communist Party bosses, government officials, and P.L.A. soldiers had grasped more keenly than most people the development of objective reality. Not surprisingly, they were, if not the true inheritors of Tibetan culture, certainly the people best placed to make money out of it.

On one occasion when I met Woeser, she was accompanied by her partner, Wang Lixiong. Wang had risked much, not only by finding fault with Chinese rule over Tibet — something no prominent Han Chinese writer or intellectual in China was known to have done — but also by meeting the Dalai Lama. Like Woeser, Wang had been born into China's privileged class. Then, in 1968, at the height of the Cultural Revolution, his Moscow-educated father, denounced as a "capitalist-roader and Soviet-revisionist spy" and imprisoned for months in a cowshed, had committed suicide; his mother, an editor at a film studio, had been sentenced to hard labor in the countryside. Naturally, the Cultural Revolution had given Wang a deep distrust of China's political system. It also brought him and Woeser together, he told me. Shortly after they started an e-mail correspondence, she sent him some photographs taken by her father in the late sixties of rampaging Red Guards in Tibet. He encouraged her to interview the people in the pictures, which showed mob fury and personal humiliation, and to write a commentary to go with the photographs.

Together, Woeser and Wang radiated a bemused happiness, as though they were still savoring the extraordinary luck of having found each other. They had corresponded by e-mail for a year before finally meeting, in 2000, when Wang visited Lhasa to research an article. Wang described it as a case of "love before first sight."

Wang told me that he thought the Communist system in China was in serious peril, that the Party's control over China was in danger of being broken. This did not make him hopeful about the future of Tibet, however. He told me that he had taken the train to Lhasa last November. On the journey, he met a Tibetan woman who had left her Tibetan village to see the world and had ended up as a singer and dancer in a traveling show run by a Han Chinese. Realizing after some years that she was getting old, she had opened her own show, in the city of Yangzhou. She told Wang that she was returning to her native village to find more girls there who could be "ethnic exhibits."

Woeser thought that these privileged and ambitious Tibetans did not exceed 10 percent of the Tibetan population, but Wang seemed more pessimistic. He said, "The most important change the train will bring about is in Tibetan self-perceptions. Back during the Cultural Revolution, the Red Guards smashed everything, but they left Tibetan hearts unchanged. But now Tibetan attitudes are being changed by the new cultural revolution of modernization and globalization. You can't resist this new materialism."

Woeser, in one of her essays, recounts a conversation with a young Tibetan entrepreneur seeking to develop Tibet's tourist industry, who grandly proclaims, "We are going to be the city eating up the villages." But it seemed that few young Tibetans were well placed to take advantage of the new economic environment. The infusion of Han Chinese, privileged by both ethnicity and language, had left the teahouses and barbershops in the Tibetan quarter thick with the unemployed and the idle. One evening in a restaurant near the Jokhang temple, I met five young English-speaking Tibetans so overwhelmed by bitterness at their situation that they forgot, briefly, about the punitive consequences of talking to foreigners.

Dressed in jeans and big fluffy jackets, they appeared as if they might have been more at ease in the Chinese quarter's discos than in the Tibetan quarter. But an old-fashioned courteousness lay behind their coolly modern appearance; they belonged to a very different class from the Tibetans I had seen in the night clubs near the Potala Palace on my previous visit. Children of barley farmers in villages north of Lhasa, they lived crammed in small rented rooms in the city.

Looking for an unobtrusive place to talk, we went up to a restaurant's second floor. A young Chinese couple were already seated there, and a moment of unease followed. The couple were most likely tourists; romantically self-absorbed, they barely glanced at us. The Tibetans, after a few appraising glances, became indifferent to them, probably confident that the Chinese wouldn't be able to follow a conversation in English. But I found myself nervously surveying the menu, remarking, pointlessly, on its variations on yak meat, and then abruptly talking of the Dalai Lama's embrace of vegetarianism during his exile in India. None of the Tibetans ordered meat, and they declined my offer of beer; they did not drink alcohol. I asked if they were religious, and they nodded. Did they go to temples? They nodded again. Conversation flowed only after the Chinese couple left.

The Tibetans had known one another since their early teens, when they left Tibet and made a dangerous journey together across high mountain passes to India. They spoke nostalgically of their time in India, especially of the school run by and for Tibetan refugees in Dharamsala. Their stay abroad had expanded their sense of possibility, but it had also brought a painful awareness of their place in the world. They had learned English in India, but this skill, valuable anywhere else in China, had proved to be of little use when official pressure on their families forced them to return to Tibet. Speaking passionately, and often all at the same time, they described how Chinese authorities worked hard to prevent Tibetans from escaping to India — some three thousand succeed annually — and how they periodically harassed Tibetans who had returned.

In any case, my companions couldn't have benefited from Tibet's market economy without fluency in Chinese. Even exams for the job of tour guide were conducted in Chinese and covered Chinese rather than Tibetan history. Higher education in China was far too expensive for this group, and they had none of the connections that Tibetans, however well educated, needed in order to obtain good government jobs, or to avoid being posted to the cold border regions. Their only option was to eke out a living off tourists in the summer season, as translators and guides, and then spend much of the winter on their families' farms.

They had, they told me, almost no contact with the local Chinese, and they saw Lhasa as a city divided, as much psychologically as physically, into the Chinese and Tibetan quarters. Mutual wariness, rather than outright hostility, had so far governed the relationship between the two communities. But the train, they felt, could change that. They had little doubt that it was meant to benefit only the Chinese. Travel by road and air had been too arduous or expensive for likely Chinese migrants, who mostly tended to be poor. The train had already speeded up Han Chinese immigration to the city, where Tibetans were now in a minority. Every day, according to the Tibetan government in exile, more than five thousand visitors came to Lhasa, of whom some two thousand stayed. The effect on the local economy was already being felt. Rent for modest rooms of the kind they lived in had doubled.

Our voices resonated in the empty, dimly lit restaurant. It was New Year's Eve, but the lanes near the Jokhang had acquired a wintry desolation early in the evening. When we emerged into the night, there was a long wait for a taxi, but the Tibetans insisted on seeing me off. Quietly standing in the cold dark lane, they suddenly appeared adrift in their own city.

Returning to my hotel, I found P.L.A. cars and green-uniformed soldiers blocking the driveway. Alarmed, I went in to discover ballroom dancers crowding the lobby, which had been cleared of much of its Tibetan decorations: the hotel had decided to celebrate the Western New Year. Local Chinese officials in suits sat stiff-necked on sofas, watching women in long black gowns solemnly twirling around the marble floor as a synthesizer produced an approximation of the "Blue Danube" waltz. The uncertain and experimental nature of the event became more evident when the dance floor abruptly emptied and a heavily made-up Nepalese girl, not more than sixteen years old, in a white miniskirt began a kind of pole dance to the tune of a Bollywood film song. As if completing a scene from a colonial past, the Tibetan and Nepalese staff looked on blankly from the sidelines.

I left after the Nepalese girl threw off her jacket. In my hotel room, I switched on CCTV's New Year's show to find an overweight woman in an orange tracksuit singing a song about the railroad to Lhasa titled "The Road to Heaven." Woeser later told me that "The Road to Heaven," an adapted folk song sung by a half-Tibetan pop star named Han Hong, had been played interminably on radio and television in Tibet for a whole year before the train arrived in Lhasa. In 2004, Han had also performed in Potala Square. In fact, she had planned to helicopter onto the roof of the Potala Palace for the performance, and had been dissuaded only after a campaign on one of Woeser's influential blogs, which has since been shut down. Judging by the English subtitles, "The Road to Heaven" consisted of a series of slightly ominous banalities: "people of all nationalities come together," for the train "was like a dragon crossing the mountains," "bringing warmth of the motherland to the frontier," whose arrival would make "barley and butter tea taste sweeter."

On my last day in Tibet, I visited a young farmer in his rural home, some sixty miles from Lhasa. The Tibetans I had met had sent him to accompany me to the Ganden Monastery, on one of the hills near Lhasa. On the way, I asked him if I could visit his village instead. Much to my surprise, he immediately agreed. It was a bright morning, cloudless, with only a few wisps of mist lingering around the hills in the remote distance. The farmer joked about Chinese attempts to get families in his village to fly the Communist flag and display pictures of China's president, Hu Jintao. Tibetans were apparently still required to take seriously the old-fashioned propaganda that much of inland China has outgrown.

It was with something like pride that he showed me around his old family house and introduced me to his parents and younger siblings. The courtyard where a huge Tibetan mastiff sat tethered, the hay-strewn shed where cows were being milked, the long living room with the coal stove and a fridge and a television set (both emblems of modernity covered decorously with embroidered cloth), the flat roof with an unrestricted view of the hills: this, he seemed to say, was the life that he and his family had created, without any help from the Chinese.

Nowhere was he more self-assured than in the prayer room, to which he took me last. Pausing in what was evidently the best-tended part of the house, he let me absorb its aura of sacredness. The Tibetan love of color and baroque decoration was on full display in the paneled chests painted with floral designs, the thick frescoed columns, the *thangkas* representing scenes from the life of the Buddha, the sashes hanging from the ceiling, the pile of Tibetan scriptures bound in bright yellow silk, and the row of silver lamps before an extravagantly gilded shrine.

On one relatively bare wall was a poster, the mandatory portrait of Hu Jintao. It was even bigger than the largest of the *thangkas*, but in this portrait the Chinese president had been Tibetanized: he wore a *khatag*, and his figure was superimposed over images of the Potala Palace and ecstatic Tibetan dancers in traditional costumes. Smiling conspiratorially, the farmer pointed to one of the paneled chests. Inside, he said, was a picture of the Dalai Lama. It is illegal to possess one in Tibet, but the farmer, growing more cheerful by the second, told me that all his neighbors had one, too.

It was a defiant gesture, like that of the nomad who had watched from outside his tent as the train went past. And when I returned to Lhasa later that morning the city, overwhelmingly defined by the Chinese, appeared more clearly to be an exception. It seemed that there were many more Tibetans like the young farmer, asserting traditional ways of life against change imposed from Beijing — Tibetans whose loyalty to their faith and identity had been tested by successive political setbacks, and who would now struggle to survive the arrival of the railroad in Lhasa.

The Most Expensive Road Trip in the World

FROM *Details*

OUR CONVOY IS ROARING through the endless rocky desert, kicking up a dust storm that announces our presence for miles around. Barreling through southwestern Pakistan, our five tricked-out Toyota Land Cruisers are getting nicked, jolted, and thrashed, and they're performing like champs. Each vehicle is rigged with thousands of dollars' worth of GPS trackers, satellite phones, and gleaming rifles. An American filmmaker named Wendy is stretching through the sunroof, shooting with a Panasonic DVX100B video camera, and I'm hanging partway out a back window, my headscarf whipping my face. The screws are literally rattling out of my camera's shotgun mike.

Sitting at the steering wheel, Zakaria, an Egyptian falcon breeder in his thirties, speaks urgent Arabic into his walkie-talkie. (No full names appear in this story.) He's an expert wheelman, but it's impossible to be at ease when you're traveling with one of the world's most dangerous hunting expeditions. After one accident on a recent trip, an injured passenger had to be medevaced out. And not long ago, the caravan was crossing back over the border from Afghanistan when U.S. troops checking for arms detained the hunters for several hours — releasing them with an apology after checking their license plates. While in custody, the party had to head off a potentially explosive scenario after hundreds of tribal villagers showed up to support the chief who had arranged the hunt. But these hunters are invited dignitaries who have the kind of clout that can get them out of almost any trouble — the kind that would turn a villager's Kalashnikov attack on their caravan into an international incident.

Perched between Wendy and me in the back seat is a regal peregrine falcon named Diva. Apart from us humans, she's the most valuable cargo in the Toyota.

"Why is she bobbing her head?" I ask.

Zakaria is scanning the sand among the rocks, searching for bird tracks, and he replies distractedly, "She does that when she wants to fly." I wonder, To fly? Or to rip another bird's throat out?

The stereo is blasting an undulating Arabic song. "What's he singing about?" I ask.

Zakaria laughs. "How his wife is jealous that he loves his bird more than her." Then he mutters, "I can't talk now. I have to hunt."

Up ahead, a woman is walking miles from her village to fill a bucket of water, and a camel is approaching, loaded down with firewood. An impossibly thin man, heading toward a mud shack, is trailed by a vulture. Our SUVs thunder past them all, enveloping them in dust.

Zakaria must have followed my gaze. "These people who live here have nothing," he says. "No electricity, no water, nothing. My only hope is that they are close to nature, their minds are clear, and they are happy."

Abruptly, the convoy swerves and splits into two groups, crisscrossing the arid terrain with military precision. One of the other Land Cruisers roars up next to us. The driver, whose head is covered in a blindingly white kaffiyeh held down by a special black *agal* that indicates he's descended from the Prophet Mohammed, is Prince Hamad, a dashing man blessed with classic movie star looks. But he's no spoiled young playboy — he's the manager of several hospitals. He's been hunting since he was a young child and racing around in Land Cruisers since he was fourteen, and he has absolute reverence for Arabic tradition. His English is limited, but his spirit translates perfectly — he's forever approaching our back window with dates and bread and baklava.

Prince Hamad waves to Zakaria with contagious exuberance. "Your falcon is trying to kill mine!" he exclaims. Then he tears off, his tires spitting dust at us.

We've veered far off course by now, and Zakaria points to a field of tiny struggling plants. "We are very careful to never drive near a farmer's crops," he explains.

Another SUV crosses in front of us, cranking "Dragostea Din Tei," a thumping disco hit by a Moldovan band, O-Zone. At the wheel is Sheikh Mohammed, a commercial real estate developer in Prada shades and rippling white robes who's picking up the tab for this year's Pakistan trip as a gift to his friends.

And what a gift it is. Our expedition's camp employs a small army: dozens of cooks, launderers, mechanics, and marksmen. Sheikh Mohammed invests in the areas where he hunts every year, paying for wells to be dug and schools and mosques to be constructed. Plus, there are formal payments, made through a fixer, to the provincial tribal leaders who allow the hunters to use the land and provide their own men for protection.

Nobody keeps precise track of what this trip costs — not even Sheikh Mohammed. I don't dare ask, but he's been known to shrug and say, "I stop counting after a million and a half."

The men in the caravan know the region well, but they're not from around here. They're mostly royalty and businessmen from Qatar, the tiny, oil-saturated Persian Gulf nation known both for its lavish ways and for its generosity. (The country donated $100 million to charity after Hurricane Katrina devastated New Orleans in 2005.) And they let off steam for a month or more every autumn, packing up their gorgeous falcons and driving through the craggy desert hills near some of the world's most politically inhospitable regions. Their wealth lets them engage in this otherwise impracticable tradition.

The agile Prince Hamad bears little of Sheikh Mohammed's solemn gravity. At twenty-six, he's one of the youngest hunters here, the newest link in a chain of cultural identity stretching back through the generations. Islamic tradition holds that the Prophet's uncle converted to the faith after spending time in the desert with his raptor. It's hard to get Prince Hamad to talk about anything apart from the birds. When I ask him whether he's married, he nearly shouts, "I am married to my beautiful falcon."

More than a thousand years ago, Prince Hamad's ancestors rode into the desert by camel, with spears, arrows, and wild falcons. The prey then, as it is now, was the sly, elusive houbara bustard, a long-necked, wide-eyed, fat-bodied real-life cousin to the cartoon Road Runner. From late October through March, the houbara migrate to Egypt from Mongolia. The falcons intercept them — or try to — in this anarchic corner of Pakistan. The houbara is an endangered species, and hunting it in Pakistan requires hard-to-obtain government permits. Sheikh Mohammed is funding a project to repopulate both species — until recently, the peregrine falcon was also endangered — and Zakaria says the campaign has cost Sheikh Mohammed $26 million to date.

The party happens to have chosen a region enduring one of the world's gravest political crises. The Taliban haven't seized this secular Muslim corner of southwestern Pakistan, but they've resurfaced in eastern Afghanistan to the west and in the violent Waziristan region to the north, where they've reportedly killed at least one hundred tribal chiefs. Taliban leaders already have homes near the brick red mountains outside Quetta, a dusty city choked by mopeds and donkeys in Pakistan's tribal province of Baluchistan, where hospitals routinely patch up wounds sustained in hillside skirmishes.

But the real threat to peace is the fighting over regional autonomy between Baluch tribes, who once fought one another but have recently united, and the Pakistani military. Baluchistan is blessed with vast reserves of gold, copper, coal, and natural gas, and the national government is trying to keep its grip on the region through bombings and kidnappings.

Pakistan is a tinderbox. And the hunters could lose their power to ward off danger here at any time.

In Karachi, Pakistan's most populous city, the Qataris' falcons live in their own house. This home away from Qatar is spacious, decked out in glorious Persian carpets, plush red drapes, and enormous crystal chandeliers. Spread across the carpet are a dozen perches where the falcons sit impassively, their long black talons and leather hoods making them look like patrons at an underground bondage club. Some of the birds are worth tens of thousands of dollars. Each has a microchip embedded in its chest, a wire transistor in its tail feathers, and even its own passport.

Tonight a few falcons are watching TV, and we join them, eating pizza and drinking Coke. Out in the yard, a breeder arrives with three falcons for sale. The seller tosses a pigeon to excite the falcons. When they're riled up, they defecate, and Zakaria checks the scat under a microscope for parasites.

"This sport is something that our grandfathers did to feed their families," Sheikh Mohammed says. "We hunt to be together, to travel. We see how other people live. It gives us experience, and we need it. But at the end of the day, this is about friendship and tradition."

Although most of these falcons are female, for centuries the Qataris have referred to their birds only as male. The hunters still have trouble accepting that the females are larger. "My grandfather loved falcons, my father loved falcons, and I love falcons," Prince Hamad tells me.

He glances over at a black, brooding bird. "Except that one," he says. "That one is mean. You know how you can look at a person and not like them right away? That's how I feel about this bird. I hate him."

Zakaria is no longer staring out the window at the ground, checking for houbara tracks. His eyes have wandered up to a hill, watching an expanding dust cloud that mirrors our own. The cloud approaches slowly at first, and then motorcycles burst out of it, their riders loaded down with AK-47s.

Our motorcade is armed, but not heavily enough to win a gun battle. Sheikh Mohammed has paid to secure the hills — sentries with automatic weapons are watching over us. But you never know.

We stop, and Prince Hamad and Sheikh Mohammed emerge from their SUVs to climb the hill where the motorcycles have stopped. "Hope they're friendly," Zakaria says, looking at Wendy and me in the back seat. "Well, as American women, perhaps you are my protection." He pauses. "Or perhaps they will kidnap you." Before I can determine whether he's joking — and maybe he's not sure himself — he steps out of the Toyota and joins the others.

The tribal norms are tough for an outsider to evaluate. Out here, land disputes and criminal offenses are settled in tribal council meetings. "Years ago," one Baluch told me, "when one tribe killed the men of another, blood compensation was made with money, land, and women. If warring tribes intermarry, they have ties that lead to peace."

As I watch through the Toyota's window, my mind races through the possibilities: a rival tribe demanding money for driving through its chief's land; the police or the military, demanding to see our hunting permits; bandits. But as the hunters and the fixer approach the motorcyclists on the hilltop, I watch the postures of the men in the distance relax. Whatever just happened, it's been defused. There's a round of handshakes, and Zakaria, Prince Hamad, Sheikh Mohammed, and the rest of the party head back down the hillside toward their SUVs.

Several times a day, the men stop on the side of the road. As the dust settles around the convoy, they unroll mats and place them on the ground. They check their compasses, face Mecca, and kneel. Their gorgeous prayers rise and roll over the desert. And then we're off, starting the next bone-crunching three-hour drive.

The trackers are watching the patches of sand, and one deftly spots a wispy, telltale three-toed print. *"Houbara! Houbara!"* The SUVs scramble to reach coordinates pinpointed by the tracker's satellite phone. Up ahead, a vehicle's sunroof slides open, and a falcon named Samir rockets from her perch. Zakaria guns our Land Cruiser, and all the vehicles zigzag toward the battleground to watch the dogfight.

For the peregrine falcon, the houbara is a worthy competitor: a master of camouflage and a great sprinter, reaching twenty-five miles per hour. Falcons, though, can hit two hundred miles per hour in a dive, and Samir has the advantage. She snatches her prey and swoops up again, and the two birds tumble through the air.

Watching the hunters as they gaze at this primal battle, I see that falconry has the power to transcend tradition, sport, art, and pastime as a consuming passion. In the instant of combat, time shudders backward and becomes a moment from earlier centuries and generations, free of incendiary local politics and of the business pressures left behind in Qatar.

Then the birds hit the ground, and Samir tears off the houbara's head. The hunters erupt in a lusty cheer. *"Shabash!"* Wonderful! It's the first kill of the day — the first houbara of the trip. Over the coming weeks, the hunters and the falcons will get many more kills, *insh'Allah.*

One Qatari falconer, Rashid, sprints to the scene and feeds Samir the houbara's heart. "A falcon needs to taste his prey," he says, "or he loses his instinct to kill." Cautiously, he hoods the falcon, soothing her as he tucks her away for the next chase. Rashid's intimacy with his falcon is tender and disarming, but with the other men, he's competitive, keeping spirits high with a boastful swagger. He rejoices in the kill, and cell phones start chirping with braggadocio relayed back to fellow enthusiasts.

On the road again, Rashid continues his teasing via walkie-talkie, blasting us with boasts and the Pakistani pop on his sound system. Although most orthodox mullahs discourage music, it blares exuberantly out of every SUV during the hunt. After all, the Koran, like the Bible, is open to interpretation. Drinking is illegal in Pakistan, unless you're a foreigner having a nip in a hotel room. Early on, in Quetta, I worried about breaking a rule and offending my Baluch hosts, until one scolded me: "Oh, don't go all Taliban on us — have a drink."

And then we spot a herd of gazelles, stunning in their grace. The convoy slows and stops. Nobody pulls out a gun. Sheikh Mohammed is a conservationist, and he understands that this is the meat that feeds local tribesmen. After we watch in awe, he permits his party to shoot a single gazelle.

Everyone fires. Everyone poses with the gazelle. Everyone claims the kill as his own.

That night, the men unfurl rugs and mats by a bonfire, warning me to keep an eye out for jackals, wild dogs, leopards, snakes, and scorpions. Maybe they're joking, but I know we're at least protected from any human predators.

The Qataris are in a jovial mood — indeed, Prince Hamad is leading his falcon in an improvised waltz. My hosts point to the mats they've laid on the sand, calling this patch of desert a five-star hotel. Pointing to the sky, I volley back: "No, it's a million-star hotel."

One guy gets the last laugh, gesturing to a bush: "Yeah, well, there's your bathroom."

Zakaria is drinking chai and reclining on pillows. "What I want most of all on a hunt," he says, "is to turn off my phone, be with my friends, and disappear."

We dine on the day's kill: gazelle, houbara, and two sand grouse

— compliments of Sheikh Mohammed, who saw what none of the other hunters did, and neatly squeezed off two shots. Zakaria revisits the gazelle hunt. "'Run for "deer" life,'" he says. "Is that where the phrase comes from?"

"God knows," I say.

"Allah knows," Zakaria says solemnly.

"Google knows," Wendy says, and the laughter is explosive.

Chewing a mouthful of roasted gazelle, I bite down on something hard. It's not bone. I pull it out of my mouth. A single buckshot pellet. I tuck it away, like a tiny black pearl.

Kabul Nights

FROM *Gourmet*

WE'D BEEN LURED into the dwindling light and rising dust of Kabul's streets by the rumor of barbecued pork. Our driver aimed the van down a street with so many ruts that our conversation continued in hiccups. We rattled past a herd of goats grazing on a mound of garbage, then veered onto a busy street where the driver zigged and zagged around other cars, turbaned old men on bicycles, water buffalo, and women in burkas hurrying to get home before dark. We flew past butcher shops where sheep were still dripping blood onto the street, past one of the now closed Chinese "restaurants" notorious for trafficking in a different kind of flesh, past one of the glittering new villas going up behind the walls of a compound. We passed the heavily barricaded avenue leading to the American Embassy and mounted the bridge over the Kabul River where there were still a few cars idling on the shore, their drivers tossing buckets of water to wash away the dust. We passed bullet-riddled, bomb-ravaged apartment buildings, then skirted a vehicular graveyard where smashed blue buses were stacked five high.

"I think it's over there," said Gay-LeClerc Qader, one of my companions. She spoke to the driver in her soft Dari.

The driver pulled into what looked like the entrance to a prison, except for the giant red chile pepper mounted on a pole over the gate. Two guards were lounging on white plastic lawn chairs, cradling their machine guns. One of them made the universal sign for eating, pressing his fingers together and raising them to his open mouth. When our driver nodded, he opened the gate and waved us through. We drove across several hundred feet of torn-up terrain that could have been either a construction site or a minefield and came to another gate. When the guard threw back that gate, we saw a green lawn and outdoor benches and the painted brick walls of the Red Hot Sizzlin' restaurant. Inside, we settled into our seats and the tables around us filled up — one with bulky security guys, another with an international cast of idealists from some aid organization. The rumor of barbecued ribs — happily true — had drawn many pork-starved, *haram*-heedless foreigners from their isolated compounds in this Muslim country.

I was a wide-eyed visitor on my second trip to Afghanistan, in spring of 2006. I was there to help Debbie Rodriguez, my other dining companion, put together a book about running a beauty school and salon in Kabul. And she and Qader — both American — were in the final weeks of preparation for a joint enterprise with their Afghan husbands. They would soon open the Cabul Coffee House and Café, the first Western-style coffeehouse in Kabul, complete with blues musicians, Wi-Fi, piles of books, and honey-nut lattes, as well as kebabs and burgers. They were eager to check out some of the other dining establishments in town and to talk to the proprietors. Or, at least, that was our excuse as we ventured out night after night.

Not all of Kabul's restaurants were as tucked away as the Red Hot Sizzlin', but most were still tough to find in a city with few named streets and no addresses. One night, we drove in circles looking for the now-closed Samarqand and finally made an educated guess after spotting a gate with an onion-shaped dome and a knot of men with machine guns. The guards opened the gate to a lovely garden and restaurant. Another night, we went looking for a Middle Eastern restaurant called Taverne du Liban. Again, we drove up one street and down another, then finally pulled up in front of a compound with a cluster of guards and the aroma of roasted meat. Upon closer inspection, we saw that there was a sign. It wasn't much bigger than the luggage tag on my suitcase.

Western-style restaurants — meaning those that adhere to Western standards of sanitation and quality, serve alcohol, and allow men and women to mingle — keep a low profile in Kabul. Most foreigners themselves keep a pretty low profile, either because they don't want to impose their presence on a country struggling to rise from the ruins of nearly three decades of strife brought on by foreign meddling — or because they're afraid. And they have some good reasons for their fear. One foreign doctor told me that a warning circulated through the international community last year that terrorists were focusing on soft targets, including Westerners frequenting restaurants. He continued to go out to eat, but the nongovernmental organization that employed him insisted on having guards on motorcycles patrol the block to make sure that no one was idling just around the corner, waiting to snatch him away.

It wasn't always like this. Before the Soviets invaded, in 1979, and the fighting began, Kabul was called the Paris of the East. In *An Historical Guide to Afghanistan,* from 1977, Nancy Hatch Dupree wrote that "tall modern buildings nuzzle against bustling bazaars, and wide avenues fill with brilliant flowing turbans, gaily striped *chapans,* miniskirted school girls, a multitude of handsome faces and streams of whizzing traffic . . . Travelers have written glowingly of Kabul for centuries, and modern visitors continue to be captivated by its lively charm." Her book listed twelve Afghan and European restaurants in Kabul, most with bars and several offering dancing.

A few of the restaurants attempted to stay in business after the fighting began — first the mujahideen against the Soviets, then the civil war that followed the Soviet withdrawal in 1989. Those that lasted until the Taliban victory, in 1996, quickly closed their doors, since alcohol and mixed-gender gatherings were now strictly forbidden. Kebab shops continued to draw customers, but they offered little more than kebabs, rice, and naan, and they served only men.

After the fall of the Taliban, in 2001, a few Western-style restaurants opened to serve the thousands of foreigners and diaspora Afghans who had begun to pour into Kabul. There are now more than twenty such places. While the government tolerates — albeit uneasily — the drinking of alcohol by foreigners, it prohibits restaurants from serving alcohol to Afghans. This bifurcated policy creates a great deal of awkwardness when someone who looks and sounds Afghan — and presumably Muslim — arrives at the gates of a restaurant. The guards often demand to see a passport. If the prospective customer doesn't hold a foreign passport, they deny entry. Sher Dil Qader, who is Gay-LeClerc's husband and a former mujahideen fighter, lived in the United States from 1989 until shortly after 9/11. He holds a U.S. passport. On the one evening he joined us at a restaurant, he was grudgingly granted entry by the guards and looked uncomfortable all night.

The Qaders met in a refugee camp in Pakistan in the mid-1980s while working with a program that trained field medics. They left Pakistan at the beginning of the Afghan civil war. Sher Dil had no formal restaurant training, but he found a job in Washington, D.C., working with an up-and-coming chef. By 2000, the couple had moved to Reno and opened their own place: One-Stop Burgers and Kabobs. Sher Dil managed the restaurant and occasionally worked the grill, and Gay-LeClerc served customers when the restaurant was busy. The two returned to Afghanistan after 9/11 to distribute donated school supplies and clothing to orphanages. Eventually they started a community health program in Bamyan. Later, in Kabul, they opened a hamburger kiosk at the American military base. Then they hit upon the idea of the coffeehouse with Rodriguez, imagining the kind of mellow yet hip atmosphere that tends to be in short supply in conflict zones.

While Rodriguez and the Qaders met at the coffeehouse to address a few final details before their grand opening, I sat at one of the tables and admired the compound's yard. The walls were freshly painted a creamy white, the tables were arranged under green canopies, the rosebushes were blooming, and the guards were chatting amiably near the gate in matching blue bulletproof vests. A smiling young man hustled through the gate with a wheelbarrow full of gravel, which he raked onto one of the pathways. He then ran back out the gate for another load. Suddenly, the coffeehouse partners looked out the window and stared at him.

"Who is that guy?" Rodriguez asked the Qaders. "Did you hire him?"

"I didn't hire him," Gay-LeClerc said, looking quizzically at her husband. He shook his head.

This is one of the challenges of opening a restaurant in Kabul. The city is swarming with impoverished refugees, and the unemployment rate is around 40 percent; locals desperate for a job will simply start working and hope someone decides to pay them. I was glad I didn't have to be the one to tell this young man that all the jobs there had been filled.

There were many other challenges as well. Electricity was intermittent at best, so the Qaders needed a generator to keep things running. They may eventually have to harden the place with barbed wire on the walls, blast film on the windows, and rocket barricades along the top of the building so that people who work for organizations that are bullish on security can come. "And everything has to be brought in from outside the country," Gay-LeClerc said. Except the chairs we were sitting on. The partners couldn't find an Afghan company that made or imported restaurant furniture, so they decided it would be cheaper to have a carpenter make some rather than ship it from Dubai — the source of almost everything else they were using. They ordered walnut from a lumber dealer and had a carpenter craft the wood into tables and chairs out in the compound's yard.

Supplying the coffeehouse will continue to be a challenge, because many things have to be ordered a month in advance. The partners can't afford to run out of coffee or Equal or stirrers, and they can't call a local restaurant-supply store (there aren't any) or run out to Costco for necessities. Even when they start serving kebabs and burgers, the meat will be from outside the country. "The local butchers hang meat outside in the dust and flies," Sher Dil said. "People get sick, but they don't care. They're always sick — they think this is just the way life is."

On my last night, Rodriguez and I and a friend went to one more restaurant. First, we sat in Rodriguez's salon — now under new management, as she has left the country — and shared a bottle of wine, which is a fabulous hostess gift in a country where only a few places sell it. The city's power was down, and the generator wasn't working, so we talked and sipped by candlelight. Then we set out for the restaurant. It took the usual amount of driving around in circles, this time in total darkness. The friend finally spotted an alley where a few guards were hunkered down. They peered into the car and waved us through. The restaurant was down the alley, behind a hidden wall. When we walked inside, it was as if we were in another city.

When we left, a few hours later, our driver bore down on the gas pedal and we streaked through the empty streets. Every once in a while, I realized that certain compounds must have had generators running because I saw the flickering light of a television or rooms that glared with brightness. Then I noticed that the driver was slowing down. Two men were standing in the middle of the dark street waving us down with flashlights.

"Why are they stopping us?" I asked, my heart pounding just a little.

Rodriguez shrugged. "They probably just want to make sure we're not being kidnapped. Look happy."

So when they shined the light on my face, I smiled.

DAVID SEDARIS

Journey into Night

FROM *The New Yorker*

THE NIGHT FLIGHT TO PARIS leaves J.F.K. at 7 P.M. and arrives
at de Gaulle the next day at about 8:45 A.M. French time. Between
takeoff and landing, there's a brief parody of an evening: dinner is
served, the trays are cleared, and four hours later it's time for
breakfast. The idea is to trick the body into believing it has passed a
night like any other — that your unsatisfying little nap was actually
sleep and now you are rested and deserving of an omelette.

Hoping to make the lie more convincing, many passengers prepare for bed. I'll watch them line up outside the bathroom, some
holding toothbrushes, some dressed in slippers or loose-fitting pa-
jama-type outfits. Their slow-footed padding gives the cabin the
feel of a hospital ward: the dark aisles, corridors; the flight attendants, nurses. The hospital feeling grows even stronger once you
leave coach. Up front, where the seats recline almost flat, like beds,
the doted-on passengers lie under their blankets and moan. I've
heard, in fact, that the airline staff often refers to the business-class
section as "the ICU," because the people there demand such constant attention. They want what their superiors are getting in first
class, so they complain incessantly, hoping to get bumped up.

There are only two classes on the airline I normally take between
France and the United States — coach and something they call
Business Elite. The first time I sat there, I was flown to America and
back for a book tour. "Really," I kept insisting, "there's no need." I
found the whole "first-to-board" business a little embarrassing, but
then they brought me a bowl of hot nuts and I began to soften.
Pampering takes some getting used to. A flight attendant addresses

me as "Mr. Sedaris," and I feel sorry that she's forced to memorize my name rather than, say, her granddaughter's cell phone number. On this particular airline, though, they do it in such a way that it seems perfectly natural, or at least it does after a time.

"May I bring you a drink to go with those warm nuts, Mr. Sedaris?" the woman looking after me asked — this as the people in coach were still boarding. The looks they gave me as they passed were the looks I give when the door of a limousine opens. You always expect to see a movie star, or, at the very least, someone better dressed than you, but time and time again it's just a sloppy nobody. Thus the look, which translates to "Fuck you, Sloppy Nobody, for making me turn my head."

On all my subsequent flights, the Business Elite section was a solid unit, but on this particular plane it was divided into two sections: four rows up front and two in the back. The flight attendant assured everyone in my section that although we were technically in the back, we shouldn't *think* of it as the back. We had the same rights and privileges as the passengers *ahead* of us. Yet still they were ahead of us, and I couldn't shake the feeling that they'd been somehow favored.

On the way to New York, I sat beside a bearded Frenchman, who popped a pill shortly after takeoff and was out until we landed. On the leg back, there was no one beside me, at least not for the first half hour. Then a flight attendant knelt in the aisle beside my seat and asked if I might do her a favor — that's how they talk in Business Elite. "I'm wondering, Mr. Sedaris, if you might do me a favor?"

Chipmunk-like, my cheeks packed with warm nuts, I cocked my head.

"I've got a passenger a few rows up and his crying is disturbing the people around him. Do you think it would be okay if he moved and sat here?"

The woman was blond and heavily made up. Glasses hung from a chain around her neck, and as she gestured to the empty window seat beside me I got a pleasant whiff of what smelled like oatmeal cookies. "I believe he's Polish," she whispered. "That is to say, I think he's from Poland. The country."

"Is he a child?" I asked, and the flight attendant told me no. "Is he drunk?" It didn't matter one way or the other. I was just curious.

Again, she said no. "His mother just died and he's on his way to her funeral."

"So people are upset because he's crying over his *dead mother?*"

"That's the situation," she told me.

I'd once read where a first-class passenger complained — threatened to sue, if I remember correctly — because the blind person next to him was traveling with a Seeing Eye dog. He wasn't allergic, this guy. Labrador retrievers on the street didn't bother him, but he hadn't paid thousands of dollars to sit next to one, or at least that was his argument. If that had seemed the last word in assholiness, this was a close second.

I said that of course the man could sit beside me, and the flight attendant disappeared into the darkness, returning a few minutes later with the grieving passenger.

"Thank you," she mouthed.

And I said, "No problem."

The Polish man might have been in his midforties but seemed older, just as people in my parents' generation had. Foreign blood, or an abundance of responsibility, had robbed him of the prolonged adolescence currently enjoyed by Americans of the same age, so his face, though unlined, seemed older than mine, more used. His eyes were red and swollen from crying, and his nose, which was large and many-faceted, looked as if it had been roughly carved from wood and not yet sanded smooth. In the dim light, he resembled one of those elaborate, handcrafted bottle stoppers — the kindly peasant or good-natured drunk who tips his hat when you pull the string. After settling in, the man looked out the darkened window. Then he bit his lower lip, covered his face with his remarkably large hands, and proceeded to sob, deeply. I felt that I should say something, but what? And how? Perhaps it would be better, less embarrassing for him, if I were to pretend that he wasn't crying — to ignore him, basically. And so I did.

The Polish man didn't want dinner, just waved it away with those king-size mitts of his, but I could feel him watching as I cut into my herb-encrusted chicken, most likely wondering how anyone could carry on at a time like this. That's how I felt when my mother died. The funeral took place on a Saturday afternoon in November. It was unseasonably warm that day, even for Raleigh, and returning from the church we passed people working on their lawns as if nothing had happened. One guy even had his shirt off. "Can you beat that?" I said to my sister Lisa, not thinking of all the funeral processions that had passed me over the years — me laughing, me throwing stones at signs, me trying to stand on my bicycle seat. Now here I was eating — and it wasn't bad, either. The best thing about this particular airline is that after dinner they offer you a sundae. The vanilla ice cream is in the bowl already, but you can choose from any number of toppings. I order the caramel and chopped nuts and the flight attendant spoons them on before my eyes. "Is that enough sauce, Mr. Sedaris?" she'll ask, and "Are you sure you don't want whipped cream?" It would be years before I worked up the courage to ask for seconds, and, when I finally did, I felt like such a dope. "Do you think, um . . . I mean, is it possible to have another one of those?"

"Well, of course it is, Mr. Sedaris. Have a third, if you like!"

That's Business Elite for you. Spend $8,000 on a ticket and, if you want an extra thirteen cents' worth of ice cream, all you have to do is ask. It's like buying a golf cart and having a few tees thrown in, but it still works. "Golly," I say. "Thanks!"

In the years before I asked for seconds, my sundae would be savored — each crumb of cashew or walnut eaten separately, the way a bird might. After those were gone, I would recline a bit and start in on the caramel. By the time the ice cream itself was finished, I'd be stretched out flat, watching a movie on my private screen. The control panels for the seats are situated on a shared armrest and it would take me a good three or four flights before I got the hang of them. On this trip, for instance, I kept mashing the buttons, wondering why they failed to work: feet up, feet down, head back, head forward. I was two seconds from calling the flight attendant when I looked to my right and saw the Polish man keening and bucking against his will. It was then that I realized I had the wrong control panel. "Sorry about that," I said. And he held up his pan-sized hand, the way you do when you mean "No hard feelings."

When my empty bowl was taken away, I leafed through the inflight magazine, biding my time until my neighbor's dizziness wore off and he could fall asleep. In an effort to appear respectful, I'd already missed the first movie cycle, but I didn't know how much longer I could hold out. Up ahead, in the cheerful part of Business Elite, I heard someone laugh. It wasn't the practiced chuckle you offer in response to a joke but something more genuine, a bark almost. It's the noise one makes when watching stupid movies on a plane, movies you'd probably never laugh at in the theater. I think it's the thinness of the air that heightens your reactions — and not just to comedy, either.

Take my seatmate. The man was crying again, not loudly but steadily, and I wondered, perhaps unfairly, if he wasn't overdoing it a bit. Stealing a glance at his blocky, tear-stained profile, I thought back to when I was fifteen and a girl in my junior high died of leukemia, or "*Love Story* disease," as it was often referred to then. The principal made the announcement and I, along with the rest of my friends, fell into a great show of mourning. Group hugs, bouquets laid near the flagpole. I can't imagine what it would have been like had we actually known her. Not to brag, but I think I took it hardest of all. "Why her and not me?" I wailed.

"Funny," my mother would say, "but I don't remember you ever mentioning anyone named Monica."

My friends were a lot more understanding, especially Barbara, who, a week after the funeral, announced that maybe she would kill herself as well.

None of us reminded her that Monica had died of a terminal illness, as, in a way, that didn't matter anymore. The point was that she was gone, and our lives would never be the same: we were people who knew people who died. This is to say that we had been touched by tragedy, and had been made special by it. By all appearances, I was devastated, but in fact I had never been so happy in my life.

The next time someone died, it was a true friend, a young woman named Dana, who was hit by a car during our first year of college. My grief was genuine, yet still, no matter how hard I fought, there was an element of showmanship to it, the hope that someone might say, "You look like you just lost your best friend."

Then I could say, "As a matter of fact, I did," my voice cracked and anguished.

It was as if I'd learned to grieve by watching television: here you cry, here you throw yourself upon the bed, here you look in the mirror and notice how good you look with a tear-stained face.

Like most seasoned phonies, I roundly suspect that everyone is as disingenuous as I am. This Polish man, for instance. Given the time it would take him to buy a ticket and get to J.F.K., his mother would have been dead for at least six hours, maybe longer. Wasn't he over it yet? I mean, really, who were these tears for? It was as if he were saying, "I loved my mother a lot more than you loved yours." No wonder his former seatmate had complained. The guy was so competitive, so self-righteous, so, well, over the top.

Another bark of laughter from a few rows up and it occurred to me that perhaps my sympathy was misplaced. Perhaps those tears of his were the byproduct of guilt rather than sorrow. I envisioned a pale, potato-nosed woman, a tube leaking fluids into her arm. Calls were placed, expensive ones, to her only son in the United States. "Come quick," she said, but he was too caught up in his own life. Such a hectic time. So many things to do. His wife was getting her stripper's license. He'd been asked to speak at his son's Alateen meeting. "Tell you what," he said, "I'll come at the end of dog-racing season." And then . . . this. She rides to her death on a lumpy gurney and he flies in Business Elite to her funeral. The man killed his mother with neglect and because of that I can't watch a movie on a plane?

I pulled my private screen from its hiding place in my armrest, and had just slipped on my headphones when the flight attendant came by. "Are you sure I can't get you something to eat, Mr. . . . ?" She looked down at her clipboard and made a sound like she was gargling with stones.

The Polish man shook his head no, and she regarded me with disappointment, as if it had been my job to stoke his appetite. *I thought you were different,* her eyes seemed to say.

I wanted to point out that at least I hadn't complained. I hadn't disrespected his grief by activating my screen, either, but I did once she'd retreated back into the darkness. Of the four movies playing, I had already seen three. The other was called *Down to Earth,* and starred Chris Rock as an aspiring standup comic. One day, he gets hit and killed by a truck and, after a short spell in Heaven, he's sent back among the living in the body of an elderly white man. The reviews had been tepid at best, but I swear I've never seen anything funnier. I tried not to laugh, but that's a losing game if ever there was one. This I learned when I was growing up. I don't know why it was, exactly, but nothing irritated my father quite like the sound of his children's happiness. Group crying he could stand, but group laughter was asking for it, especially at the dinner table.

The problem was that there was so much to laugh at, particularly during the years that our Greek grandmother lived with us. Had we been older, it might have been different. "The poor thing has gas," we might have said. For children, though, nothing beats a flatulent old lady. What made it all the crazier was that she wasn't embarrassed by it — no more than our collie, Dutchess, was. Here it sounded like she was testing out a chainsaw, yet her face remained inexpressive and unchanging.

"Something funny?" our father would ask us, as if he hadn't heard, as if his chair, too, had not vibrated in the aftershock. "You think something's funny, do you?"

If keeping a straight face was difficult, saying "No" was so exacting that it caused pain.

"So you were laughing at nothing?"

"Yes," we would say. "At nothing."

Then would come another mighty rip, and what was once difficult would now be impossible. My father kept a heavy serving spoon next to his plate, and I can't remember how many times he brought it down on my head.

"You still think there's something to laugh about?"

Strange that being walloped with a heavy spoon made everything seem funnier, but there you have it. My sisters and I would be helpless, doubled over, milk spraying out of our mouths and noses, the force all the stronger for having been bottled up. There were nights when the spoon got blood on it — nights when hairs would stick to the blood — but still our grandmother farted, and still we laughed until the walls shook.

Could that really have been forty years ago? The thought of my sisters and me, so young then and so untroubled, was sobering, and within a minute, Chris Rock or no Chris Rock, I was the one crying on the night flight to Paris. It wasn't my intention to steal anyone's thunder; a minute or two was all I needed. But, in the meantime, here we were: two grown men in roomy seats, each blubbering in his own elite puddle of light.

GARY SHTEYNGART

To Russia for Love

FROM *Travel + Leisure*

"ONLY LOVE IS MATTER," some besotted loverboy has scrawled along one of St. Petersburg's ethereally romantic canals. Whether this is merely bad English or some newfangled law of physics we will never know, but one thing is certain: it's summertime in Russia's loveliest city, and everyone seems to be tying the knot. They couldn't have picked a better place. Petersburg's over-the-top czarist architecture obliges even the humblest newlywed with pomp and drama. Wedding parties composed of tall, gangly men in short sleeves and pretty girls aglow in makeup crowd beneath the hooves of the famously airborne Statue of the Bronze Horseman, AKA Peter the Great. Grooms sweep brides off their feet and smooch them on cue beneath the fifteen-foot-tall granite Atlases stoically holding up the roof of the New Hermitage's portico. The streets are crowded with flower-bedecked Hummer limos and, on at least one occasion, a motorcycle wedding escort whose yuppie members have misguidedly christened themselves "The Busy Riders." Everywhere mothers are weeping with joy and terror, and papas are panning the pale summer beauty of their children and their native city with video cameras, while "witnesses," the Russian equivalents of best men and bridesmaids, uncap bottles of cheap but effective "Soviet" champagne and fill the air with cloying sweetness.

I come to St. Petersburg on a chilly week in early August for the wedding of my good friend K. and his betrothed, Yana. They are two progressive smarties with their share of diplomas from the prestigious St. Petersburg State University, not to mention an unusually diverse couple: he has Russian and Ukrainian blood, and she is one of the fewer than a half million Yakut, an Asiatic people many time zones away from Petersburg and Moscow, whose frozen landscape is rife with diamonds, reindeer, and throaty shamanistic arias. Baby-making seems to be at an all-time low in Russia — even President Putin has spoken out about a "demographic crisis" — but while they are loath to multiply, Russians still marry young. "When I came here I was twenty-six," a Dutch expatriate tells me, "and they thought I was old. Now I'm thirty-three and they've lost all hope for me. There's not even a word for 'boyfriend' in this language."

Having just crossed the Rubicon of thirty, K. is ripe for a band of gold. He certainly is taking the traditions and rituals of matrimony seriously. Whenever I return to Petersburg, K. and I usually go on a rampage, consuming vodka by the bottle and eating skewers of lamb and hunks of lard. This time he takes me to a vegetarian Indian restaurant and orders some puri bread. He explains to me that tomorrow he will be in church taking confession with Yana, and so, according to custom, he cannot consume meat, milk products, or alcohol. It's touching to hear this brazen carnivore say to a young waitress in some faux-Indian getup, "May I have the soy-based substitute, please?"

After the confession comes its diametric opposite: K.'s bachelor party. We're hanging out with a friend of K.'s who claims to be a descendant of Russia's beloved poet Pushkin. He's got several gold teeth and worships Deep Purple. After getting kicked out of the suburban Klub Kangaroo for reasons I cannot discern (maybe K.'s antigovernment T-shirt set off the meathead bouncers), we end up at Fireball, at the edge of town. It's a rockabilly joint festooned with Confederate flags where a clientele that looks like it's been imported from the worst disco in England grooves along to '50s standards. Disturbingly, a large woman comes out to show the crowd her breasts. The women at the club try to mimic the stripper's thrusts and parries, as if taking notes for their lovers. Perhaps they too dream of dragging their men to Wedding Palace Number One, where K.'s wedding will take place the next day.

The palace sits magnificently on the English Embankment by the Neva River, an unparalleled vista of the sun-burnished city unfolding from its steps. Since Soviet times, this elegant former mansion has seen countless weddings, known for their gilded backdrops and thirty-minute assembly-line haste. Beneath an enormous chandelier, guests sit on a set of couches, the striking Yakut girls resplendent in their green dresses, Yana's mother in slacks and a traditional amulet and shawl. In Petersburg, like anywhere else in the world, no romantic gathering would be complete without a piped-in rendition of the score from *Titanic.* The ceremony takes place in a great mirrored hall beneath the insignia of the double-headed Russian eagle. The government's emcee, who looks like a younger Judge Judy, gives a rather rambling speech along the lines of "One day . . . love comes. The weak become strong. And then come the responsibilities." The appropriate documents are signed at an ornate desk, the cameras zoom in for the kill, the organist mysteriously plays Abba's "The Winner Takes It All," a tender kiss is exchanged, and with little fuss but with many sincere wishes from their international friends, the smiling K. and Yana have become a family.

But this is only the beginning. The next twenty-four hours are given over to drinking, endless toasts, and shouts of *"Gorko!"* meaning "Bitter!" which inspires the newlyweds to make the wedding wine sweeter with a kiss. We head downstairs to the reception, where a table is packed with salmon and cold veal sandwiches and plenty of champagne. The young men up the ante by passing around a bottle of vodka. "You're young, you're beautiful. I hope you have a full set of children," Yana's mother tells the assembled.

"How many is that?" K.'s mother asks.

"Four."

A tearful aunt sounds the typical Russian lament: "Please . . . please, don't forget the parents."

"To our Siberian princess, our diamond," one so-called nonconformist friend says, raising a glass to Yana, then adds a political coda: "May the clouds lift over our homeland, so that your lives may be well."

With more champagne in hand, we crowd into a limousine of the non-Hummer variety and circle the town. First, we go to the beautiful campus of St. Petersburg State University, the couple's alma mater. We hew to tradition by visiting the bronze Peter the Great rearing up on his steed, and then, in a bit of a departure from the usual, we head to the Stalinist-era Moscow Square, where we pose beneath the mighty Lenin statue in various mock-heroic revolutionary poses (K. has brought along a suitably Leninesque worker's cap for the occasion). Teenage skateboarders popping ollies at Lenin's feet ask us for a sip of our celebratory champagne, and, this being Russia, we oblige.

Yana's mother lives nearby, and once we enter her snug little apartment, we are treated to a variety of Russian and Yakut customs, not to mention a king's ransom in booze. The Russian bread-and-salt ceremony is performed, part of which involves the bride and groom tearing off a piece of bread, the larger hunk supposedly determining the head of the household. The mother, who is a Yakut shaman, uses black and white horse's tails, symbolizing water and fire, sky and earth, to purify the couple. Then there is the kidnapping and ransoming of the bride, an ancient ritual that once symbolized the passing of the bride from one family to another, but now mainly entails guests dumping 500-ruble notes into a hat for the wedding fund. We dig into a freshly hunted duck, pieces of pellet still lodged in its succulent flesh, and drink Yakut vodka that was reportedly made from an iceberg. The celebrants get rowdier and begin to express themselves. "I've written some poems," a sweet old lady tells us. Another begins a mind-bogglingly long speech with the familiar Russian words: "My husband, well, he is sitting on a pension." Then Yana's mother, red-cheeked and proud, the traditional Yakut silver draped around her neck, sings a polytonal song in her language, which hushes us with its sinuous beauty. If this isn't a mournful ballad about love and its consequences, I don't know what is.

The next day the ceremonies continue, this time with a religious bent. A thermos of coffee gets me to the church on time. The bearded, ponytailed priest tells any lightly dressed women to cover their bellies, and the rest of us to turn off our cell phones. We are at a recently built church, the freshly painted cupolas glowing brightly amid the drab Soviet-era surroundings. K. wears a traditional Ukrainian shirt embroidered around the cuffs and collar. Small Yakut women huddle together, adjusting their headscarves. The choir sings brightly, adding light to the multitude of flickering candles and golden icons. "God have mercy," the priest chants. Bride and groom cross themselves. Holy water is drunk from a little golden cup. Hanging on to the priest's heavy saffron robe, K. and Yana circle the altar three times, a symbol of eternal marriage. The priest gives a speech centering on the Adam and Eve–rib story. The idea seems to be, "Man has dominion over women, but, hey, don't go nuts with that dominion." Exhausted by the ceremony, I walk out into the paltry northern sunshine, knowing that the party will now resume at Yana's mother's house. More iceberg vodka and happy toasting await. Russian weddings remain the maximalist and sentimental affairs they have been since the time of Ivan the Terrible. Regimes come and go, lives worsen and improve and worsen again, global warming may yet cause the Neva River to cascade out of its granite banks, but in the end "only love is matter."

SETH STEVENSON

Looking for Mammon in
the Muslim World

FROM *Slate.com*

I REALIZE I'M LATE TO THE PARTY: Dubai is long past its media moment. The flurry of breathless write-ups — in Sunday travel sections and glossy lifestyle magazines — has come and gone. We're on to the next destination already. (Laos. Yemen. Low-altitude space orbit.)

Still, I remain determined to see Dubai for myself. It's too curious to ignore. What sort of mania drives this small, lonely desert outpost to begin construction on the tallest skyscraper in the world? To carve an indoor ski slope from the side of a shopping mall? To pour dirt into the ocean, forming man-made island chains into a Mercator projection of Earth?

There is profound wackiness afoot here. But I wonder: Is something more interesting happening, too? Because I can't help but find reason for hope in this crass spectacle. The cultures that produced Dubai and Las Vegas surely must have *something* in common. If the Arab world's starry-eyed dreams are just like ours — full of schlock, gluttony, and elaborate theme hotels — perhaps we can get along after all.

I'm not saying that out-of-control capitalism will defuse the clash of civilizations. But I'm eager to find out what it looks like when Islam gets mixed up with reckless expansion and tacky greed. These are the sorts of ambitions the West has no difficulty understanding.

The clichés begin springing to life the moment I arrive in Dubai's gleaming airport. Whirring along on the people-mover, I pass an endless stretch of ads for high-rise condos and high-tech office parks. Each promises greater swank than the last. None has been fully built yet. The ads are conceptual drawings: crosshatching sketches in the outlines of seventy-story towers, newly dug harbors, bustling helipads . . .

At the end of this gantlet, I'm deposited in a cavernous immigration chamber. I fall in line behind a crowd of South Asian men, here to get jobs as construction workers. (Someone has to build all these shiny developments.) The men in front of me are Bangladeshi, I gather from the passports they clutch nervously in their hands. They all wear matching bright yellow T-shirts and cheap baseball hats bearing the words MID-EAST STAFFING. These impromptu uniforms were no doubt handed out by some wrangler from the employment agency — here to usher the newest subcontinental fodder through the bureaucracy.

International-arrivals halls offer interesting first impressions of a place. (I remember the last time I flew back to Washington, D.C., from a trip abroad. As I stood in the snaking line at Dulles, waiting to be admitted into America, I noticed the overhead televisions were all tuned to Fox News. The customs clerks behind the desks wore police-type uniforms, with badges and epaulets. A sniffer dog wandered among us, at the end of a leash.) Here in Dubai, the immigration clerks are all women in abayas — those long, loose black cloaks. They cover their hair with headscarves, of course, and some wear a face veil, too. While the tough guys in D.C. look you hard in the eye as they grill you on the purpose of your trip, these women make only fleeting eye contact (if any) as they quietly stamp our passports.

My hotel (after an air-conditioned cab ride through choking traffic) turns out to be a tad more Western-friendly than I'd have preferred. Across the street are a McDonald's and a KFC. The lobby bar is packed with drunken Brits watching soccer by satellite. (Though alcohol is technically a no-no in the United Arab Emirates, restaurants and bars attached to hotels are allowed to serve it.)

The only hint I'm somewhere unfamiliar is the gold-colored arrow affixed to the desk in my hotel room. It points to Mecca — unless perhaps a Hindu maid has unknowingly shuffled the room's furniture, in which case the arrow might well point toward some alternative holy shrine. (Jerusalem. Stonehenge. Jim Morrison's grave.)

Around dawn, I'm awakened from my fitful, jet-laggy sleep by the sound of prayer. It blasts from a loudspeaker mounted atop a nearby mosque. I love this sound — the calm, low voice intoning "*Allahu akbar*," or "God is great."

But while I strive for respectful tolerance in all things religious, I take issue with the final line of the morning prayer. It makes a controversial claim: "*A-aalaatu khayrun mina-naum*": "Prayer is better than sleep." I've no doubt Muslims truly believe this as they chant it each morning (still bleary-eyed, not yet having enjoyed their first sumptuous gulp of Moroccan tea). But me, I could never pledge fealty to such a notion. I honor the infinite by yielding myself to the spirit realm of dreams. (Also, I'm really lazy.)

When I finally rouse myself, I stumble out into the ninety-five-degree heat of a winter afternoon. I'm in the older Bur Dubai neighborhood, far from the glitz of the modern towers just down the coast. Here, the winding streets are lined with squat, humble buildings — cramped storefronts at ground level, apartment balconies with drying clothes flapping in the wind above.

The architecture and feel are not unlike what you'd find in some poor Third World cities. But there are no beggars here. No homeless families. If you're a local, you're taken care of by your fantastically rich government. If you're an immigrant . . . those construction sites are hiring.

Since it's my first day, I decide to visit the Dubai Museum for an overview of the city's history. As it turns out, there's not much history to speak of (though I'll have more on this). It's certainly astonishing to look at pictures taken before oil was discovered in 1966. They show a tiny settlement on the banks of a twisting creek. Some of the houses are little more than tents. The creek is shallow and dotted with sandbars.

When I go back outside, I walk the lovely promenade of this same creek and marvel at the changes. Water taxis float a steady stream of workers from shore to shore. The creek has been dredged to improve shipping, and dhows loaded with commercial goods crowd the teeming docks. Beyond, glass office buildings and five-star hotels rise from the sand.

As the sun sets, I walk back to my hotel, the sound of evening prayers echoing out from the mosques. In my room, I flip on BBC World. They're showing footage of a massive blimp, circling the skies above London. On the side of the blimp is an advertisement. It's the logo of the Palm — a new island development here in Dubai. Luxury homes are available now . . . though, of course, construction has not yet been completed.

Before diving into the plate-glass heart of modern Dubai, I decided it might be wise to establish some context. I wanted to learn more about the Bedouin culture that once existed here before the construction cranes and money-chasing expats arrived. Thus I found myself, on a weekday afternoon, catching a taxi to the Falcon Center.

The guidebook says the Falcon Center is a complex devoted entirely to the noble sport of falconry. (Falconry was a staple of the ancient Bedouin desert lifestyle and remains a hobby for some Emiratis.) In my head, I'd pictured a giant aviary bustling with high-intensity falcon training. Falcon obstacle courses. Midair targets, with falcons violently attacking from every angle. A miasma of shrieking and clawing. As it turned out, the Falcon Center (located on the sandy outskirts of town) was just a large building with some retail stores inside. These stores sold falcons (and falcon accessories).

When I wandered into one, I found several live falcons perched on stands, their heads covered by tiny leather hoods. The birds were silent, occasionally grooming a loose feather with a talon. As I leaned in closer for a better look — emboldened because the falcons couldn't see me, and thus were unlikely to shred my face to ribbons — a shopkeeper quietly entered from a backroom.

"Would you like some tea?" he asked. I was not expecting this, but tea sounded lovely. So, he returned to the backroom and emerged with a teapot and some elegant little glasses, which he filled. I thanked him, took a sip or two, and then began to pepper him with questions. What were the specs on these falcons? What exactly were they capable of?

By way of response, he pulled out his cell phone, punched some buttons, and held the screen in front of my face. On the small display, I could make out a film of a falcon flying in the desert, its wings pumping up and down. A few seconds in, the bird swooped and totally blitzkrieged a helpless animal that appeared to be — I swear to God — some sort of small antelope.

At this point, I realized: I must have a falcon. I inquired as to the cost. The shopkeeper explained that this depends on the size of the falcon and its skill. But in general, they'll run you about five grand apiece.

Which is clearly worth it, when you think about it. I had my eye on the fierce-looking bird in the corner. I planned to name him Shrieky. I'd haul him out on my balcony in D.C., turn him loose, and wait for the freshly killed game to pile up. Perhaps a neighbor's Shih Tzu. Or infant.

Of course, I couldn't really justify purchasing a falcon. (Nor did I relish the thought of getting it through customs. Or keeping it fed — the shopkeeper had now begun to place raw chicken drumsticks in the falcons' talons, and they were munching away with wet, flesh-ripping sounds.) So, instead, I opted for perhaps the oddest souvenir I've ever bought: a falcon hood.

It's leather, with little rawhide straps to tighten it over the bird's eyes. I'm not sure what I'll use it for, though it might come in handy if I had a pet guinea pig that was really into bondage sex games. But I felt I had to buy *something* after this shopkeeper was so kind and hospitable.

Hospitality — along with falconry — is one of the proud pillars of Bedouin society. (It's the Bedouin people who roamed these deserts for centuries and who are the root source of Gulf Arab traditions. I'm talking here about the countries of the Arabian Peninsula, such as the United Arab Emirates, Saudi Arabia, Bahrain, and Qatar. They have a history and mood distinct from other parts of the Arab world.) In fact, based on my reading and my visits to Dubai's museums, I'd argue that Bedouin culture boils down to the following elements: hospitality; falconry; camels (and camel racing); fancy, engraved daggers; deserts (and desert wandering); and covering up your women.

And that's about it. When you're a nomad on a constant hunt for water, there's not so much time for dabbling in the delicate, nonfunctional arts. It's all about weapons and animals.

As for the Bedouins' manner of dress, it's fascinating to me that Emirati men still wear their traditional long, white robes. (They're called *dishdashas* — and *wow* is that a fun word to say.) Nearly all

U.A.E. nationals — even the ruling heads of state — continue to resist trousers and other Western clothes. It's a little bit badass, and it speaks to serious cultural pride. I suppose if your people survive in the harsh desert for millenniums, you don't let some pansy foreigner tell you what to wear.

You do, however, tell your women what to wear. And I have a few raw chicken bones to pick on that score:

1. It seems horribly unfair that the men's *dishdashas* are white, while the women's long cloaks (called abayas) are black. I ask you: Which would you rather wear beneath a blazing desert sun? If Arab culture weren't otherwise so progressive on gender issues, I might say this was a clever means of discouraging women from leaving the house.
2. The unfairness becomes crystal clear when you go to the beach here. The Emirati women keep their abayas on. Meanwhile, their husbands strip down to tight, short bathing suits — exposing their flabby stomachs and hairy backs.
3. I'm fine with the headscarf that covers the hair. (This seems not unlike wearing a yarmulke.) But the face veil is fundamentally different and, in my view, not okay. One cannot happily contribute to society when one has no face. The veil transforms women into a pair of downcast eyes. And again, it seems, more than anything else, like an enticement to stay at home.

I realize some Muslim women will talk about the face veil as an empowering, female-driven choice. This seems like the same kind of empowering, female-driven choice that sorority sisters make when they choose to become bulimic together.

All of which brings me back to falconry. At one of the museums, I saw an old photo of a sheik with his prized falcon. The caption read, "The key to falconry is the relationship between the falcon and the falconer," which seems reasonable enough. The text also observed that the falcon was wearing one of those little leather hoods, and in parentheses it noted the Arabic word for these masks: *burqa.*

Suddenly, the thought of those birds, forcibly hooded, tied by the ankle to their master's wrists, gave me a small chill.

On a glaring, scorching afternoon in downtown Dubai, I wiped the sweat from my brow, turned to my friend, and said, "Wanna go skiing?"

We'd been considering this idea for a while. The enormous Mall of the Emirates features an indoor slope. And skiing inside a mall just seems like a very Dubai thing to do. Besides, I'm always up for a new sporting adventure: I've tried surfing in Baja, cricket in India, and skeet shooting in West Virginia, but I've never shooshed a graceful S-turn next door to an H&M.

The tricky thing about skiing in a desert is that no one owns the proper clothes. And indoor snow may be man-made, but it's still cold and melty when you fall. Luckily, Ski Dubai includes a rental parka and snow pants with your lift ticket. (They do not, however, include hats and gloves. That's how they getcha. Although I'm secretly pleased that I now own "Ski Dubai" mittens.) All told, the clothes, equipment, and ticket cost $45 for two hours on the slope. Which is not bad, given what it would cost to get to the nearest outdoor skiing.

Once we'd suited up, we walked through a revolving door into an enormous, chilly warehouse with fluorescent lighting. A four-person lift sped us to the top of the slope. And just like that, with a dig of my poles, I was on my way down — trying hard to avoid the three-story wall to my immediate left.

Ski Dubai offers two short runs side-by-side — a gently undulating beginners slope and a steeper hill for the more experienced. If you tuck, you'll reach the bottom of either one in about twenty seconds. Nothing here will rev your engines if you've skied for real before. But I will say this: Having grown up in New England, I've definitely seen worse snow and lamer trails.

Also, I've had a few "yard sales" before (wipeouts so disastrous that my hat, goggles, skis, and poles were strewn across the slope). But Ski Dubai, with its mid-mall setting, offers a unique opportunity for the reckless skier. Should you lose control wildly enough, it is possible to explode through the window of a T.G.I. Friday's.

On the slope with us were mostly expats. (Not surprising, as 80 percent of Dubai's population is foreign-born.) At one point, we shared a lift with a pair of European teens who go to high school here. These kids told us they come to the mall nearly every weekend to snowboard. Which suggests that there's not a whole lot to do if you're a teenager in Dubai. By that point, I'd navigated the expert run three times, and already I was getting bored of it.

As for locals, I don't think I spotted any Emiratis on skis or snowboards. But there was an adorable scene going on in the little "snow park" at the bottom of the slopes. Emirati girls and boys — wearing loaner parkas over their *dishdashas* and abayas — were riding inner tubes down a tiny hill. Small children, some of them no doubt encountering not just snow but *coldness* for the very first time, were having a cheerful snowball fight. Also, there were Arab guys who work there adjusting bindings all day and operating the chairlift. Yeah, that's right: Dubaian ski bums. (And they've already got that aloof, barely tolerating the tourists thing down pat.)

Everyone I've met in Dubai tells the same basic story to explain why wacky ventures like an indoor ski slope have come to exist in this once-quiet corner of the world. As the tale goes, Dubai's royal family realized early on that their oil riches (not nearly as vast as those of neighboring emirate Abu Dhabi) would at some point run dry. So, with great foresight, these sheiks decided to broaden Dubai's economy with a two-pronged strategy: First, they would create a friendly business environment — where Westerners could feel comfy and secure as they grubbed after Arab wealth. Second, they'd transform Dubai into a world-class tourist destination.

With not much indigenous culture to promote, it would take some modern sort of attraction to bring in foreign visitors. But how on earth do you lure rich tourists to a desert in the middle of nowhere? It seems like an impossible problem . . . until you remember that someone's already solved it. Viva Las Vegas!

Of course, the nominal draw in Vegas is the gambling. (Which isn't gonna happen in an Islamic country.) But is that what's really bringing people to the Strip — even folks who could make a short drive to an Indian casino back home in Connecticut or wherever?

I'd argue that it's more the sheer nuttiness of Las Vegas that packs 'em in. Its replica Eiffel Tower, and the indoor Venetian canals, and the scale model of the New York skyline. It's the over-the-top excess that truly fascinates us all.

This is the brand identity Dubai is cribbing from. The announcement of each new fantastical project (man-made islands in the shapes of continents; the tallest tower in the world; a theme park where the theme is to aggregate theme parks) keeps Dubai in the news. And it all sounds so very strange that we simply *must* see it for ourselves. Hey, that's what brought *me* here.

In another shrewd marketing move, Sheikh Mohammed keeps the media abuzz with a lineup of international events. (Just during my ten-day visit, there were an automotive rally, the Special Olympics, and an exhibition tennis match between Bjorn Borg and John McEnroe.) Other than a twelve-night run of shows from Barbra Streisand (which really isn't out of the question), how else might Dubai emulate Vegas? I suppose it could become a hub for prostitution — but, like gambling, that would never fly with an Islamic government in charge.

Or would it? Before I left, I got this e-mail from an acquaintance — a guy who works on Wall Street and has done business in Dubai:

> If you want to see the shady side of the city, go to Cyclone. The place looks like a typical club, but in actuality it's all hookers. I don't mean like the typical hookers-at-the-Oak-Room thing you see in NYC. I mean essentially a whorehouse in disguise. Hundreds of women of every flavor proactively pursuing their prey. Mostly businessmen traveling thru, but a share of the ex-pat community and Gulfy Saudis in town as well . . .

For research purposes, it seemed imperative that I check this out. So, late one night, after a couple of drinks, a friend and I asked a cabbie to drive us there. Naturally, the cabbie knew exactly where the place was. After paying a $20 cover each (and won't *that* be fun to expense to *Slate*), we bought a couple of $10 beers and took a lap around the club.

Our first sign that something was off was that there were dozens of attractive women — and each one was standing by herself. This simply does not happen in the real world. Also, the men here were generally older, pudgier, and balder than at other clubs we'd gone to. The scent of their desperation battled for prominence with the equally strong scent of a Hungarian hooker's perfume. Huge security goons roamed the room, keeping an eye out for anyone attempting to consummate transactions on the premises. The whole scene was disturbing — and not in a fun way — so we jetted after fifteen minutes or so.

But, let it be said: I have witnessed sexual deviance being tolerated — or at least ignored — within the borders of a Muslim country. And I'm declaring it a promising sign. If there's one thing the West and the Middle East can come together on, it's a Hungarian hooker.

(Though that, of course, would cost extra.)

I was walking into the Fairmont Hotel on Sheikh Zayed Road — planning to view an art exhibition of Arabic calligraphy — when, a few steps into the lobby, I got flagged down by a woman in a business suit. "Are you here for the press conference?" she asked me.

Well, no, to be honest. But what self-respecting journalist turns down a press conference that falls in his lap? Moments later, the woman was ushering me into a function room filled with TV cameras and notebook-flipping journalists. I grabbed a pen and a pad of paper from the table by the entrance, found a seat near the front, and settled in to figure out what the hell I was reporting on.

Turns out it was the announcement of a major business deal. A deal involving a vitally important resource here in Dubai. No, not oil. Water.

According to the suits up on stage (they represented a private equity firm and a water-supply company — both based in the United Arab Emirates), there is a potential water crisis looming in this region. The scare stat: MENA (the Middle East and North Africa) contains 5 percent of the Earth's population, but only 1 percent of its accessible fresh water. The equation is particularly grim in Dubai, where the population is exploding in the middle of a desert. An estimated $117 billion will be invested in water supply over the next decade — mostly in desalinization projects. An executive from the water company explained that "it's the vision of Sheikh Mohammed to make Dubai a world center for desalinization excellence."

When the Q and A session began, I made my exit and headed to the calligraphy exhibit. (Which was mind-blowing, by the way. If you have a moment, check out the work of Mouneer Al-Shaarani.) But given the dire forecasts I'd just been listening to, I couldn't stop thinking about Dubai's insane growth. Is there any way this pace is sustainable?

There's ongoing construction literally everywhere you go. Neighborhoods are being invented from thin air. New buildings sit eerily empty, with no inhabitants. By day, you can see which towers are missing plates of glass at random intervals. (They look like badly pixilating LCD screens.) One street has a row of skyscrapers without tops. (These look like deadheaded flowers in a window box.)

I am firmly convinced that a real estate crash is due. The rate of expansion just doesn't make sense and seems driven more by the royal family's fantasies (they're the money behind much of the construction and harebrained theme-park-type ideas) than by a genuine level of demand. Besides, there's no price-boosting shortage of land here — there's just more empty sand waiting beyond the city's edge.

Meanwhile, the traffic grows unbearable. (As a Pakistani cab driver told me: "Traffic! Every people is headache!") The foreign labor force gets exploited. (Fliers taped to the side of phone booths advertise for "Filipina bed-spacers." I thought this sounded racy, until it was explained to me that it refers to women working coordinated shifts so they can use the same bed.) The expansion rolls on, with little indication of a prudent central plan or a grand design.

One day, I was walking with a friend when — glancing around at the honking traffic, the construction cranes, the rebar, and the miserable, hot dust — my usually upbeat pal suddenly spoke from a deep chasm of ennui. "I want to call in the airstrike," he said.

Of course, we instantly saw the inappropriateness of this, on all sorts of levels (and here I should admit I'd had similar thoughts). But we couldn't shake our basic disgust with Dubai. Which suggested it was time for a break.

So, we rented a car and hit the open road. After twenty minutes of driving, the city faded out and the desert began. After an hour, we pulled over at a rest stop. It was like we were in *Lawrence of Arabia* — if Lawrence had a rental car. There was nothing here but a lonely power line and a few brave outcroppings of scrub.

Eventually, we reached our destination: an ancient oasis in the town of Al-Ain, at the Oman border. As the guidebook notes, this trip once required a five-day camel trek. Now it's a ninety-minute scurry in a Honda Civic. (Soon, no doubt, the relatively nearby Rub' Al Khali — the vast Saudi desert known as the "Empty Quarter," in my view perhaps the most romantically desolate place left on Earth — will be tamed by paved highway and power lines, too. Progress sort of sucks sometimes.)

We parked the car and took a walking path into the heart of the oasis. It was the precise opposite of downtown Dubai. A lush forest, thick with date palms. Leaves rustling in a gentle breeze. Precious shade now suddenly abundant. It's not difficult to imagine the joyous miracle this would have seemed to a thirsty Bedouin coming in from the desert. No desalinization machines necessary here.

Granted, there is a Pizza Hut a few hundred yards away, which does dampen the natural wonder of it all. But Al-Ain is a delightful little town. No skyscrapers. No cranes. No expats in pinstripe suits.

Instead, there's an outdoor market where people sell goats from the backs of pickup trucks.

On the heels of a week in Dubai, it's a true oasis, in every sense.

Through a friend of a friend of a friend, I was put in touch with a guy named Ahmad who lives here in Dubai. Ahmad graciously invited me to dinner at Al-Hallab, his favorite Lebanese restaurant. Over scrumptious grape leaves, hummus, and chicken with garlic paste, I asked him to tell me his story.

Ahmad is a Palestinian refugee. He was raised in Lebanon and then went off to college in the United States, earning a degree in engineering. He lived in California for a while, started his own business, and married (and later divorced) an American woman. Things were going okay. Until 9/11 happened.

Living in the United States suddenly became uncomfortable, he says. In the weeks after the attacks, Ahmad became frightened to let his mother leave the house — because she wore clothes that marked her as a Muslim. "Who knows what some cuckoo was going to do," as he puts it. He also found it harder to do business. "They'd rather deal with a guy named Jim than a guy named Ahmad," he claims. (If you doubt there is truth in this assessment, consider the Dubai Ports World debacle — in which some fairly naked racism drove a Dubai-based, Arab-owned firm out of America.)

The irritations accrued, and Ahmad decided it was time to move back to the Middle East. He chose Dubai, because it seemed a perfect compromise — Islamic, with a big dose of Western tolerance and First World amenities. He's now launching his own technology business here. He dreams of making millions and using his riches to fund education grants for other Palestinian refugees. As the baklava desserts arrived at our table, and the Emiratis around us sucked on their hookahs, I asked him if he felt Dubai might be viewed as a hopeful vision of a cooperative future between the Arab world and the West.

To my surprise, this question occasioned anger. "Dubai isn't a good example," Ahmad said dismissively. "It ducked the problems of the other Arab countries," he argues, because it never suffered from the same kind of "Western interference." Britain pulled out of the emirates around the same time that oil was discovered, and — armed with riches and independence — Dubai was left to make its own way in the world. If anything, according to Ahmad, Dubai is a vision of what might have been had the West stayed out of the Middle East from the start. At this point, of course, there's no erasing bitter history and, take-home message, we're all screwed.

This isn't quite what I'd hoped to hear from Ahmad. Yes, in some ways, Dubai is a grotesquerie: Hordes of white guys in suits trying to get their paws on Arab money; a monarchy with comic, megalomaniacal ambitions; a semi-indentured labor force; social problems swept under the rug in the name of profit. Still, I see things happening here that I like to pretend are good signs.

Look at the "Letters to the Editor" sections in the local newspapers. Every week, someone complains about the skimpy attire on the beaches. Someone else writes that this is what happens when you welcome heathen foreigners into your country. Another person chimes in with some words about harmonious diversity. And so on. It's a never-ending argument — and, granted, the stakes are sort of low — but if this leads toward a dialectically achieved compromise (instead of, say, a fatwa), then hey, we're making progress.

To me, here's what's promising about the cultural dynamic in Dubai: It throws very different people together within a peaceful and prosperous setting. That, I think, can be a good recipe for breeding tolerance. Even watching the TV commercials here gave me some perspective I think we're missing back in the States: I saw happy Arab families, traditionally attired, smiling as they were enjoying processed-cheese spread together. I can't remember seeing this kind of humdrum, positive portrayal of Arabs on American television. The fact that Westerners here are exposed to this everyday stuff, and the other way around (Arabs having nonterrible interactions with Westerners), should, over time, cement a mellower coexistence.

Of course, sometimes the two different Dubais bump up against each other in unsettling ways. One afternoon, I got lunch at a bistro on the ninth floor of the Fairmont Hotel. (By the way, this was the third-nicest hotel I saw in Dubai. The second-best was the One & Only Royal Mirage, and champ was the Burj Al Arab — the sail-shaped tower that is the one truly beautiful, iconic creation Dubai has given the world. I had a drink in the Burj Al Arab's top-floor bar and was not disappointed by the view or by the stylish clientele.) This restaurant had windows overlooking the outdoor terrace of the hotel pool. But the windows were one-way glass. A pair of gorgeous, sunbathing European women by the pool did not realize this, and they began admiring themselves in what they thought were harmless mirrors.

This came as a delight to the American businessman sitting at a table next to the windows. The women came toward the glass until they were no more than two feet away from his widening eyes. As the gals leaned in toward him and peeled their bikini tops back from their cleavage to check for tan lines, the man literally choked on his glass of water and performed a perfect spit take. It was like a Benny Hill episode come to life. And it was hilarious to everyone in the restaurant who saw it . . . save for the nearby pair of Muslim women covered in black from scalps to shoe tops. Okay, it was a tad awkward, but it was still no big deal — and that's the idea.

Of course, perhaps I'm naive, and these two worlds haven't a prayer of ever finding middle ground. I hate to end on a bleak note, but I have to share my most depressing moment in Dubai.

I was on the chairlift at the indoor ski slope. I was sharing a ride up with a pair of snowboarding teens, and I asked where they were from. Turned out one was from Britain and the other from Holland, but they went to high school together in Dubai. Their parents were expats who had moved here for work.

"What do you think of Dubai so far?" the U.K. kid asked me, making small talk. I told him I was still making up my mind. "You grow to hate the locals," he said. I raised my eyebrows. "For one thing, they can't drive."

I smiled at this, as I must admit I'd seen my share of inventive maneuvers on Dubai's crowded roadways. But I fear I emboldened him to get nastier. Because now this little blond twit (with apple cheeks and wire-rim eyeglasses, wiping his snotty nose with his snowboarding mitten) unleashed some good old imperialist invective. "And they should really treat us with kindness and respect," he said, in his pipsqueak British accent. "They're rather cheeky. You know, if we went home tomorrow, this whole place would turn back to sand."

At that point, to my relief, the lift ride was over, and we went our separate ways. But I was left to ponder his comment. Ignoring the incredibly insulting assumptions embedded in what the kid said, I wonder if some Emiratis wouldn't gladly make that trade.

THOMAS SWICK

Have Book, Will Travel

FROM *The Weekly Standard*

TRAVEL WRITERS, regularly dismissed as trivialists, rarely indulge in the popular book tour whine. It's not just that we have bigger trips to fry, we have fewer bones to pick. We don't see what novelists find so objectionable about a diet of fine hotels, especially when the rooms all come reserved and generously paid for. We are puzzled by the memoirists' complaint about living out of a suitcase because to us it's infinitely preferable to living in the past. And, needless to say, we don't quite grasp the horror of going out and meeting readers. Those sensitive souls who flaunt their lack of social skills are as pathetic as people who boast that they are bad at math. A signing in Dubuque is not a journey into the heart of darkness.

The only possible trauma of a book tour is the potential encounter with apathy: The empty chairs of a ghostly chain at the short end of a mall in a town without pity. But for this, too, travel writers are much better prepared. We tend not to enter MFA programs, teach at universities, or live in New York City, so we are in constant touch with the great unread. From our hours spent in airports we know that most Americans, when presented with large chunks of free time and removed from demanding home entertainment systems, will still find almost any excuse — a cell phone, a laptop, another bag of chips — not to pick up a book. To travel is to be continually reminded of the growing homelessness of the written word.

So, unburdened by illusions and still out of the house, travel writers are the happiest authors on tour. (Not to mention the most symmetrical.) Some may give the impression, often by their wardrobes, that they'd be much more content sharing gourds of gazelle blood with Masai tribesmen, but don't believe them. A book tour provides us with a focus, not always a given in our all-over-the-map trade. ("No one," Paul Theroux once wrote, "has ever accused me of traveling with a theme.") And the focus, in another pleasing twist, is us.

Travel writers are, by nature, in search of the other — which, by definition, is not oneself. Some memoirists manqués have wandered into the field, and appropriated place as nothing more than a scenic backdrop to the more important story of themselves. But the majority, the best (it goes without saying), project their interest outwards. It is only on a book tour that we stand front and center.

True, that position is difficult to define — not to mention enjoy — in an empty store. But all day long the evening reading gives us a sense of purpose, a handy response to Bruce Chatwin's ever-present "what am I doing here?" And if it turns out to be a wash, there's always the sympathetic staff to chat with, and pump for local color. A stood-up author still beats a doubting travel writer, especially when they're one and the same.

I know because I've played the part. When my collection of travel stories came out in paperback, I traveled to the Midwest to revisit some of the places that appear in the book. It was a self-guided tour — my publisher is small; I am even smaller — which, to the bestseller pashas, probably sounds as uplifting as a solo honeymoon. But they're not travel writers flying coach with their first paperback.

The shuttle from Midway buzzed with raves for warring weekend attractions. The young woman behind me announced that she had come to see the Red Sox play, in a rare Wrigley Field appearance, while two other women talked excitedly about the Blues Festival. It was good preparation, which I wouldn't have gotten in a chauffeured limo, for the Printers Row Book Fair.

The thing about great cities is that they have enough people to go around. On Saturday afternoon, crowds of nonfrequent fliers grazed the book tents on Dearborn Street. "Everybody's carrying about fifteen extra pounds right now," Carlos Cumpian, a local Chicano writer, explained to me as we sipped iced tea at a sidewalk café. "During the winter they're able to hide it under coats. Chicagoans look their best in October — after the summer, and before they've had their Halloween candy."

The evening VIP party was held in a parking lot. The unassuming locale carried a certain appeal which apparently only I appreciated, as almost no other authors attended. This was a disappointment. At the Miami Book Fair there had been a cocktail party in a downtown office tower which most of the featured authors attended. In Austin, the Texas Book Festival featured breakfast at the governor's mansion and a dinner and dance band Saturday evening. The Arkansas Literary Festival in Little Rock hosted a black-tie gala that included a postprandial game of "Name That Tome" (my team lost to Roy Blount Jr.'s). Each had seemed a kind of glittery reward for the cloistered life which every author could treat as a personal celebration.

In Chicago, for whatever reason, authors felt no need to congregate. At least not in parking lots. I searched in vain for the black-and-white Hawaiian shirt of Paul Theroux, whom I had listened to in an airless tent a few hours earlier. He had flattered his audience, comprising about two hundred people (in a city of three million), congratulating them for being readers. They were, he said, "like the early Christians, gathering in tents." He told of talking to a young woman recently, a college graduate, and mentioning a book by Robert Louis Stevenson. She had never heard of him.

"Didn't your parents read to you when you were a child?" Theroux had asked her incredulously.

It occurred to me that writers' concerns about the decline of reading stem from more than just a self-preservation instinct; they are tied, as well, to the nearly-as-powerful need to connect. You don't have to read me, but read so you can talk to me. All writers were readers first, and most continue their lives as more prolific readers than writers; with fellow readers — unlike with fellow writers — we feel a noncompetitive bond. (There are no prestigious workshops, or covetous magazine assignments, or Pulitzers for readers.) Tell a writer you write and depression sets in; tell a writer you read and gratitude blossoms. Especially now, in the Blog Age, when it seems that more people want to write than to read (not realizing that you need to read in order to write anything that is worth reading, or hasn't already been written). But this is the inevitable result when a culture prizes self-expression over learning. It is the written equivalent of a room in which everyone is talking and nobody is listening, particularly to the dead. Literature, like French, has ceased to be the lingua franca for the so-called educated crowd.

But this wasn't what I wished to discuss with Theroux. I wanted to ask him why he ignored my book, which my blurb-seeking publisher had sent him, after choosing one of the chapters for *The Best American Travel Writing 2001*.

I carried my plate of hummus and bruschetta and sat down at a table of secondhand booksellers. Used books were more a part of the Printers Row Book Fair than of the other fairs I'd been to. One of the sellers said there used to be even more secondhand stalls, before the chain bookstores became involved and inevitably changed the character of the fair. A woman with short brown hair and dirty fingernails told me, too, that many older, even middle-aged, secondhand booksellers (middle-aged and secondhand — a dire combination in the country of the next new thing) gave up on book fairs because of the physical labor involved. Ultimately, there is a lot of heavy lifting in literature.

On Sunday, I woke up well before my 2:30 presentation. I was scheduled to appear with a professor of Buddhism who had written a book about the religion and his experiences teaching it in Cambodia. I was ambivalent about panels, not just because the audience is doubled for your potentially one-bettered performance, but because they had produced, at previous fairs, my greatest public debacle as a writer, and my finest hour.

In Miami, I had followed the author of a book about her multicultural neighborhood in Queens. She had brought slides, recordings, and her sizable talents as an actress and mimic, re-creating accents that ranged from street black to Ukrainian immigrant. It was an impressive performance, and a long one, as the coauthor, her husband, hadn't been able to make the trip and she took the time allotted to (at least) two speakers. When she finally finished, and the lights came back on, a crew appeared to dismantle her audio and visual aids. During the lull a large portion of the audience, either having seen what they'd come for or believing the session now over, got up and walked out, heartlessly passing in front of me as they went. The moderator, inexplicably at a loss, made no announcement. I watched the agonizing faces of friends who stayed to lend their support and thereby magnified my humiliation by being witnesses to it. Eventually I took the podium, and read a short section in a voice of controlled hurt.

In Austin, things worked out differently. As viewers of Book-TV know, readings at the Texas Book Festival take place in the state capitol. My panel, probably because it contained two Texans, was put in the House Chamber. The three of us looked out from our hillock over a plush plain of leather swivel chairs, all of them occupied by make-believe legislators. Lesser would-be officials speckled the balcony.

Once again I went last, after another dramatic reading, this one by a young Hispanic woman who used not just her voice but her body to evoke a night of rumba in Havana. After she sat down, and the other Texan read — about the founder of a sailing ship company — I pulled out a newspaper column I'd written, inspired by recent campaign speeches. (The book fair took place one week before the presidential election.)

"My fellow Americans, as your next president I will ensure that every working man and woman receives one month of vacation a year."

Applause rang through the chamber.

"I will approve discounts on Prozac for flight attendants.

"I will make any hotel with attitude host a weekly Rotary Club luncheon.

"I will convince the manufacturers of suitcases to come up with a new black.

"I will pass through Congress a bill mandating that any passengers who fail to fit their carry-on bags into the overhead compartment on the first try must turn said bags over to a flight attendant and, before landing, write letters of apology to all the people seated in rows higher than their own."

The vote in the House was clear: I had carried Texas.

In Chicago, I met the professor of Buddhism in the authors' lounge. I had envisioned a man who brought a bemused detachment to the huzzah of the marketplace, so I was relieved when he seemed as concerned about sales and publicity as I was. We were taken to a small classroom where about twenty people sat. This time I read first, from my chapter on Comiskey Park, and then the professor read about Cambodia — two subjects that quite possibly had never been paired.

And probably never should be again. Afterwards, I signed three books and then looked on as the line, made up almost entirely of comely young women, grew in front of the professor's table. The majority of readers are female, of course, just as the majority of sports fans are male. (The percentage of women at a ball game is no doubt comparable to the percentage of men at a book fair.) The fact that I was in Chicago was no excuse for my choice of reading; people don't want to be transported to the homegrown. And as a meaningful way of life, Buddhism will always surpass support for the White Sox.

For ten long minutes I not only encountered apathy, I also watched its opposite turn its perfumed back to me. Panels. Then I remembered that I was a travel writer and I did what travel writers do: I left. I walked out of the book fair, picked up my rental car, and pointed it toward Iowa.

I was looking forward to my first trip to the state since 1992. That also was an election year, and as in every election year, commentators were talking about the heartland. I had never been to the heartland. I flew to Des Moines, rented a car, and discovered a miscellany of intimate Americana: the Surf Ballroom in Clear Lake, where Buddy Holly, Ritchie Valens, and the Big Bopper gave their last performance; the National Hobo Convention in nearby Britt; the "Field of Dreams" in Dyersville; the limestone buildings of Grant Wood's old artists' colony in Stone City — everything connected by rolling fields of tall green corn. I thought of all the people who had said "Huh?" when I had told them where I was going next. Iowa taught me a valuable lesson of travel, or at least travel writing: Often, the less glamorous the destination, the more rewarding the journey.

The sun disappeared as Copland's "Red Pony" played on the radio. Just across the Mississippi a SUPER 8 MOTEL sign pierced the gloaming. I dropped my bags in my room and headed into Le Claire. A 1923 Rolls-Royce sat in front of Sneaky Pete's.

"That's my car," said one of the two men sitting at the bar. "A Silver Ghost." He and his friend had left New Hampshire and were on their way to Montana for a little fly-fishing. In 2007, he said, they were going to ship the car to China and then drive it in the Beijing-Paris rally.

Hundreds of neckties hung from the ceiling of the dining room. "We cut them off customers," the bartender told me, before mentioning that Buffalo Bill Cody had been born in Le Claire (somehow I had missed the town on that first trip). Minutes later he brought me my buffalo burger, which I washed down with a glass jar of beer.

"Where you staying?" he asked. "Out at the Super 8? That's too bad. I've got a B & B," and he handed me a card for the Hog Heaven Bed & Breakfast. And I sat there struck (once again) by the limitless riches of the road — in fifteen minutes I had found four travel stories, that of a biker B & B being almost as marvelous as that of the future Eurasian road racers — and also by the brute similarities between the lodging and the publishing industries. The franchises — Super 8, David Sedaris — get prominent placement along the highway and just inside the door (and with it ever-increasing business), while the little guys — the B & Bs and midlist authors (while often charming, and full of personality) — fight a losing battle tucked away on side streets and back shelves where they are invisible to all except those who specifically seek them out. That night I cut my ties with the chain motels.

In Iowa City, I found a handsome bed-and-breakfast in the middle of a leafy academic street. Though it was a good walk from the university, you could still imagine professors heading off in the morning to disseminate knowledge. A visiting professor of mathematics, in fact, occupied the room next to mine. In the morning we were joined at table by an innkeeping couple from Minneapolis. And in that easy familiarity of boarding house breakfasts, they asked about me. B & Bs, it was clear, give go-it-alone book tour authors not only a warm feeling of solidarity but also an excellent opportunity for self-promotion. Front and center once again. And many people, moved either by a brush with celebrity or a bout of sympathy, will buy a book if they've met the author. At least they say they will.

A sign in the upstairs café at Prairie Lights (independent booksellers get the same professional courtesy as B & Bs) informs customers that they are on the site of the old literary society, The Times Club, that brought Robert Frost, Carl Sandburg, e. e. cummings, Langston Hughes, and Sherwood Anderson to town. Black-and-white photographs of them and others decorate the walls. Downstairs, Paul Ingram talks books like the one-man literary society he is.

My reading was hosted by a local radio personality and carried live on WSUI. (As are all readings at Prairie Lights, giving them an unexpected air of import.) About fifty people filled the chairs, while a blessed handful stood in the back. Thanks be to college towns with famous writers' workshops. Ignoring the lessons of Chicago, I read about Iowa, though I ended with some helpful travel advice for runaway brides (inspired by the memory of a town that embraces drifters) and a soliloquy on the beauty of unsung places. When the hour-long program was over, a number of people came up to chat (it was me or nothing). One was a boy, no older than fourteen, who gave me my book to be signed and then, just as endearingly, his hand to be shaken.

The next morning I stopped in Anamosa to visit Grant Wood's grave, leaving a postcard of my book with the woman in the Chamber of Commerce office. (After verifying that I had correctly identified in it his final resting place.) That night's reading in Dubuque was turned into a signing as the space before the microphone remained dishearteningly vacant. Friendly staff made like a grounds crew and swiftly moved my table out of the café and into the center aisle.

An author at a signing is like a picture at an exhibition — passively open to public scrutiny, ridicule, approval, dismissal, avoidance. The difference being, of course, that the author perceives and registers (or, frequently, tries not to register) the reactions she inspires. But sometimes he is simply an information source for a customer looking for the latest Palahniuk.

Our culture has no accepted etiquette for dealing with writers sitting alone with their books. People bring to the experience, even in large cities, no helpful guidelines or learned behaviors. Which is why I remember with such awe and affection the young woman in Dubuque.

She walked by, trailing her husband and two children.

"So, you're an author?" she said, slowing her pace but not coming to a stop.

"Yes," I said.

"Congratulations."

JEFFREY TAYLER

The Woman in the *Kuffiya*

FROM *WorldHum.com*

THUNDER RUMBLED FROM PURPLE-GRAY autumnal clouds gathering over the village of Harran, where I was headed. Ethnically Arab, Harran lies tucked away in southernmost Turkey, just a few miles from the Syrian border. It is ancient: the Book of Genesis says Abraham stopped there on his way to Canaan from the Land of Ur. The bus from the nearby town of Urfa had left me at the turnoff on the highway; I had six miles to cover on foot down a road that cut through sweeping fields of barley and cotton. I walked alone, lost in thoughts about history and the Bible.

But then I heard hoofs on asphalt, the tongue clicks of a female driver commanding a horse. Soon, a white mare dragging a wooden cart pulled up beside me and halted: sitting cross-legged on the cart was a young woman swathed in turquoise and black robes. A *kuffiya*, or red-and-white-checked Arab scarf, was wrapped around her head. She was gripping its end between her teeth so that it covered all but her eyes like a veil.

"Itlaʾ!" (jump aboard) she said, releasing the *kuffiya* as she spoke to unmask a comely, full-lipped mouth and clear bronzed skin. Her eyes were jade green and arrestingly radiant; I looked at them and looked again, but then averted my gaze — I was in an Islamic country, after all.

I climbed onto the cart and took a seat beside her.

"Sss! Gaaʾ!" she shouted to the horse, hitting it with her switch. We rolled ahead. "You're a Turk?" she asked me in Arabic. American, I told her, also in Arabic. Her head lolled sensuously with the bumps in the road. "Ahh, Ameerka! President Boosh!"

She meant George Herbert Walker, not George W. This was in 1996; even then, news reached this remote part of Turkey slowly. But I didn't care; I couldn't help stealing glances at her. Her hair was raven black; it framed her cheekbones and cascaded down her back under her *kuffiya* and robes. Her eyes remained fixed on me even when I looked away. She told me her name was Hawa', or Eve in Arabic, and she lived in Harran. I told her I was a writer. She nodded, but a minute later asked me what a writer did. She worked the village's cotton fields; that was all she knew, that was her world, an ancient world where little changed and needed to be read about.

We rocked down the road, with lightning flickering from the vaulted clouds ahead. I felt uneasy about riding alone with her in this conservatively Muslim part of Turkey where, in the local Arabic dialect, women were known as *hareem,* or the forbidden ones. So I tried not to look at her, but I failed. She was just too beautiful.

I asked if she was married.

"Ahh, our men are our grief!" she exclaimed. "Yes, I am."

At this she reached behind herself, twisting around and pulling at the blankets on the cart. To my surprise, she uncovered another young woman lying with a baby in her arms.

"My sister, 'Aysha!" Hawa' announced. 'Aysha handed her a shard of pita bread. "Try this," Hawa' said to me. "It's *khubz al-'Arab*" — Arab bread — "and I baked it myself." Her eyes sparkled green. She covered 'Aysha again. I took the bread. It tasted like clay, but I ate it anyway.

She clucked and hissed to the horse, and we rolled on toward the thunderclouds. We passed a group of men huddled in the fields around fruit and jugs of water; they called out an invitation to me to come eat with them. Hawa' shouted to them that I must get to Harran immediately. She chuckled; she seemed happy to keep me to herself, and, to put it mildly, I was happy to stay with her.

"You're married?" she asked me. No. "Praise be to God!" she said, smiling. "As for us, our men are our grief. Before we had the irrigation water, they did nothing at all while we worked the fields. Now they harvest cotton but complain about how they have to work."

"Our grief!" shouted 'Aysha from her blanket. "Our grief, by God!" chimed Hawa' again, laughing.

Her clucking and hissing to the horse, her lyrical, wild-sounding Arabic, her grace with the switch, her eyes and the glimpses of her figure captivated me. I couldn't resist looking at her, I almost felt bewitched. We trundled toward Harran for the next hour, carrying on a sparse dialogue of charged words and subtle gestures, reveling in each other's company. When we neared the outskirts, she slowed.

I jumped down and thanked her. We stared into each other's eyes, communicating something wordless and visceral and shared: repressed lust. Then she wrapped the *kuffiya* around her face again and gripped it with her teeth. With a cluck and a hiss-hiss she was off, and I was alone once more, my heart thumping in my chest.

As I entered the village it began to rain. I watched her cart pull away into a maze of mud-brick houses. I was soon wondering at just how little I had seen of her charms, yet how exciting I had found them. The fiercest lust smolders under wraps, but expires in the open. The oft-maligned Islamic custom of purdah does much to preserve passion in its most urgent and ineffable form. No topless beach has ever, to me, looked the same after Harran.

MATTHEW TEAGUE

While the King Sleeps

FROM *National Geographic*

THE ROYAL GUARDS slouched a little, and wore pith helmets. They stood looking at their feet, so that their faces disappeared behind the helmet brims. One guard swept a boot across the gravel, as though an explanation might lie hidden underneath.

"I'm sorry," he said. "It could be a while."

The crown prince of Tonga had sent word earlier that morning that he would grant me an audience. Now the sun stood high overhead, and we all sweated in the royal driveway, clearing our throats and crunching the gravel underfoot.

The prince's mansion sat on a high hill overlooking much of the kingdom. It's the last true monarchy in the Pacific, and one of the last in the world. A few weeks earlier in the summer, the beloved and ancient king had checked into a hospital in New Zealand. Now his unloved son, the prince, prepared to ascend the throne.

Prince Tupouto'a could live at the royal palace by the sea, but he prefers the sprawling hilltop redoubt. Tongans call it "the villa," when they speak of it. It's a neoclassical affair, with marble columns and a pool where he sometimes plays with toy boats. On this particular day the guards washed the crown prince's cars: a jaunty Jaguar, a sport-utility vehicle, and a London black taxicab. His Royal Highness had seen the taxi in England, a guard explained, and decided to ship one back home. No one seemed to know why, and I promised to ask the prince.

From the villa a great white driveway descended the hill, sweeping past a fountain and a guardhouse. There it joined the road into Tonga's capital, a hot and dusty town called Nuku'alofa, home to a third of the country's one hundred thousand inhabitants. At the base of the hill, on the road to town, a woman sat making brooms from palm fronds, hoping to trade them later on in this largely barter economy. Farther toward town, a little yellow food stand bore the slogan "Democracy, not Hypocrisy." Farther still, the royal tombs stood vast and ageless, where workers prepared for the king's imminent death. Farthest of all, beyond the prince's hilltop view, squatters lived at the island's garbage dump, scrounging for anything salvageable.

There's a movement afoot among Tongan commoners. While the Western world struggles to plant democracy other places around the globe, in Tonga it's sprouting from the soil. Its growth has been nurtured by the forces of modernity, which have crashed into Tonga in a relative instant: the ease of air travel and the improvement of technology. Geographic distance no longer means ideological isolation.

So the country now finds itself at a moment of decision: stuck midway between the past and future, monarchy and democracy, isolation and global engagement.

The apologetic, pith-helmeted guard trotted away, and returned a few minutes later. "I'm sorry," he said again. "His Royal Highness is asleep. Everyone is afraid to wake him."

Tongan royals deserve a measure of fear. Starting about nine hundred years ago, a long lineage of kings used war and diplomacy to spread Tonga's influence to other gentler island neighbors, including Samoa and perhaps Fiji. Even today Tonga remains the only country in the Pacific never to be governed by a foreign power.

The country's history is one of relative isolation, and Tongans are among the most ethnically homogeneous people on the planet. But the culture has been buffeted by waves from afar — explorers, missionaries, swindlers, and suitors all leaving their mark. Captain James Cook arrived in the 1770s, and impressed by the hospitality of the locals (and unaware of their plans to try to kill him), dubbed it the Friendly Isles, a nickname that stuck. When swimming, many Tongans wear clothes, often black, instead of swimsuits, modesty that reflects the nation's large and conservative Methodist and Mormon populations. Tonga has a literacy rate of 99 percent and claims to produce more Ph.D.'s per capita than other nations in the region, but the country's largest source of income is money sent home by Tongans who have moved overseas. And Tonga has a thirty-two-seat parliament, but only nine members are elected by the people. The others are selected by the king and the nobles, and all decisions are subject to the king's approval.

The king during my visit, Tupou IV, enjoyed respect from his people for decades. He even looked royal from a distance — six feet two inches tall and weighing up to 460 pounds. When he was younger, he surfed and dived, and the islanders adored him. But in recent years, as the king's health failed and his attention wandered, the royal family stumbled into a series of schemes that can only be described as wacky.

The king, for instance, committed millions of dollars trying to convert seawater to natural gas. His oldest son, the crown prince, proposed making their islands a nuclear waste disposal site. The monarchy led an expensive search for oil, despite slim geologic evidence there was any oil to find. They registered foreign ships with giddy abandon, including some that turned out to be, embarrassingly, part of al Qaeda's fleet. The list goes on.

But the plot that really angered the kingdom's subjects started in the 1980s, when the king hit on the idea of selling Tongan passports. The world's most unwanted citizens — and sometimes "wanted" — jumped at the opportunity. Imelda Marcos, for instance, became a Tongan citizen. The sale ultimately rang up $25 million before protests ended it. But that's when the deal took its weirdest turn: The king turned over the money to an American schemer named Jesse Bogdonoff, whose previous business dealings included selling magnetic bracelets. The king appointed him official court jester. He was the only one in the world, and a royal decree pronounced him "King of Jesters and Jester to the King, to fulfill his royal duty sharing mirthful wisdom and joy as a special goodwill ambassador to the world."

His first turn as jester was a vanishing act: He invested the kingdom's money in an insurance scheme and lost it all, then disappeared. The Tongan people, feeling less than mirthful, started to question the role of the royal family. The monarchy seemed increasingly out of touch. The crown prince, for instance, had spent much of his upbringing abroad, educated at Sandhurst and Oxford. He wore impeccably tailored tweed suits and sometimes a monocle. He spoke with a precise British accent, and liked to collect toy soldiers. In 1998 he quit a cabinet position to pursue business interests, and soon he owned the brewery, electric company, a telecommunications company, airline, and more. Watching it all, his people were incredulous, but the prince didn't seem to care. He told newspapers that without royal guidance, Tongans would "urinate in elevators." He dismissed Tongan livelihoods, such as "basket weaving or whatever it is these people do." Increasingly, many Tongans wondered whether the prince hated them. Or more to the point, whether they hated the prince.

In the 1980s a young man named 'Akilisi Pohiva emerged as a voice of dissent. He stood in public and railed against the monarchy. Other Tongans laughed at him. He thought differently than they did, and even looked different: Among round people with round features, Pohiva looked like a hawk, with eyes that gazed down either side of a sharp nose. He was jailed twice for speaking against the government.

But after years of royal goofs, Pohiva's calls for political reform have slowly taken hold, culminating in open unrest in 2005. It started as a strike by the country's civil employees, who wanted pay increases. But the protest grew into a full-on demand for democracy. Rioters overturned cars, marched the streets, firebombed a royal residence, and — unthinkably, in Tongan culture — threatened bloodshed.

After my first attempt to meet the crown prince, his secretary told me it might be a while before he would see me. So while I waited, I set out to see the kingdom.

At the airport outside the capital city, a languorous clerk checked bags for island-hopping flights by Peau Vava'u, the crown prince's airline. "Please place your luggage on the scale," she said, noting the weight with a pencil. It brought strange comfort, in an age of plastic explosives and sniffer dogs, that somewhere in the world an airline still depends on longhand arithmetic.

"And now you," she said.

"Yes?"

"Please step on the scale."

The prince's plane, she explained, was "not new," and so it was crucial that she total all cargo, from luggage to passengers to pigs.

Out on the tarmac I saw just how "not new" the prince's airplane was: There sat a gleaming Douglas DC-3, left over from the Second World War. Dwight Eisenhower flew in one when he was just a general, and these days they're rarely seen outside museums, much less flown in daily commercial use. But the prince loves them. After a white-gloved attendant waved the passengers aboard, the ancient Pratt & Whitney radial motors sputtered awake and strained to heave us skyward, riding up and down the waves of wind like a ship on water. I realized, as ukulele music floated through the cabin, that we were flying aboard the prince's favorite toy airplane.

From high above, Tonga looked like green flecks against a blue background. Its islands are tiny and far-flung: five hundred miles from one end to the other, and almost all water. The islands fall into three main groups — Vava'u, Ha'apai, and Tongatapu — each so different that to the visitor they lack any meaningful connection. Traveling between them feels less like a geographic journey than a chronological one; each island group seems to exist within a different point in the country's history.

My first destination was the Vava'u Group: Tonga of the future.

Yes, yes, the boat captain said. We've got a couple of sharks off the bow, but they're only "little ones." Which would have sounded a good deal more reassuring if we hadn't just pushed several tourists off the stern.

The sharks disappeared underwater, and the captain, a New Zealander named Allan Bowe, grinned. "They'll be fine," he said, laughing. Bowe is a whale hunter, of a peculiar sort. His long gray beard whipped in the wind, and sunlight got lost in the wrinkles around his eyes. Meanwhile the tourists bobbed in the deep water like chum.

Humpback whales migrate north each year from cold Antarctic waters and spend five months among the islands. Big and strong, the whales look like they could swallow a dugout canoe without a burp. Bowe, though, saw an opportunity. On a boating trip to Vava'u about fifteen years ago, he took a leap, diving into the water to splash around with the whales. "It scared me witless at first," he said. But the humpbacks just nosed around like enormous underwater basset hounds, and in an instant Bowe conceived a new industry: swimming with whales.

Vava'u draws in dreamers and sailors from around the world; tourists park their yachts in the Port of Refuge and come ashore to sip coffee at The Mermaid. Yachts sail in easily from New Zealand or Hawaii, but to leave they've got to sail far east or west to catch homeward trade winds. So, often they simply never leave. Some yacht sailors have stayed anchored off Vava'u for years, or even lifetimes.

After Allan Bowe's epiphany about swimming with whales, he bought a boat, outfitted it for the business, and sparked a debate among conservationists and thrill seekers. Scientists haven't agreed on the impact of swimming with whales. Some people say it disturbs them and their environment, while others argue anything that brings attention to the whales helps save them from hunting.

On Bowe's boat, batch after batch of tourists plunked into the water and survived despite the sharks. Again and again they climbed back into the boat with tales of a mystical experience. They had communed with nature, they said, and felt the wonder of the moment. So I pulled on a pair of flippers and hopped off the stern along with three other swimmers. We paddled toward a pair of humpbacks, a mother and baby, and almost immediately they turned away. With one mighty *swoosh* they were gone.

We saw grace there, and beauty and awe, but overwhelmingly I sensed something else. I felt like a man walking on an empty beach, who happens across a couple reclining together on a towel, and suddenly decides to plop down beside them.

The whales seemed, more than anything, annoyed.

The prince's antique airplane rattled into tiny Lifuka, the main island of the Ha'apai Group, and parked at the one-room airport. As soon as the pilot cut the engines, a deep silence saturated the island. After the touristy bustle of Vava'u, Ha'apai felt like a patch of some other era: Tonga of the past.

A lone car sat outside the airport, with a barefoot man standing beside it, grinning. "Ride?" The island is only a few miles square, and the driver crossed it at little more than a walking pace. This happens all over Tonga, where cars only caught on in recent years, and people drive them as if they were horses. But in Ha'apai cars barely outnumber horses. The island group is flat, unspoiled, and quiet. The people live simple lives, fishing and farming. They care little for politics and have little exposure to tourism. Many live on Lifuka and keep animals on a nearby island, Uoleva. At low tide they can cross on horseback.

One day I met a young man named Roni who offered to let me come along for a pig feeding on Uoleva. We rode bareback with homemade rope bridles, and the outgoing tide washed over the flanks of the horses. They tripped across a coral seafloor, angling their bodies to lower their profile against the current. We emerged onto the Uoleva beach, and the horses surged from the water, so that we felt like the conquerors of some tiny and faraway new world.

At the grove where he keeps his pigs, Roni climbed a tree and knocked down some coconuts, which we cracked open and drank. He filled a water bowl for the animals and scattered some food. Then he ran and leaped at his horse, vaulting onto its back. Before we left, he trotted around a bit, awash in a sea of tranquility.

The troubles on Tongatapu, the kingdom's main island — Tonga of the present — seemed centuries away.

After sundown the village of Houma, like every other village on Tongatapu, goes well and truly dark. And on this particular night, dozens of villagers emerged from the blackness into a tin-roofed meeting hall to plot a democracy.

The room was lit only by a few weak fluorescent bulbs, with murals on the walls. The women sat on metal folding chairs with their hands folded in their laps. The men sat in an oval on the floor, around a great six-footed wooden bowl of kava. It's a gently narcotic drink, made from a local root and served in halved coconut shells. Tongan men drink it down to the bitter residue at the bottom of the shell, then fling the shell toward the big bowl for a refill. Kava tends to slow down time for its drinker, so such sessions often last all night.

The men at the democracy meeting invited me to sit and drink. I did, and worked to keep pace, but it didn't matter because the drink didn't seem to have any effect. Everyone just laughed and told jokes about the crown prince and his wealth, and we drank kava. Someone complained about taxes, and we drank kava. Then slowly the eyes of the men in the oval seemed to soften, and their smiles lingered long after each joke had faded. An old man danced in the corner to no music, and another old man with purple hair sat singing softly to himself. Someone gave Prince Tupouto'a the new name of Prince Tippytoes.

'Akilisi Pohiva strode into the room, and immediately stood out from his stoned compatriots. Time has not dulled the edges of his hawkish face, or his rhetoric. No one laughs at him now; he's one of the few members of parliament elected by the people, and the longest serving. As the men and women gathered around, he spoke. "Last year I was charged with sedition," he told the crowd. The penalty for speaking out, he said, "is indicative of their pressure. They are putting pressure on us."

Pohiva grew up on a tiny island in the Ha'apai Group. His parents died when he was a child, so his brothers raised him. There had been no school for boys previously in Ha'apai, and young Pohiva was one of the original twenty-five students at the first school. He did well, and later attended the University of the South Pacific in Fiji. He told me that's where he started to question the Tongan royal family, and learned about democracy. "At the university," he told me on another day, "I was exposed to the alternatives. The history of other countries, democracy, communism, socialism. That really helped widen my knowledge."

After several hours of speeches from the meeting attendees, thoughts blurred by kava had resharpened their edges. One of the democracy organizers set a document on a table at the front of the room. It was a petition to wrest power from the royal family by giving more seats in parliament to the people. The organizers didn't want to destroy the royal family, but to set it aside, after the British model.

One by one they stepped up to the desk, picked up the pen, and signed their names. And so among these strange surroundings, saturated in kava and singing old songs, the Tongans shaped democracy in their own image.

The crown prince, after some weeks, granted an audience.

The guard at the entrance to the property waved me in, and I climbed the hill toward the villa. I waited on the lawn while His Royal Highness finished a meeting with the ambassador from the Netherlands; the king of Tonga was ill in New Zealand and would die within a few weeks, so the crown prince was serving as the country's interim ruler. Scores of guards lounged in the sun with a variety of brass instruments. When the ambassador emerged, they snapped to attention and played a march until she had climbed into her car and pulled away.

The crown prince's personal secretary brought me to the villa's front door. It opened onto a breezeway that separated the house's two wings. The day was warm, but the villa sat atop a hill, and a cool breeze swept in. The sound of the secretary's shoes echoed off marble floors and columns. The walls were mostly bare, but painted in the trompe l'oeil style to convey the illusion of depth.

The secretary left me alone in a sitting room that seemed to belong to three or four different people. Ancient religious icons lined the mantel of the fireplace, a collection of Japanese art filled one corner, abstract art hung elsewhere. A piano sat in another corner; the prince plays jazz, and once formed a band in England. The electric outlets were all of the American type, instead of the local current, because the prince prefers appliances bought in the United States.

A few minutes later the prince entered the room. "Hello," he said, in a British accent as rich as plum pudding. He extended a hand, with a palm so soft it felt wet. He sat on an ottoman, unbuttoning the jacket of a gray tweed three-piece suit. A woman appeared. She crossed the room with what appeared at first to be an empty silver serving tray, but when she bent toward the prince, he picked up a cigarette.

We chatted for a while about his background and upbringing in England. I asked him about the taxi imported from London, and his desire for it. "Practicality, really," he said. "A London taxi is easier to get in and out of when you're wearing a sword."

There's another practicality: The cab features curtains in the windows, which the prince pulls shut as he rides around his country, so that his people can't see him, and he can't see them. I asked if things would change, once he ascended.

"I think we'll probably carry on doing things the way we have in the past, which has been very successful," said the future king.

A few days earlier I had visited Tonga's school for disabled children, where the computers were donated by Australia, and the vehicle was donated by the people of Japan. It seems unfair, I said, sweeping a hand toward the Japanese art and the view beyond, for the royals and the nobles to have what is relative opulence and wealth, while other, less fortunate people rely on foreign help. Is that an unfair criticism?

He dismissed it with a wave of his hand, noting that despite America's reputation for wealth and power, it also has poor people in inner cities and rural areas. "Lubbock, Texas," he said, "and such places."

His hand rose slowly, and he pulled a long breath from a new cigarette. "Foreign aid is foreign aid," he said. "So how you treat other people's kindnesses is not their business, it's yours."

I pondered that statement for a bit, and decided I had been told off, in the royal way. The audience didn't last much longer. At the end I thanked the prince for his time, and for . . .

"Goodbye," he said. The sharp interruption stood in such contrast to the warm smile on his face that I didn't realize for several moments that I had been dismissed. The prince turned his back and walked away, leaving me alone.

I wandered back outside into the sunlight, where the prince's driver, Harry Moala, washed the royal vehicles. He saw me and smiled, and asked if I needed a ride back to town.

"Sure."

"How about in the Jaguar?" he said.

We flew down the long royal driveway and reached breakneck speeds on the byroads of Nuku'alofa. Two months later, in November 2006, most of the city's downtown would go up in flames during a second wave of political riots. Thick black smoke would hang over the city, as crowds flipped cars, set fire to offices, and threw stones at government buildings, demanding more democratic representation. Eight people would die, hundreds would be arrested, and five democratic leaders — including 'Akilisi Pohiva — would be charged with sedition.

For now, though, Moala dodged slower cars and reflected on His Royal Highness.

"Up to one week I don't see him. He just stays in his room. He gets the food taken to his room, up to one week," he said. "The HRH stays lonely in his room. Maybe he likes to stay by himself. But busy on computer. Stays on the computer all day and night."

I knew what he meant: The new king remains asleep, and everyone is afraid to wake him.

PAUL THEROUX

The Golden Man

FROM *The New Yorker*

TURKMENISTAN, from the time it gained independence from the Soviet Union, in 1991, until the end of 2006, was a tyranny, run by a madman, Saparmurat Niyazov. He died of heart failure last December, at the age of sixty-six, but while he lived he was one of the wealthiest and most powerful lunatics on earth. He treated Turkmenistan as his private kingdom, a land in which everything belonged to him, including the country's plentiful natural gas — much of which issued into the air from his own person in the form of interminable speechifying.

With the mountains of Iran and Afghanistan stacked up on its southern border, Turkmenistan was once a land of nomadic horse breeders in search of grazing pastures. It attracted conquerors — Alexander the Great, the Parthians, the Arabs, the Mongols — but because of its considerable size (it is almost a hundred and ninety thousand square miles), its inhospitable terrain, and its fierce tribalism it was not easily governed. Russia's first military expedition into the region, ordered in 1717 by Peter the Great, ended in disaster; the czar's men were massacred by local khans. By the late-nineteenth century, though, the territory was under Russian control. The country did not have a defined border of its own until 1924, when it became a Soviet republic. "The Turkmen S.S.R. was always a backwater," a seasoned American diplomat told me. "It was the sleepiest, most remote, least favored of the U.S.S.R.'s republics." Niyazov, a career bureaucrat, was named First Secretary of the Communist Party of Turkmen S.S.R. by Mikhail Gorbachev in 1985. After the breakup of the Soviet Union, in 1991, he gave himself the name Turkmenbashi, "Leader of All the Turkmen," and put himself in charge.

I was lucky to get a visa to travel to Turkmenistan in the middle of last year, at a time when Turkmenbashi was still alive, and many of his people cringed at his name, he was jailing dissenters, and his roads were mostly closed to people like me. Turkmenbashi famously hated writers, and Turkmenistan, during his reign, was one of the hardest countries in the world for a solitary traveler to enter. Apart from its gas pipeline, it had few links to the rest of the world. Only the truly privileged had access to international phone service, the Internet, and cell phones. When I arrived, Internet cafés had been closed for more than three years. Newspapers, radio, and television were all under state control; there was no real local news and little access to news from elsewhere. My BlackBerry, which had worked in Baku, Azerbaijan, and in Tbilisi, Georgia, went dark. People tended to whisper when they spoke, and no wonder. In a typical case, reported by international sources, a fifty-eight-year-old journalist, Ogulsapar Muradova, a reporter for Radio Free Europe/Radio Liberty and a mother of three, had been arrested on a trumped-up charge, tried secretly without a lawyer, and given six years in jail. In September, a month after she was imprisoned, she was found dead (she appeared to have suffered a "head injury"), and her body was handed over to her daughters.

I took a fifty-minute flight from Baku to Turkmenistan's capital, Ashgabat, and passed, in the process — or so it seemed — through the looking glass. Few planes landed at the casino-like airport, which was staffed by officials with a very slim idea of how to do their jobs — a characteristic common to officials in most dictatorships, where fear of retribution inspires indecision and incompetence. Men in handsome uniforms stood around, delaying the processing of passengers, most of them foreign workers in the gas industry — British, Malaysian, Filipino. The officials grinned at one another, but when they met my gaze they glowered and looked fierce. One official, in a wide-crowned and shiny-visored cap, looked at me and sucked his teeth and said, *"Problyema."*

"What's the problem?"

"Shto eta?" What is this? He tugged at the offending object in my bag. (He spoke Russian with me, although Turkmen is the official language of the country.)

"Icon," I said. It was a silver icon, with an oil portrait of Jesus staring out from a lozenge at the center, which I had bought at a flea market in Tbilisi and wrapped in a T-shirt so that it wouldn't get scratched.

"*Eta starinnaya,*" he said.

"No, it's new."

"*Ochen' dorogaya.*"

"Not really. It was cheap."

"*Antikvarnaya!*"

"An antique?"

"*Da. Problyema!*" he said. He showed me the flat of his hand. "*Zhdi zdyes'.*" Wait here.

I waited almost an hour. A team of men returned. One spoke English while the rest of them clucked approvingly.

"Why you bring this eekon here?" he said slowly. "Why you not bring it khome?"

"I am bringing it home," I said.

He raised his hands. "This Ashgabat, not khome."

"I'm on my way home," I said. Which was, in the larger sense, true. "To give this to my mother."

"*Mat',*" the man explained to the team. "It is for his mother."

Mention of one's mother is useful in such situations, particularly in a country whose leader, I was to discover, encouraged a cult of motherhood.

But the man seemed baffled as to what to do next. I explained that, since a section of the customs form asked for "Description of Objects," we could fill out that portion, and I would show it at the border when I left, to prove that I wasn't smuggling antiques. He and his team seemed to think that this was an appropriate compromise, and so after two hours I was riding into Ashgabat.

The city was an example of what happens when absolute political power, money, and mental illness are combined. Turkmenbashi's acolytes had recently pronounced him the "national prophet," a harmless enough conceit if you're a civilian, but a pathological, if not fatal, one in a despot. In support of this claim, Turkmenbashi had written a sort of national Bible, called *Ruhnama* ("Book of the Soul"), and he regarded himself as an accomplished writer — a clear sign of madness in anyone. He had also recently built a vast space-age mosque, which he'd named after himself — Saparmurat

Hajji Mosque — and he encouraged his people to visit it annually, in a kind of local haj.

Ashgabat was filled with gold statues of Turkmenbashi. In these statues, which had an ecclesiastical aura, Bashi was El Dorado, the Man of Gold, all-powerful, all-knowing. People were meant not to gape at them but to venerate them. One revolving statue, showing Turkmenbashi with his arms raised, rotated according to the sun and seemed to guide it across the sky, from dawn to dusk. It stood upon a gigantic marble apparatus called the Neutrality Arch, which looked like — and was referred to by some as — a toilet-bowl plunger. Other statues showed him sitting, striding, waving, saluting, and smiling a twenty-four-karat smile. One even showed him as a precocious golden child, seated in the lap of his bronze mother. He once said to a journalist, "I admit it, there are too many portraits, pictures, and monuments [of me]. I don't find any pleasure in it, but the people demand it because of their mentality." A statue of Lenin in Neutrality Square was bronze and life-size, its message LENINISM IS THE WAY TO FREE THE PEOPLES OF THE EAST; it was modest and charming by comparison. The irony of Ashgabat was that nowhere, among the gold statues and the white marble plazas, was there a place to sit down. It was a city without benches — the subtle message: *keep walking*.

There were also portraits of Turkmenbashi, several of them measuring hundreds of square feet, everywhere in Ashgabat. In some, he looked like a fat and grinning Dean Martin; in others, he was a truculent C.E.O. with a chilly smile. A common image showed him, chin on hand, squinting in insincere bonhomie, like a lounge singer. A heavy drinker, a bully, and a wearer of bling — two or three diamond rings on each hand — he had Italianate features, and was sometimes portrayed with a stack of books, like an author on a book tour.

Everything Turkmenbashi did seemed to indicate that he was out of his mind. He'd had parliament declare him "President for Life"; it was the will of the people, his ministers had said. He'd banned beards and ballet; he'd denounced gold teeth as unhygienic. A London newspaper reported that he had renamed bread after his mother. No one I met in Ashgabat had heard about this, but he had done something even nuttier. He had renamed the months of the year — January after himself, and April for his mother. The days of the week and the names of the years were also new, Turkmenbashi's innovation. The year 2003 was named after his father, 2004 after his mother, and 2005 was "The Year of *Ruhnama.*"

"He was on TV last night," my driver said. "Well, he's on almost every night." Turkmen almost never said Turkmenbashi's name aloud. "He said, 'If you read my book three times, you will go to Heaven.'"

"How does he know this?"

"He said, 'I asked Allah to arrange it.'"

Ruhnama is a farrago of memoir, Turkmen lore, potted history, dietary suggestions, Soviet-bashing, boasting, wild promises, and Turkmenbashi's poems. He seemed to regard it both as a sort of Koran and as a how-to guide for the Turkmen people, a jingoistic pep talk. In fact, it is little more than a soporific, "chloroform in print," as Mark Twain described *The Book of Mormon.* I read it once. Turkmenbashi would have to promise more than Heaven for me to read it two more times.

In his confused and patchy exposition, Bashi reaches back five thousand years (or so he says). After the flood of Noah, he explains, the original ancestor of the Turkmen, Oguz Khan, emerged. Oguz's sons and grandsons produced Turkmenistan's twenty-four clans. The figure of Oguz is key to *Ruhnama;* his name, according to Bashi, was set upon many features of the earth and the sky. Turkmen called the Milky Way "the Oguz Arch," and the Amu Darya River "the Oguz River," and the constellation Taurus "the Oguz stars." Oguz also "implemented . . . the use of the national Oguz alphabet." *Ruhnama* might as well be subtitled "The Second Coming": Bashi sets himself up as a reincarnation of Oguz Khan, every bit as powerful and wise — which was why he chose to name cities, hills, rivers, and streets after himself and to dedicate his life to his country.

Turkmenbashi was an orphan. He makes much of this in the book, and the passages about his childhood have a clumsy tenderness. "I have borne many difficulties throughout my life," he writes. He tells how his father was killed in the Second World War, fighting for the Soviets in North Ossetia, and how, in 1948, when he was seven, his mother was killed in an earthquake that leveled much of Ashgabat. In adversity, Bashi was made stronger. "When I considered my situation, I understood that I was not an orphan!" he says. In place of parents, he had a nation and a cause — and, in Oguz Khan, a father in history. Later in the book, he waxes emotional about mothers. "The mother is a sacred being," he writes. "One can understand the value of sacred things only after one has lost them." He recalls a Turkmen saying — "Fatherless, I am orphan; motherless, I am captive" — and concludes, "Fate decreed two pains for me. I was both an orphan and a captive."

A lost childhood seems essential in a dictator's biography; it is a determining factor in the development of a political tyrant. As far as abandonment complaints go, *Ruhnama* resembles (sometimes almost word for word) the tale of the Austrian paperhanger in the first part of *Mein Kampf,* who wrote, "In my thirteenth year I suddenly lost my father . . . When my mother died, Fate, at least in one respect, had made its decisions." But the orphaning is more sentimentalized in Bashi's book, and the list of obligations and duties he provides for the Turkmen people includes the not exactly Hitlerian "Maintain a smiling face." Turkmenbashi was emphatic about smiling. "A smile can make a friend for you out of an enemy," he writes. "When death stares you in the face, smile at it and it may leave you untouched." Smiling is a form of conversation: "Talk to each other with smiles." It is a way of delaying aging: "'There will never be any wrinkles on a smiling face,' as the saying goes." And, in memory, it is a source of comfort to him: "I often remember my mother. Her smile . . . is visible to me in the dark of night, even if I have my eyes shut." This was perhaps why many of the portraits of Bashi showed him with a smile, though he never looked less amused than when he was grinning; his smile — and this may be true of all political leaders — was his most sinister feature.

At Bashi's command, *Ruhnama* is studied in all the schools of Turkmenistan; a thorough knowledge of it is still an entry requirement for colleges and universities and for advancement in the civil service. (Elections held in February, which were widely criticized as neither free nor fair, brought to power Bashi's former Deputy Prime Minister Gurbanguly Berdimuhammedov. Berdimuhammedov promised to stay true to the spirit of his predecessor, and, since then, conditions in Turkmenistan have changed little.) The immigration officials who gave me a hard time had little idea how to handle a simple customs matter, but they probably could have quoted "A smile can make a friend for you out of an enemy."

In the memoir parts of *Ruhnama,* Bashi fails to mention that, after overcoming the difficulties of his childhood and completing his education in Leningrad (he studied electrical engineering), he became a party hack. In the 1970s and '80s, he rose through the ranks to the Soviet Politburo. He was one of the educated provincials who Gorbachev hoped might serve as agents of reform. Also not mentioned in *Ruhnama* is the fact that Bashi spent a great deal of time in Leningrad and Moscow, or that he married a Russian, who lived apart from him, in Moscow, or that he had a son and a daughter who lived out of the country. (Turkmenbashi's son, Murat, was reportedly one of the people vying to replace him after his death.)

Another significant omission in recent editions of *Ruhnama* (more than a million copies have reportedly been printed, in more than thirty languages, including Zulu and Japanese, and in Braille) is any mention of the assassination attempt against Bashi. In 2002, in what was possibly a failed coup, he was shot at as his motorcade sped through Ashgabat. This attack resulted in a wave of repression; the alleged perpetrators and their helpers were hunted down and either killed or imprisoned. Whole families were jailed, and nothing was heard of them afterward. The word was that some disgruntled and ambitious former officials had schemed to get rid of Turkmenbashi. The caper failed, but it understandably enhanced his paranoia; his delusions of grandeur were joined by delusions of persecution. He ordered a clampdown on what was already limited contact with the outside world, and stripped the country of the few freedoms that remained. He also intensified another inconvenient feature of most tyrannies: roadblocks. These were installed throughout all Turkmen cities and every few miles on the roads leading out of those cities. On an eight-mile journey to see some ruins, I was stopped three times by well-armed men in spiffy uniforms who didn't have the slightest notion of what to do with the cars they stopped. They examined papers, they looked into back seats, they scowled and shouldered their rifles, but really they were foxed.

I made the trip to the ruins with two Turkmen I'd met through a mutual friend, who told me that they knew something of Turkmen history: a man I'll call Mamed, whose English was shaky, and a woman I'll call Gulnara, who was fluent. In the car, I asked them about Turkmenbashi's passion for renaming. They told me that he had made so many changes they were unable to keep the names straight.

"January is now Turkmenbashi," Gulnara said. "February is Baýderk — the flag. March is Nowruz. April is Gurbansoltan Eje — his mother. June is Oguz — our hero. But May is . . . What is May?"

Mamed said, "May is Sanjar."

"No, that's November."

"Are you sure?"

"I know September is Ruhnama," Gulnara said.

"August is Alp Arslan," Mamed said. "He was sultan."

"You forgot July," Gulnara said.

"I don't remember July. What is it?"

Gulnara shook her head. She squinted and said, "Then there's October."

Mamed said, "Garaşsyzlyk."

"Independence," Gulnara said.

They were just as vague on the days of the week, though Gulnara started confidently, "Monday is Bashgün — Main Day. Tuesday is Yashgün, Young Day. Wednesday is Hoshgün."

"Tuesday is Hoshgün," Mamed said. "Wednesday is Yashgün."

"I don't think so," Gulnara said.

Their confusion was funny but odd, given that by government decree all ministries, schools, colleges, the police, the army, and all citizens had not only to demonstrate a knowledge of the changes but to use them, too.

"He renamed ketchup," Gulnara said. "He made a big speech. 'Why do we say "ketchup"? This is a foreign word. We are Turkmen. We must have a Turkmen word for this!'"

"So what is it?"

"Ketchup is *ümech*."

"If I looked up *ümech* in a Turkmen-English dictionary, what would it say?"

"It would say 'ketchup,' except we don't have any new dictionaries in Turkmenistan."

All this talk of their obsessive president made Mamed and Gulnara self-conscious, and when they fell silent I said, "Does it bother you that the president has made all these changes?"

"Most people don't think about it," Gulnara said. She meant, Most people don't want to think about it, because it will only make them miserable.

"What about the gold statues of himself that he puts up?"

Mamed made a face, shook his head, and became suddenly alert. It was said that hotel rooms and offices were bugged. Surely his car could be bugged, too?

But Gulnara had an opinion. She was confident and bright, qualities that she shared with many of the Turkmen women I met. She said, "The statues. The slogans. The five-year plans. We have seen this before. Stalin — and others. This will pass away."

It was, it seemed to me, the right way to view the autocracy, for of course this domineering man would die, and likely sooner rather than later — he was seriously afflicted with heart disease, possibly caused by diabetes, and had undergone at least one bypass operation. In the meantime, Turkmen often expressed their disaffection through jokes. "Why is Turkmenbashi the richest man in Turkmenistan?" Answer: "Because he has five million sheep."

We had passed a number of state-owned vineyards. One of the oddities of Turkmenistan — which first encountered Islam in the seventh century and is now almost 90 percent Muslim — was its vigorous wine industry, both for export and for local consumption. Turkmen Muslims, at least the ones I met in Ashgabat, were for the most part moderate in their faith and had a surprising taste for wine. Turkmenbashi himself, who had made the haj, was also a notorious boozer.

At the edge of the desert, we approached some rising ground, more a mound than a hill, on which there was a broken structure of mud bricks. This was Anau, the ruins of a fifteenth-century mosque, which strangely showed a Chinese architectural influence. In its bright mosaics, there was imagery that I had never seen before in Islamic art, and over the archway of the entrance were some fragments of a still sinuous dragon.

Much of Turkmenistan is desert wasteland, scrubby bushes, and dusty boulders; lizards skitter through a landscape like cat litter. In Soviet times, Turkmenistan's few towns and cities were outposts, as benighted as those of any imperial colony, where people in colorful clothes surrendered their reserves of gas and oil to the Russian overlords. This exploitation was one of the injustices denounced in *Ruhnama*. But the dragon on the mosque was a reminder that this part of Turkmenistan had also been on the Silk Road, the route to China, and that some of the toughest travelers of history, some of the boldest generals, and the largest armies had passed this way. The mosque was still a place of pilgrimage, because its grounds contained the tomb of Seyyed Jamaluddin, the father of a local governor from the fifteenth century. A dozen people, most of them women with children, were praying at the pile of broken bricks that was his grave.

"They come because he has good communication with Allah," Mamed said.

There was another grave, the Tomb of the Unmarried Woman — Gulnara said that "unmarried woman" could also be translated as "virgin." Young women were praying here. Hundreds more had left behind requests to be granted. Small carved cradles indicated a woman's wish to be blessed with babies. Gulnara said that the sheep bones, carefully piled, indicated a wish for children, too, since bones were used as toys by Turkmen children. A hairpin meant that a girl was desired, as did patches of colored cloth; a toy car indicated a wish for a boy.

"In Islam, you don't usually appeal to a dead woman," Gulnara said. "You're supposed to ask Allah. But this is a powerful woman."

I pointed out that most of the appeals were for boys.

She said, "Women who give birth to girls have another way of indicating that they want a boy. They will name the daughter Enough (Besteir) or Fed Up (Boyduk). These are common names. I know many."

About forty feet from the ruined mosque was another mound, on which there were hundreds of toy huts made of broken clay tiles. It looked like a miniature city. A squatting man in a smock and a woman with a blowing headscarf were building one as we watched.

"People praying for houses," Gulnara said.

The cruelty of Turkmenbashi's policies was obvious when you contemplated the tableau of toy huts, a visible plea for housing. Homeless people abounded in this fabulously wealthy country. (Natural gas exports alone accounted for an estimated three billion dollars in revenue in 2006. This month, Berdimuhammedov signed a lucrative deal to run a new pipeline to Russia.) Bashi fancied himself a city planner; he'd ordered that hundreds of houses be bulldozed, compounds flattened, and the neighborhoods of Ashgabat dispersed, so that he could build oversized white marble apartment blocks that now stood empty because they were, in their deluxe absurdity, unaffordable. He rarely compensated the owners of the houses he tore down; nor did he rehouse them. They now lived precariously, in temporary huts on the outskirts of town.

Turkmenbashi was also a self-declared landscape artist. He promised to create a desert forest that would improve the climate and last for a millennium. He ordered the planting of tens of thousands of young trees in immensely long rows at the center of Ashgabat and on great swaths of land outside the city, a sort of instant forest. But although Bashi's trees, mostly a type of juniper, were two or three feet high when planted, the forestation was not a success. Drip irrigation had been rigged for them, but they were baked by the sun and blown flat by the wind; a full third had that peculiar rust red hue, the vivid color of an evergreen's death.

"They are called *arça*," my new guide, whom I'll call Merdan, said. (Mamed was busy that day, or perhaps wary of all my questions.) "He, um, likes them."

I was still waiting for someone to speak Turkmenbashi's name; I wanted to hear what citizens would call him. "Turkmenbashi" seemed too pompous, "Niyazov" too familiar, "the Leader" too formal, and "the national prophet" obviously hard to say with a straight face. Later, I learned that people usually referred to him as *mähriban ata*, "the dear father," or *serdar*, "tribal leader."

We were heading west, out of the city, past scores of signs reading PEOPLE-MOTHERLAND-TURKMENBASHI. On the side of a mountain, in large letters carved from marble blocks, was a sign in Turkmen that said OUR HEALTH ROAD OF OUR GREAT ETERNAL LEADER. (It was just the sort of cliff-top message that I had seen a decade earlier in Albania, and doubtless it would end up the same way, as a pile of rubble in the adjacent valley.) This one was meant to encourage people to walk on a paved path that wound through the dying dwarf forest.

"He wants us to be healthy," Merdan said.

But it was questionable whether Turkmenbashi did, in fact, want his people to be healthy. He had closed all hospitals outside Ashgabat, replaced thousands of health care workers with military conscripts, and instructed the country's doctors to pledge their allegiance to him and to *Ruhnama*, rather than taking the Hippocratic oath. Life expectancy had fallen to sixty-three, more than fifteen years below the European average, and, even though Turkmenbashi had banned the diagnosis of several communicable diseases, there had been unofficial reports of the plague in recent years.

Still, Turkmen were expected to do as they were told: never mind that you were a nomad or a villager or a cotton picker, that you spent all day on your feet; you were supposed to make the time to walk on the Eternal Leader's thirty-six kilometers of paved pathway traversing the mountainside. One of Bashi's many residences, another marble palace, lay beyond that hillside. He claimed that the lavish gold-domed presidential palace built for him in Ashgabat was not of his choosing. ("All I wanted was a small, cozy house.")

"And many people don't have jobs," Merdan said. "More than 60 percent of the population is unemployed."

"I'm surprised people aren't angry."

"Some are angry. But we have cheap things, too. Natural gas is free. Electricity is free." Gasoline, Merdan told me, cost the equivalent of three cents a gallon; he could fill the tank of his car for fifty cents.

"What do you think are the problems here?" I asked.

"We have problems, but we can't address problems, because there are no problems," Merdan said, and smiled at me, a smile that said, *Please, no more questions.*

Another day, Merdan and I went to the big bazaar outside Ashgabat, which had two names: Tolkuchka, derived from the Russian word for "pushing"; and Jygyldyk, an onomatopoeic word in Turkmen that means "babbling" or "jabbering."

Turkmen have a horror of the evil eye. Perhaps a lingering feature of the shamanism that was once part of the spiritual life of the region, this anxious reflex is apparent in every sphere of Turkmen existence. Trinkets for warding off the evil eye were on sale in many of the stalls in the bazaar — staring glass eyes, carved wooden talismans, and a sheep-horn symbol that Merdan said was effective against maledictions. Some Turkmen believed that evil could come as a withering blast from thin air, a kind of diabolical death ray. The most common antidote to this bedevilment was a charm that broke the ray into pieces, a sort of prism made of colored wool, which one wore as a necklace or a bracelet, or hung over a bed or a doorway. Some of them looked like the kind of multicolored lanyards I had made at camp when I was a boy. Still, the things worked, or so I was assured by Merdan, who bought me a length of brown-and-red rope to get me through to Uzbekistan. (Bashi was as superstitious as his countrymen; he kept an evil-eye amulet over the door to his office, and always wore an evil-eye tie tack, first a blue eye and, in his last months, a diamond.)

In most respects, the Tolkuchka Bazaar was more vital and more various than its obvious rivals, the Covered Market in Istanbul or the bazaar in Damascus or the Mall of America in Bloomington, Minnesota. It was a partly tented affair, with billowing marquees and draperies marking off the separate stalls. It was highly competitive and intensely local; there was not another tourist to be seen. It covered many acres; the horse market alone occupied what could have been an entire fairground. Buying a carpet or a melon or a sack of spices is only part of the interest of such a bazaar. The interaction of people — farmers with their families, gawky boys, shy girls — is also important. Country people may travel for a day or two on an old bus or a night train to meet city people; families rendezvous nearby for picnics; men swagger and shout while boys gape and imitate them. This bazaar was a kind of vortex, drawing in Turkmen from all over, in an ancient ceremony of encounter and negotiation, with music playing and camels howling and hawkers shouting for customers. Everything imaginable was on sale: not just Chinese clothes, shoes, belts, and blue jeans but rows and rows of traditional velveteen dresses, and the detachable white hand-embroidered collars, yoke-shaped and lovely, that are unique to the Turkmen women. Brassware, samovars, silver spoons and dishes — tables and tables of these. Russian belt buckles, military buttons, medals, and campaign ribbons. Bronze artifacts, pottery from diggings, some that looked genuine, others that didn't. Stacks of coins, too, some of them rubles from the departed regime, and lots that the sellers swore were ancient coins from the ruined cities in the desert, from the Turkmen of Afghanistan and India.

Something else attracted me at the Tolkuchka Bazaar: its multiethnic shoppers and stallholders. Most of the people were obviously Turkmen, but there were Russians, Persians, Azeris, and Uzbeks, too. For centuries, settlements across Central Asia were polyglot, and most people thought of themselves as Muslims or as tribesmen, and little else. In the 1920s, the Soviets carved the region into distinct republics, each named after a national group, but many communities remained mixed, and became more so over time. Some migrations were economic. Others, especially under Stalin, were forced, and left a number of ethnic communities stranded from their homes.

The most exotic group at the bazaar, and in Turkmenistan, was the Koreans. There were several tables of Korean women, smiling and shouting for attention, trays piled with pickled cabbage.

"Stalin sent you?" I asked one.

"He sent my father and mother," she said.

"Kimchi," I said, the only Korean word I knew.

"Yes, yes! Try some!"

"It's cheap. It's the best. Buy some."

"Take me to America!"

One afternoon in Ashgabat, I caused a diplomatic incident. I had been invited by the United States Embassy to give a harmless pep talk to some writers and journalists. About thirty men and women showed up at a sort of boardroom in a hotel that the Embassy used as an annex. They were of every physical type: stylish women in velvet dresses with the impassive faces of nomads, dark beaky men in heavy coats, young mustached men in suits, Russian aunts in blue dresses, carrying satchels, some hefty warrior types braced behind the chairs, their arms folded, a furtive man fussing with a big shoulder bag, and two pale young women, slender Slavic beauties with lank blond hair and blue eyes, standing shyly by the wall.

My topic was "the return journey," how the passage of time reveals the truth of people and places. I spoke for about twenty minutes, through an interpreter. At the end, there was polite applause. The man who had been fussing with his shoulder bag had taken out an expensive camera and begun snapping pictures.

"Any questions?"

Hands shot up.

"What do you think of Islam?" one man asked.

I made a tactful reply, commending the verses of the Koran encouraging hospitality, which I, as a traveler among Muslims, appreciated, and quickly moved to the next question.

"I am a poet," one of the Russian aunties declared. And she went on to ask how she might get her poems translated into English and published in the United States. I referred her to the fellow who had translated her question.

"How do you write a novel?" a young man asked.

I mentioned needing an idea, and characters, and a setting, and about two years of solitude.

"You are not here for very long," another man said. "How can you understand us in such a short time?"

"You're right," I said. "It's impossible. So what particular thing do you think it's important for me to understand about Turkmenistan?"

"Do you know about the pensions?"

"No, I don't. Tell me."

"The government has reduced the state pensions for some people," he said, his voice rising. "In some cases, these were people who were granted pensions by the Soviet government, but when Turkmenistan became independent these were eliminated. What do you think of that?"

As he spoke, the man with the camera leaned over and began snapping his picture.

He turned and took my picture as I said, "We have a similar problem in the United States. A lot of older people will have to work longer because the government pension fund is running out of money. The qualifying age for Social Security has risen to sixty-seven."

"But what about us?" he asked. Now his voice was strident. "This situation is serious."

"You're not getting your pension?"

"Many thousands of people are not getting it! They were workers. Now they're old, and they have nothing to live on. This is a wealthy country, but they are poor. The government has done this to us. Why don't you write about that?"

"You're a writer, all of you are writers," I said. "You are the people who should write about it, not me. You have all the facts."

"I am not a writer," the man said. "I am the chairman of the Unity and Neutrality Party of Turkmenistan."

Before this could be translated, the photographer leaped forward and snapped pictures from several angles, his shoulder bag bumping against his hip.

Then an American security officer took three strides toward the photographer, grasped his coat in one hand, snatched the camera with the other, and frog-marched the man to the back of the room and outside. This all happened so fast that the photographer did not have time to protest, though I heard him howl as the door slammed.

"Do you write about love?" one of the pretty women asked.

"Constantly," I said. I elaborated on this subject, and then declared the meeting over. The room emptied quickly.

But the harm was done. I had allowed a political dissident a forum. It turned out that this was the first anyone had heard of his underground party. And there might be collateral damage, so to speak, because the other writers and journalists who had been quietly invited (many of them unpopular with the government) had all been photographed.

"What just happened?" I asked the security officer.

I had been impressed by his deftness: without hesitating, almost without creating a scene, he had plucked the man and his camera from the room. The photographer had been a government spy, he said. In the corridor, he had erased the images from the camera.

"He should know better," the American said. "This is technically U.S. government property. Can't take pictures here."

"Is this going to be a problem?"

"We'll see," he said. "Hey, I liked your talk."

The problem developed later that day when the spy complained to his superiors at Turkmenistan's Ministry of Foreign Affairs. And the next day the Deputy Chief of Mission of the U.S. Embassy in Ashgabat was summoned to a meeting with the minister. Who is this Paul Theroux? she was asked. What are the details of his visa? Does he have permission to speak? When is he leaving? How?

I had the answers to some of these questions. My visa was in order, and in a few days I planned to take the train to the eastern city of Mary, to see the ruins at Merv. Then the train to Turkmenabat and the Uzbekistan border and, I hoped, another train.

I spent the rest of my time in Ashgabat doing what Turkmen like doing most: sitting on a lovely carpet, eating my way down a spit of lamb kebab or through a mound of rice *plov*. Always there was hard bread, sometimes dumplings; usually there was tea, sometimes wine. Now and then, these meals were served in homes that stood in empty fields, like a stage set for a Beckett play — a house in a wasteland, everything around it bulldozed to make room for a prestige project or a gold statue.

Because I was now being watched by the Ministry of Foreign Affairs, I had to be careful. But having Turkmenbashi as an enemy was also helpful, because when Western diplomats tried to explain my predicament to me they were often revealing about his quirks.

"He hates people meddling," one diplomat told me. "He hates NGOs" — nongovernmental humanitarian organizations. Turkmenbashi had banned local human rights groups and religious groups and environmental groups — all the more readily if they received assistance from foreign partners. He'd placed tight restrictions on the Peace Corps, and he refused to ask for help from the International Monetary Fund or from the World Bank, no doubt fearing that if he opened Turkmenistan's finances to international scrutiny he would be sharing information about his personal finances as well. "That's his big secret," another diplomat told me. "He's a billionaire many times over."

A person who had spent some time with Turkmenbashi in his palace said, "He's a tease. He's a mocker. He banters with his ministers and humiliates them."

"Of course his system's corrupt," a student explained. "You need to bribe a lot of people to get into college, but only Turkmen are allowed. A Russian or an Uzbek or a Korean wouldn't have a chance. They have no future here."

"He stopped education at the ninth grade for most people," a bureaucrat told me. "He was once asked about that by a foreign head of state. He said, 'Uneducated people are easier to govern.'" (One of Berdimuhammedov's first acts after coming to power was to extend school by a year.)

A former exchange student to the United States told me something else that Turkmenbashi wouldn't have wanted me to hear: that because Turkmenistan was so close to the heroin-producing areas of Afghanistan hard drugs were a serious problem in the country. Heroin addicts were numerous, and their need for money caused crime. Turkmenistan was also a transshipment route of drugs from Afghanistan to Russia. Afghan hashish was freely available.

Early one evening, I took the overnight train from Ashgabat to Mary. When I found that the sleeper ticket cost the equivalent of four dollars, I became anxious: this was the price of half a dozen melons at the bazaar, and a ticket so cheap boded ill for a long journey. I guessed that the train would be dirty and crowded, a mass of people traveling in the light of a few twenty-five-watt bulbs, and it gave me no satisfaction to be right.

The railway station itself was lovely, a classic Soviet building from the 1950s, very clean and patrolled by soldiers with machine guns. Yet no passenger was searched, and whereas travelers on Turkmenistan roads were subject to roadblocks and the arbitrary search-and-seizure rules of the security forces, train travelers, it seemed, were beneath notice.

I sat in my four-berth compartment with a soldier in a dark uniform, a student of about twenty-two, and an old man with a long chin beard, wearing traditional Turkmen dress — a cylindrical black lambskin hat and a long brown cloak over a smock, one of those national costumes which seem eternal and comfortable everywhere, in all seasons. He saw me and began to address me, using the student as a translator.

"*Salaam. Dhayf al-Rahman,*" he said.

"Welcome. You are a guest of Allah, the Merciful One," the student translated.

"Please thank him for me."

The man spoke again.

"He has a question for you," the student said. "Will you answer?"

I heard the whistle blow. The train slowly pulled out of Ashgabat Station, and within minutes we were in the desert. The old man was delivering a monologue.

"He says that some years ago an astronaut went to the moon," the student said. "He was from America. When he got to the moon, he heard a strange noise. It was an *azan*" — the call to prayer, usually issued by a muezzin chanting from a mosque. "The astronaut recorded it. When he came back to earth, the scientists in America analyzed it, and they came to think that it was the voice of the Prophet Muhammad."

"On the moon?"

"Yes. On the moon."

"Furthermore, he says that because of this the astronaut became a Muslim and began praying five times a day."

The old man was facing me, as though defying me to deny the story.

"I haven't heard this story."

"He says he believes it."

"What does he think about it?"

When this question was translated, the student said, "For him, it's good news."

It seemed to me like a Turkmen version of a Pat Robertson story: divine intervention in an unlikely place, resulting in a beatific conversion, the sun breaking through the clouds. Instead of Jesus speaking to a searcher, it was Muhammad, but it came to the same thing. Later, an Arabic scholar told me that a persistent urban myth in the Middle East is that Neil Armstrong — sometimes confused with Louis Armstrong — converted to Islam.

The best tactic on this overnight train journey, it seemed to me, was to get along, which meant staying off the subject of religion. As I was thinking this, the old man was still talking to the student.

"He asks if you believe in God."

"I have a lot of questions on this subject," I said.

"He asks, 'But do you believe in life after death?'"

"I don't know about this. No one has ever come back from the dead to tell us anything, so how can we know?"

"The holy Koran tells us."

The old man spoke directly to me in Turkmen and became very animated.

"He says, 'The grass grows. Then the grass turns brown. Then the grass dies. Then it grows again. It turns green and gets tall.'"

The old man was still staring, one skinny gnarled hand in his lap, the other gripping the long gray beard attached to his chin.

"He says, 'Life is like that.'"

"Tell him I agree. Life is like that, even where I'm from."

"Where are you from?"

"Tell him America."

The old Muslim received this information with more interest than I had expected.

"He asks, 'Do you have cotton in America?'"

"Lots of it."

"He is wondering how many hectares of cotton are growing in America."

"Tell him I'm not sure. Why is he interested?"

The man showed me his ruined hands, his twisted fingers.

"He picks cotton in the fields near Yoloten, south on the road to Afghanistan, where there are cotton farms."

The old man's name was Selim. He had been born near Mary.

He had not gone to school. As a boy, he had worked in the fields; he had picked cotton his whole life. He had married a woman from his clan and had four children.

He challenged me to guess his age. He looked about seventy, so I guessed sixty. He laughed and said that he was fifty.

At my farewell party in Ashgabat, I had been given a bag of food for the train — spinach pies, mushroom fold-overs, sticky buns, all wrapped in paper. In the dim light of the compartment, I unwrapped it and handed it around — to Selim, the student, the young soldier, and a hanger-on gaping at the doorway. Selim asked a question.

"He says, 'Ask the American if we can say a prayer.'"

"Of course," I said.

All Muslims wash before they pray. When water is unavailable, they use sand or dust to perform the dry ablution called *tayammum,* making an elaborate business of rubbing the hands and arms, and slowly wiping the face, massaging the eyes, the cheeks, the jaw, then drawing the hands downward. Selim went through this ritual as the train rushed across the desert, rattling the windows and the door handles.

Then he prayed, for almost a full minute, his eyes closed, speaking into the stifling air of the compartment. When he was finished, I asked him what he had said. Was it a standard prayer or had he improvised it?

He said that it was improvised for the occasion. "I thanked Allah for the food. I thanked the friend who gave it to us. I wished the friend blessings on his journey."

"*Sagbol,*" I said, and, in thanking him, exhausted my knowledge of Turkmen.

"'Do they pray in America at mealtime?' he asks."

"Many people do."

"Do they pray at other times, too?"

"Yes. Americans pray a lot."

A knock at the compartment door: the conductor was handing out sheets. Though it was not late, the light was so bad that there was nothing to do but sleep. We each lay down in a bunk. After the feeble light was switched off, I could see the dark plains passing, the low scrub, the boulders glowing, smooth and bluish in the moonlight.

Hours later, still in the dark, we approached the town of Mary. The others were awake and yawning.

Ashgabat had been hot and dry. Wishing to lighten my bag, I had given my sweater to Mamed and my scarf to Gulnara. Approaching Mary, I gave my heavy long-sleeved polo shirt to the student, who had been so helpful.

"It's a lucky shirt," I said.

In return, he gave me a multicolored cord to ward off the evil eye.

Selim said, "I will wait at the station until eight o'clock. Then I'll get the bus to Yoloten. It costs five thousand manat. A shared taxi costs ten thousand manat. But I say, better to take the bus and give the extra money to my children."

It was a lesson in rural Turkmen economics and paternal love: this man who'd had a fitful night of sleep on the train would crouch in the cold of Mary Station and wait for three hours wrapped in his cloak to save thirty cents to divide among his four kids.

In ancient times, the area I was now in had been called Khorasan; Merv was its noble capital. In one extravagant conceit, it was "the Soul of Kings." It is almost axiomatic that such a marvel would eventually turn into a dust bowl, and Merv had. But for centuries it had been an imperial metropolis, a center of learning, a place of citadels, a walled city, or several of them. What was left of it lay in the hard glitter of the Asian desert, about an hour up the railway line, near a town and a station called Bairam Ali, which dated from 1887, not long after the Russian empire took control of the region. A substantial villa had been built for the czar in Bairam Ali, but in the end His Highness hadn't shown up, and the villa was eventually turned into a sanatorium, which it still is now, for people with heart and kidney ailments. Mary — the adjacent city and provincial capital — was half boomtown, half slum: filled with the requisite gold statues and portraits, white marble government buildings, prestige projects (an opera house, luxury hotels, a pointless flyover), and boulevards almost empty of traffic.

Off the big thoroughfares, on backstreets, were low decaying houses and Soviet tenements. Some Russians remained, but not many. The Germans whom Stalin had relocated here from the Volga region during the Second World War had all departed.

I stayed in an inexpensive government hotel, where the other guests were all Turkmen officials. Most people came to Mary to see the ruins at Merv, or the ones at Gonur Depe, also nearby. Either that or the cotton fields.

One morning in Mary, I met Evgenia Golubeva. A sturdy woman with two daughters studying in Russia, she was a third-generation Russian in Turkmenistan, well known and loved locally. She had studied the ruins here and in Gonur Depe, and she was both knowledgeable and passionate about these flattened cities.

Ancient Merv, to my fascinated and amateur eye, resembled many fabled desert cities in decline that I'd seen. It looked like a string of sandcastles after the tide had brimmed and washed over them, simplifying and smoothing their walls, until there was only the faintest suggestion of symmetry in their slopes. But, as I kept thinking, this was a vivid metaphor for what inevitably happened to the hubristic world of wealth and power, to the world of gold statues and marble palaces, of vain slogans and planted forests. The world of armies and conquest. The world of generals and windbags. Ha! It all turned to sand and was overrun with rodents and lizards. Hawks flew above it, searching for vermin.

"This is Erk Kala, oldest part of Merv, from sixth century B.C.," Evgenia said, indicating a wide low crater of dried mud.

One of the pearls of the Silk Road, Merv had been overrun by Alexander the Great's men and Tamerlane and the Persians, sacked by Tolui Khan, son of Genghis Khan, in 1221, and later visited by Omar Khayyám. It had been Buddhist and Nestorian Christian; it had been Zoroastrian, mentioned in the Avesta as a place of strength and holiness, one of the "good lands." Importantly, Merv had been targeted by Muhammad as a staging post for Islamic conversion. The Prophet himself had sent two of his closest disciples here to evangelize, Evgenia told me. She said that he called them "my eyes in the East." They were buried here, their graves marked by a marble slab with a long inscription, which she translated: "Oh, traveler, you visit this place and you are lucky, because the people who are buried here are holy and close to God. If you have a problem, walk three times around the tomb and it will be solved."

My problem, so I had been told, was that the Ministry of Foreign Affairs was annoyed with me, thanks to the disturbance at my talk. "You might have a problem at the border," I was told. "They might hassle you. They could seriously hold you up."

So I walked three times around the tomb.

What I liked about Merv was its innocence — there were no fences, no postcards for sale, no pests, not even much respect. In this shattered and somewhat forgotten place, some visitors scrambled up and down the steep walls, kicking them apart, picking up pieces of broken pottery; others picnicked among the crenellations. Young boys genially pissed on the ruins.

In the distance, some men were grazing a herd of camels. Three boys on donkeys approached us, yelling and galloping across an ancient wall, leaving hoofprints. They had no saddles; they held on to rope bridles and kicked their skinny gray mounts.

"They are Beluchis, from Persia," Evgenia said. "They settled here many years ago."

She told me that the local people, superstitious about the aura of slaughter and conquest at Merv, tended to avoid it; they used it only to pasture their animals or to pilfer bricks. Goatherds huddled by the remaining part of the exposed wall of the complex known as Gyaur Kala. The sun was setting. The shepherds' fire scorched the ancient bricks as they cooked their evening meal.

In Mary, I was told that the Ministry of Foreign Affairs was still watching me, and that this might be a good time to head east to the Uzbek border. Someone would be sent to help me. And one morning this man showed up at my hotel. I shall call him Berdy. He said that he had been deputized to accompany me to the border. He had been an exchange student in the United States.

"What did you like about the States?"

"Good people. Clean conditions. No bribes."

"Tell me what you didn't like."

"The way that children treat their elders. Not good."

What had surprised him especially was the casual way that teenagers spoke to their parents: offhand, disrespectful, sarcastic.

"My host family was very nice to me, but one day coming home from school the daughter was smoking a cigarette. I said that her mother wouldn't like it. She said, 'My mother's stupid. Don't pay any attention to her.' Imagine that. I was shocked. A mother is holy!"

We drove through the prairie toward Turkmenabat, another renamed city — some people I met in Mary still called it Çarjou. In Ashgabat, I had asked an American Peace Corps volunteer what this part of the country would look like. He said, "Looks like west Texas," and it did.

An old shrouded woman squatted by the road, with a pile of trinkets — here in the middle of nowhere, yet another seller of amulets against the evil eye. Berdy bought me another multicolored demon-distracting cord, thinking it might come in handy.

Perhaps it did. Our driver dumped us in Turkmenabat, saying he could not go farther. We got another car, but no sooner had the old man driving it pointed out the Amu Darya River — one of the wonders of this region — than a roadblock appeared. The soldiers looked at Berdy's papers and told him that he could go no farther.

He wished me luck. I watched him through the rear window, standing in the empty road.

We came to Farap, the Turkmenistan border. I was fearful of the border formalities, but there was no problem. I was searched, my bag examined, my icon remarked upon. My passport, too.

"You live Gavaii."

"Yes."

"Gonolulu?"

"That's right."

"You stay Ashgabat?"

"Yes."

"You see beeg beelding?"

"Yes."

"Weech you like better?"

"My favorite," I said with absurd eagerness, "was the big statue of Turkmenbashi on the marble pillar. His arm is up" — I raised my arm up in a kind of Nazi salute — "and when the sun moves, the gold statue moves, like this. Beautiful. Gold!"

"Yes," the man said, smiling in satisfaction. He waved me through. "You can pass. *Nyet problyema.*"

So I walked past the barbed-wire fence on the dirt road through the desert toward Uzbekistan.

CALVIN TRILLIN

Three Chopsticks

FROM *The New Yorker*

WHEN I THINK BACK on the conversations that took place after I told people that I was going to Singapore to eat, I'm reminded of the scene in *Little Red Riding Hood* when the title character first encounters the big bad wolf. I play the wolf:

"Singapore!" Little Red Riding Hood says, in an improbable New York accent. "But Singapore is supposed to be the least exotic place in Asia. There's nothing to see there, unless you're a connoisseur of skyscrapers or container ports or obsessive street-cleaning."

"All the better for guilt-free eating, my dear. Your meals can't be spoiled by remorse over not having conducted a thorough inspection of the second-most-important cathedral."

"And isn't Singapore the place where you can get fined for chewing gum?"

"But, my dear, you can't chew gum while you're eating anyway."

From those conversations, I have concluded that the governmental ban on chewing gum, promulgated in 1992, remains the fact most strongly associated by Americans with Singapore. If Singapore tested a nuclear device tomorrow, the stories in American newspapers would mention the gum ban by the second paragraph. (Three years ago, the government relented a bit, in order to satisfy the requirements of a free-trade agreement: you can now buy nicotine gum by prescription.) There is a collateral awareness of the penalties that Singapore imposes for such malefactions as dropping a candy wrapper on the sidewalk. According to what's listed on a widely sold souvenir T-shirt emblazoned SINGAPORE — A FINE CITY, the acts that can bring you a serious fine include not only gum-chewing and littering and smoking and spitting but also carrying a durian on a public conveyance. A durian is an astonishingly odoriferous melon, much prized in Southeast Asia. Having smelled a durian, I must say that the prohibition against carrying one on a public conveyance (for which there is actually no specific fine) strikes me as a very solid piece of legislation. In American terms, it's the equivalent of a law against carrying a cattle feedlot on a public conveyance.

I'd always thought that I wouldn't go much further than that in supporting Singapore's efforts to treat tidiness as the nearly Athenian ideal of government. Still, had I known that it was happening I would have backed the government's scheme in the '70s to bring food vendors, called hawkers, off the streets and into centers that have proper sanitation and refrigeration and running water — a scheme that was inspired by a desire for tidy streets, along with public-health considerations and the needs of traffic control and, presumably, the relentless modernization that seems to have a momentum of its own in Singapore. My support would have been based on enlightened self-interest, one of the cornerstones of democracy. For years, as I've walked past food stands in foreign lands, I've struggled to keep in mind that for an American visitor the operational translation for signs that ostensibly say something like BHEL PURI or TACOS DE NOPALES is "Delivery System for Unfamiliar Bugs That You Will Bitterly Regret Having Ingested." The temptation to throw caution to the wind has been excruciating, since I may love street food above all other types of food. I have never figured out just why, although I've considered the possibility that, through some rare genetic oddity, my sense of taste is at full strength only when I'm standing up. (The fact that I particularly enjoy whatever I eat while standing in front of the refrigerator could be considered supporting evidence.) For a while, I thought about testing the standup hypothesis at some fancy Manhattan restaurant by springing to my feet halfway through the main course and trying to gauge whether that makes the roasted organic chicken with fricassee of spring vegetables and chanterelle polenta taste as good as those sausage sandwiches you get at Italian street fairs.

Gathering food vendors into hawker centers, under the purview of public health inspectors, meant that a Western visitor not only can have a safe shot at a variety of Singaporean delicacies but can do so in a setting so convenient that his energy is reserved for eating. All over Singapore, there are open-air pavilions where an island of tables and chairs is ringed by eighty or a hundred hawker stands — many of them selling only one item, like just satay or just fish-ball noodles. The government has established hawker centers in the central business district and hawker centers at the beach and hawker centers attached to the high-rise public-housing projects where the vast majority of Singaporeans live. In some of the fancy skyscrapers and department stores, private operators run air-conditioned, upmarket versions of hawker centers called food courts — a term presumably selected by someone who had never tasted what's passed off as food at an American shopping-mall food court. In Singapore, even the establishments called coffee shops are essentially mini hawker centers. They might have started as places that served coffee and the pastries that the British Empire, for reasons of its own, inflicted on unsuspecting colonials throughout the world, but these days the proprietor is likely to operate the drink concession himself and rent out two or three stalls to specialists in, say, fish-head curry or Hainanese chicken rice. It has become possible to eat in Singapore for days at a time without ever entering a conventional restaurant. Since I have never been much taken with the concept of courses — my eating habits are more on the order of a bit of this, a bit of that, and, now that I think of it, a bit of something else — it almost seems as if the Singapore government of forty years ago had arranged its hawker policy with me in mind.

I don't mean that I would check the flights to Heathrow if I heard that some entrepreneur in East Anglia had created a logistically flawless collection of food stands that allowed a diner to switch with ease from, say, bangers and mash to mushy peas to bubble and squeak. Convenience isn't everything. Singapore, though, has always been noted for the quality and variety of its street food and, not coincidentally, for having a citizenry whose interest in eating borders on the obsessive. The population combines migrants from several parts of China with minorities of Indians and Malays and people who look Chinese but are known as Peranakans — a separate ethnic group, long prominent in the government and business life of Singapore, which traces its origins to early Chinese traders who absorbed some of the culture and the genes of the local Malays. The evidence indicates that every one of these groups arrived hungry.

Soon, Hainanese were cooking Peranakan specialties and Indians were frying noodles in the Chinese manner. Old dishes were transmogrified. New dishes were invented. Eventually, Singaporeans were lining up at hawker stands to eat any number of dishes available only in Singapore. Even in New York, a famously polyglot city that has, for example, three restaurants specializing in the food of the Uighur people of the Xinjiang Uighur Autonomous Region, a yearning for Singapore hawker food is surprisingly difficult to satisfy. (Singapore *mei fun,* a noodle dish often found in Chinatown restaurants, is, it almost goes without saying, unknown in Singapore.) You can find the Malaysian version of some Singaporean dishes — *asam laksa,* a terrific soup with an unlikely sour-fish taste, has some similarity to the Peranakan version of *laksa* served in hawker centers, for instance — and some dishes in Chinatown restaurants are similar to the dishes brought to Singapore from, say, Fujian or Hainan. There are, of course, some upmarket pan-Asian places in Manhattan that do versions of street food, including Singaporean hawker food. Apparently, though, a dish that is reminiscent of what's found in Singapore serves only to make overseas Singaporeans long for the real article. Culinarily, they are among the most homesick people I have ever met.

I commiserated with a number of them this spring, when the prime minister's office organized a Singapore Day in Central Park. Singapore Day was supposed to be for expatriate Singaporeans and their guests, but I was among some New York feeders who wormed our way in when we heard that the festivities would include Singaporean dishes prepared by a dozen hawkers flown in for the occasion. Six thousand people stood patiently in line for a go at some food from home — completely ignoring the government exhibitions and the requisite rock band. As they waited, they spoke of the stands they head for when they can manage the eleven-thousand-mile trip to Singapore — the coffee shop in their old neighborhood that has the best *kaya* (a sort of coconut custard, served on toast), the fried-prawn-noodle stand in Marine Parade they always visit the first day back, the place with the best halal version of chicken rice. Nobody I spoke to mentioned any restaurants.

Even though the hawkers complained that they couldn't get all of the proper ingredients in New York, the tastes I had of *roti prata* (a sort of Indian crepe with dipping sauce) and *chwee kueh* (rice cakes topped with bits of fried preserved radish) and *char kway teow* (a dense fried rice-noodle dish that includes, among other ingredients, eggs and Chinese sausages and cockles and chives and fried lard) and *laksa* confirmed the wisdom of my plan to go to Singapore to eat.

The hawkers who came to New York had been handpicked by K. F. Seetoh, a Singaporean of Cantonese descent, whose connection to hawker food is similar, on a smaller scale, to the connection the France family has had with stock-car racing: that is, he managed to recognize a lot of scattered, unexalted activity as a cultural force and figured out how to merchandise it. An energetic, self-assured man in his midforties, with a hint of blond in his hair, Seetoh, as he's known to everybody, began his career as a photographer. But his avocation — which is eating, since he is a lifelong resident of Singapore — eventually became his profession. He started in 1998 by putting together a hawker-food guide called *Makansutra,* *makan* being the Malay word for "eat" or "food." The guide lists what Seetoh considers the best stands for about a hundred and forty traditional hawker dishes — the best being all that any book would have room for, since Singapore has what Seetoh estimates to be about twelve thousand stands in the government hawker centers alone. The ratings are on a chopstick scale, with the most distinguished stands receiving three pairs of chopsticks. Seetoh's business card now identifies him as the chief executive and "*makan* guru" of a company that is also called Makansutra. He puts out other Southeast Asian food guides, appears on television, and does consultancies. He even presides over a small collection of hawker stands in the slick marina area that's part of Singapore's modernistic performing arts center — a building that, because of its shape (though not, presumably, its smell), is sometimes referred to by the locals as the Durian. Seetoh is helped in these endeavors by his wife, Patricia. Although Patricia says that before meeting her husband she ate mostly sandwiches and French fries, she comes from a Peranakan family that had good food as a priority. According to the Seetohs, when Patricia's father was on his deathbed he whispered something that made his family gather closer, thinking that he had some final instructions or blessings to impart. What he was saying turned out to be *"laksa."* They brought him a bowl of it.

Seetoh and I had become acquainted when he was in New York for Singapore Day. The next evening, at one of the sophisticated Southeast Asian places that he'd wanted to try, the Seetohs and I sampled some of the Singaporean dishes on the menu and he responded more or less the way you'd expect a barbecue nut from Tennessee to respond to what was advertised as a pulled-pork-shoulder sandwich in, say, Helsinki or Leeds. He was moved to describe the authentic Singaporean *nasi lemak* and the authentic Singaporean chili crab I'd eat when I got to Singapore. Given the fact that I wouldn't have thrown rocks at what we'd just eaten, I could hardly wait to sample the three-chopstick versions. I told Seetoh that I'd be in Singapore as soon as I could arrange it.

In Singapore, it was clear from the moment Seetoh picked me up at my hotel that, as interested as he was in authenticity and quality, pure capacity would also be an issue. He is an enthusiast. For Seetoh, there's always another noodle dish around the corner. He's quite willing to admit that there is plenty of mediocre hawker food in Singapore, but superior hawker fare renders him rhapsodic. The icon chart in *Makansutra* translates two and a half pairs of chopsticks — one notch below the top — as "Divine." Three pairs of chopsticks means "Die, Die Must Try!," which has become a sort of motto for Seetoh and his enterprises. It's a direct translation, he says, of a Cantonese phrase that means, more or less, "to die for." In addition to Cantonese and Mandarin and Malay and Hokkien, Seetoh speaks idiomatic English plus Singlish, a slangy local patois that is spoken only idiomatically. He speaks all of these languages rapidly.

Working mainly from my samplings at Singapore Day and from dishes that had been labeled "Popular Local Favorite" in the 2007 edition of *Makansutra,* I'd come up with a preliminary list of dishes that I considered, well, must try. There were nine: *chwee kueh* (the rice cakes with radish), grilled stingray, *roti prata,* curry puffs (which Seetoh describes as, more or less, a Chinese improvement on an Indian samosa), chili crab (and its cousin, pepper crab), *laksa,* fish-head curry, carrot cake (which would startle someone who'd meant to order the dessert you might get in the sort of restaurant whose waitresses slouch around in sandals: it's fried white radish and flour cake, with garlic and eggs and scallions and other vegetables), and *charkway teow.* Seetoh looked disappointed.

"Wrong list?" I asked.

Not wrong. Insufficient. I had left out Hokkien fried-prawn noodles. I had left out *otah* — fish paste, mixed with chilies, folded into a coconut leaf, and grilled. I had left out *rojak* — a sort of salad that's held together with a sauce the color and consistency of Mexican mole, unless you get the Indian rather than the Chinese version, which is totally different and, of course, a must-try item. I hadn't mentioned *mee siam,* a Thai-sounding noodle dish that is not available in Thailand. I hadn't mentioned fish-ball noodles — which is odd, since I am devoted to fish balls. I hadn't even mentioned *bak kut teh,* a simple pork-ribs soup that is, improbably, considered a breakfast treat. (Eventually, Seetoh and I had some *bak kut teh* for breakfast — in a place next to the port that is said to be the busiest in the world — and I can say unequivocally that it beats Cheerios by a mile.) I had left out *popiah,* a Hokkien-style spring roll that includes stewed turnips. By the time we reached the Maxwell Road Hawker Centre — near where Makansutra has an office, in a row of colonial-era three-story buildings known as shophouses — my list had about twenty items, and for the next few days every hawker center seemed to remind Seetoh of a dish I had to try before I went home. "You can't leave without having it," Seetoh would say, when he instructed me to add another dish to my list. "It'll knock your socks off."

Sampling what Seetoh considers the very best rendition of each dish required some traveling around town — a remarkable chicken rice here, an amazing *chwee kueh* there, a mind-blowing *laksa* somewhere else. At one center, though — the modestly named Old Airport Road Temporary Food Centre, which was serving a public-housing project during some construction that's part of an ambitious, ten-year hawker-center upgrading program that the government launched in 2001 — we were in the presence of three vendors who had been designated by Seetoh as hawker masters. There, without descending into the realm of the merely divine, you can start with *rojak,* then tear into some chili crab, and then decide whether you might want to end the evening with Hokkien fried-prawn noodles or have the chili-crab specialist do a pepper crab as a change of pace before you end the evening with Hokkien fried-prawn noodles. I had no doubt that I was indeed eating the food of masters. In fact, while eating at the Old Airport Road Temporary Food Centre I realized that it was incorrect to think that my taste buds operated at full strength only when I was standing: we were eating this food while sitting at a table, after all, and it was knocking my socks off. One of the principles of scientific inquiry is that even an elegant hypothesis has to be abandoned if irrefutable evidence to the contrary is encountered.

Seetoh seemed quite confident about his selection of the very best stand for each hawker dish, but, as I had learned from the people I'd met at Singapore Day — people whom Seetoh had described as "deprived and depraved" — a Singaporean devotee of hawker food doesn't have to be the author of a food guide to be absolutely certain that he knows where to find the best version of just about anything. One evening, while we were eating some fish-head curry — a dish that in Singapore includes an entire snapper head staring up through the curry sauce — a friend of Seetoh's named Daniel Wang shook his head sadly when he heard where Seetoh had taken me for *char kway teow*. Wang, who retired in 2004 as Singapore's director general of public health, happened to be the Ministry of the Environment engineer put in charge of building the original hawker centers, in the '70s. At his retirement, he had just presided over a $2.5-million upgrading of a beach venue called the East Coast Lagoon Hawker Centre, which was turned into something so reminiscent of a tropical resort that Seetoh refers to it as "Daniel's Club Med." Wang's contribution to hawker centers can be seen as a monument to enlightened self-interest: given his line of work, he's quite conscious of hygiene, but he happens to be crazy about hawker food, particularly *char kway teow*. As a schoolboy, Wang regularly observed the cooking technique of a particular *char kway teow* hawker, and he remains loyal to that hawker's son — a vendor who had learned well from his father, Wang explained, how to cook the noodles in lard to keep them from sticking and how to make his stock from prawns and squid and precisely when to sprinkle on white pepper. Dismissing the suggestion that childhood nostalgia might be making him a less than objective judge, Wang went on to extol the *popiah* produced by a hawker who had not been among the five *popiah* hawkers listed in *Makansutra*.

Wang was so enthusiastic about the snubbed *popiah* that there was nothing to do but go to the Newton Food Centre and give it a try, as soon as we had polished off the fish-head curry. At the Newton Centre, Seetoh was barely polite about the *popiah* and Wang did not pursue the matter, having become caught up in a discussion of a sort of oyster omelette that we'd picked up from a nearby stall. I assumed that the *popiah* discussion was at an end. The next evening, though, while the Seetohs and I were on the way to the East Coast Lagoon Hawker Centre to have some salted vegetable and duck soup (a dish that has replaced French fries in Patricia Seetoh's pantheon), Seetoh pulled up in front of a shopping mall called the Shaw Centre. While we waited in the car, Patricia ducked in to get some *popiah,* so that I could understand what a divine — or maybe even a die-die-must-try — *popiah* is like. In Singapore, I should have realized, a discussion about the relative merits of various *popiah* stands is never at an end.

The more we ate, the longer my list got. We couldn't seem to stay even. On my last evening, while we consumed some *mee siam* and the Indian version of *rojak* with Daniel Wang and a couple of his friends, Seetoh was still lamenting the dishes I hadn't had — steamboat (a sort of hot pot) and a Malay noodle dish called *mee rebus* and *lontong* (an Indonesian dish of rice cakes with tofu and vegetables simmered in a coconut curry) and *nasi briyani* (a dish of Middle Eastern origin) and a Hakka tofu dish called *yong tau foo* and Indian *mee goring.* One of Wang's guests said that when she gets back to Singapore on the flight that arrives around dawn she stops for *kueh chap* before she even goes home — *kueh chap* being a bowl of broth with sheets of rice-flour noodles served with pig intestines, or what Wang calls "spare parts." Seetoh said, almost apologetically, that he hadn't taken me to a *kueh chap* stand, and I said, "My mother used to say that it's always good to save something for the next trip."

I was, indeed, thinking about the next trip as I studied my list on the plane home. I deeply regretted having had *char kway teow* only once, for instance, and I didn't see how I was going to repair that deficit without returning to Singapore. I was also thinking of how convenient it would be if other cities — New York, for instance — had hawker centers serving the local specialties. New York's current mayor does not disdain tidiness, after all, and New York mayors have thought of street vendors as congestion at least since the reign of Fiorello LaGuardia, who gathered some of them in places like the Essex Street Market.

A hawker center could be set up by the next time the Seetohs visited New York. I could imagine us at a place that looks a bit like the East Coast Lagoon Hawker Centre, Daniel's Club Med, although it would overlook the Hudson rather than the Strait of Singapore. There's a stand selling Italian-sausage sandwiches, of course, and a stand selling Vietnamese *banh mi* sandwiches. The mayor has persuaded the *dosa* man of Washington Square to come into the operation and leave the Washington Square cart in the hands of a trusted cousin. There are stands run by the vendors from the Red Hook ball fields — one selling *pupusas* and one selling ceviche and one selling Honduran tacos. A couple of Belgian French-fry vendors are there, with fries good enough to make Patricia Seetoh consider reverting to her former eating habits. The mayor's people have persuaded the legendary Arepa Lady of Jackson Heights to give up the chancy weather of Roosevelt Avenue for the Hudson River Hawker Center. There's a jerk-chicken stand and two competing falafel stands. I've been in nearly constant movement between our table and the vendors all evening, bringing back, say, *bocconcini* or two kinds of fish balls — the plain ones and the ones with meat at the center, familiar from Eldridge Street noodle-soup restaurants like Sheng Wang and the exquisitely named Young City Fish Balls. Seetoh is saying that he's getting a bit full, and reminds me that he and Patricia have to get up early for the long flight back to Singapore. "But you haven't had a calzone yet," I say. "You haven't had a *zeppole*. We still haven't gotten you a classic New York pastrami sandwich, not to speak of a knish. I'm not talking about one of those nasty commercial knishes that look like vinyl coin purses. I'm talking about an authentic New York potato knish. You can't go home without eating a knish. It'll knock your socks off."

CATHERINE WATSON

Where the Roads Diverged

FROM *WorldHum.com*

I WAS IN ECUADOR, on my way to a folklore performance, sharing a ride with two other tourists — a middle-aged Canadian woman and a young computer guy from California. They started comparing notes on their Latin American travels. I didn't join in. I'd seen the continent edge to edge during the previous twenty-five years, but I didn't want to interrupt their conversation by saying so. I just stared out the window, only half listening.

Then I heard something that snapped me alert — something that made me feel as if I'd been kicked in the chest, as if my heart had stopped, as if I couldn't breathe.

"You know the place I liked best?" the young guy said. "Easter Island!"

The Canadian gushed in agreement. There was so much to do there! New hotels! The new museum! All the tours there were to take! And they've put so many of the statues back up.

My God, I thought, suddenly strangled by memories. My God, my God. They're talking about Easter as if it's a place. Just another place.

At the folklore show that night, I applauded when the rest of the audience did, but I wasn't there. I'd been thrown a quarter century into my own past, back to a forty-five-square-mile triangle of black lava and wind-blown grass in the middle of the Pacific Ocean, 2,200 miles from Chile, 2,400 miles from Tahiti.

La Isla de Pascua. Rapa Nui. Te pito o Te Henua. The navel of the world. "The place farthest from anywhere . . ."

By any of its names, Easter Island felt like home to me, the only place in the world that ever truly did.

I had been under its spell since before I could read, ever since my father first showed me its pictures in books — haunting pictures of giant stone heads perched on grassy slopes, lips pursed, eyes blank, staring out to sea.

I was a shy child then, and I grew into a shy adult, ill at ease with people, lonely but most comfortable alone. I took refuge in daydreams — always about somewhere else, somewhere distant and strange, where a stranger like me might better fit. When I was old enough, I started traveling, trying to make my dream world real.

By the time I got to the South Pacific, I was in my early thirties, and I'd been looking for home all my life — for the place I really belonged, the place where I should have been born. I felt I'd found it on Easter Island the instant I stepped off the plane. It was as if the island had been waiting for me, all that time, the way I'd been waiting for the island.

Yolanda Ika Tuki met me at the airport. Actually, she just met my plane, she and a pickup truck full of other island women, all hoping to rent out rooms to tourists. There were only a couple of flights a week from mainland Chile and not many visitors. Most of them were already booked into the island's only formal lodging, a six-room motel, but the local women met the plane every time anyway, crowding up to the stairs before passengers had a chance to get out, piling luggage into the pickup, and pleading for guests.

Yolanda met the plane, met me, met my eyes. It felt like fate.

Her small house stood on a shady, sandy lane on the outskirts of Hanga Roa, the island's only village. She had one room to rent, a sunny, recently added annex that felt instantly familiar. The walls were varnished plywood, like a summer cabin up north, and the furniture looked like the stuff in the government clinic where my father worked — chrome tubing, green leatherette cushions.

The reason made me smile. Everything in that room — walls, furniture, and louvered windows — was indeed U.S. government issue, liberated by the locals after our air force abandoned a satellite-tracking base on the island in the 1960s. Even the varnish smelled like home.

Yolanda Ika Tuki was short and thick-bodied, like most of the older island women, with dark skin and black hair. She might have been forty or fifty or even sixty. I never knew. Yolanda cooked for me, interpreted the island for me, introduced me to her neighbors and friends, included me in her household. It felt like a family but wasn't quite, so I fitted right in.

There was a quiet man I assumed was her husband, whom I saw mainly at dinner. A pretty little girl who was a neighbor's out-of-wedlock child — Yolanda said the mother's new husband didn't want the girl around. And the child of another neighbor, a slender boy of about eleven whose history had a different twist.

He was half-American, one of about thirty youngsters that the U.S. airmen had managed to father while they were here. It was a noticeable number, out of a population of less than two thousand, six hundred of them kids. The islanders loved children — people joked that babies were "our biggest product" — but this boy wasn't happy. He yearned to find his father and go live with him in the States.

"I know my father loves me," he said, "because he wrote to my mother once." One day the boy showed me the precious letter. The American man had promised nothing, hadn't included his address or even his last name. He was just saying goodbye.

This is what outsiders have always done in Polynesia, starting with the first European explorers and their crews — love 'em and leave 'em, down through the centuries. It made me feel ashamed, but the islanders didn't seem to mind. All good stories, in fact, seemed to begin, "When the Americans were here . . ." They had brought the modern world with them — electricity, piped water, Coke in cans, movies, the airport. "We loved the Americans," one islander told me.

Islanders didn't feel that way about people from Chile, which has governed Easter Island since 1888. They said Chileans couldn't be trusted, were lazy and given to stealing. Chileans said the same things about them.

Among themselves, the islanders spoke their own language; it was soft, rounded, and full of vowels, like all its cousins across Polynesia. With me, they spoke Spanish, the island's second language and mine as well. But while I heard about local problems — feeling discriminated against by mainlanders was mentioned often — no one dragged me into them. I think it was because I was under Yolanda's wing — not a part of the community, but not an ordinary tourist, either. She treated me more like a daughter.

Sometimes, when she called me for breakfast, she would come in and perch on the foot of my bed and chat. She also gave me advice. It wasn't always wise, but it was always the same: *Disfrute su vida, Catalina,* she said. Enjoy your life, Catherine. And I did.

I began to exist in the present tense, as if I had no past regrets and no future fears. It was something I'd never done before. That, and the incredible distances surrounding us, lent me an exhilarating freedom. I likened it to hiding in a childhood tree fort with the rope pulled up. No one knows where I am, I kept thinking. No one can find me.

My days quickly fell into their own gentle rhythm: Go out walking after breakfast. Explore a cave, a volcano, a vista. Take pictures. Talk to people. Go home for lunch. Nap or write or poke around Hanga Roa. And in the late afternoon, walk over to Tahai — the row of giant statues, called *moai,* that stood closest to town — and watch the sunset paint the sky in the direction of Tahiti.

After supper, the island's only TV station went on the air, and I joined Yolanda's household around the set. The programs, flown in once a week, would have been odd anywhere, but here in the uttermost corner of Polynesia, the mix was especially peculiar: decades-old *Beanie and Cecil* cartoons, a British-made series of English lessons ("Why are there no onions in the onion soup?"), a quiz program on Chile's fishing industry, and American reruns, subtitled in Spanish — *The Six Million Dollar Man, The Rockford Files.*

"Is there a lot of that in the United States?" an adult asked reasonably after one of Rockford's chronic car chases. The children thought the Six Million Dollar Man was real. I couldn't get over the station's signature logo: three dancing *moai,* wiggling their world-famous bellies on the screen.

One evening I stayed in my room, writing. Between gusts of wind that rattled the trees, I caught gusts of soft music. In the church down the lane, people were singing Polynesian hymns. If I'd known nothing about this culture, that music alone would have told me they'd been seafarers. There was a canoeing cadence in it, like the throb of waves or the steady beat of paddle strokes.

There was distance in it too, and a touch of sadness. It made me think of the complicated, crisscross navigations that populated the Pacific in ancient times, and the vast emptiness that early voyagers sailed into without knowing what lay ahead, and how many must have been lost before others happened upon this tiny fleck of land.

"Wind and music and nothing to do," I wrote in my journal that night, "Sunday on Easter Island." But it didn't feel like Sunday. It felt like Saturday. Every day on the island felt like Saturday.

I knew what my favorite place would be before I saw it — Rano Raraku, the extinct volcano where the giant statues had been quarried and carved. They were already old friends. Face to face, they looked exactly as they had in the books of my childhood — an army of elongated heads frozen in mid-journey down the grassy slopes.

This was where, in the late 1600s, the ancient carvers put down their stone chisels and never picked them up again. The reasons aren't fully known, but shrinking resources likely led to warfare, devastating the old culture.

The heads at Rano Raraku were the ones that never reached their destinations, travelers stranded in midtrip. Islanders said these *moai* were blind. They had not yet received or gotten their stone topknots, and they would never stand on an altar like Tahai's.

The cylindrical topknots — like top hats the size of corn cribs — were quarried at another volcano, Puna Pau, where the lava rock was rusty red instead of grayish black. Abandoned topknots lay on the ground like giant red boulders. They all had been hollowed out inside, the better to fit onto a statue's head. One afternoon, I curled up inside a topknot and spent an hour watching white clouds drift across brilliant blue sky, over a landscape of yellow grass; it reminded me of a Kansas prairie.

The weather reminded me of Hawaii — frequent showers, followed by clearing skies and rainbows. But the resemblance stopped there. The island was a big pasture edged by cliffs. It wasn't tropical, and it wasn't lush. Outside of gardens and protected valleys, there were almost no trees, and the beaches were black rocks.

Yolanda told me there was another American on the island, a woman about my own age. I ran into her one sunset at Tahai, and we struck up a friendship. She had visited the island before, drawn by its archaeology, but she was back this time because of a boyfriend, an islander. She wanted to see where that relationship was going to lead. I soon knew what she was wrestling with.

One night, Yolanda took me to Hanga Roa's little disco — about half the village was there — and I found an island boyfriend too. That meant I was swept into another extended family — parents, sisters, cousins, and armfuls of little nieces and nephews. There were more gatherings in homes, lots of talking, loud card games that I usually couldn't follow. Their favorite was a complicated four-person game called "bree-hay"; it turned out to be bridge, pronounced in Spanish.

From the beginning, Yolanda had been urging me to stay longer. I'd only planned on a week, but as plane day got closer and she kept talking, I weakened. Yolanda was right, I decided. There was really no reason to leave so soon. The only thing waiting for me was a small internship on a newspaper in Buenos Aires, and the start date was more than a month away. Besides, there was no penalty for changing my reservation. What harm could it do to wait?

I missed one plane. And then another. And another . . .

And while I waited, my newly simple life grew complicated. I was enmeshed in a love affair, all right, but it wasn't exactly with the man I'd met. It was with Easter Island itself. My island.

I could see a different future opening up for me here, and every time I cuddled one of the little nephews on my lap, it seemed more real, more possible. How many people, I wondered, get to live their dearest wish? How many people really find paradise? How many dare to stay once they find it?

That was the biggest question, and the longer I stayed, the harder it was to answer, and the less like paradise my paradise appeared. I loved the "wind and music" part but I was no longer sure about "nothing to do."

I watched the men and began to understand why every day felt like Saturday. It was because so few of them had real jobs. I watched their wives and noticed that the idle men didn't help them with all those babies. I saw how few options there were for everyone, even the children, and wondered how many options there would be for me.

Yolanda kept on telling me to enjoy my life. But my Minnesota conditioning had begun to kick in. Be careful what you wish for, it whispered in my ear. Be careful.

My American friend confided that she and her island boyfriend were having problems — sometimes he drank too much, and then they argued. It scared her. It scared me too, and I started to undermine myself with questions:

What would I do when the magic wore off? Who — what — would I turn into if I stayed? Could I really grow old here? Would days of childcare and evenings of bree-hay be enough? This wasn't just some other town — this was another world. It had taken me a lifetime to reach it. What if it took that long to get away?

I couldn't tell whether I was being realistic or just a coward, didn't know what I wanted to do, let alone what I should do. Maybe I preferred daydreams to reality, after all. Didn't I, on almost every trip, imagine what it would be like to live there? And didn't I always go back to normal, back to family, house, job, no matter how tempting the place was? Yes. Yes, I always went back.

I made the final decision fast, on almost no notice so I couldn't be talked out of it by my boyfriend, by Yolanda, or even by myself. I must have said goodbye to the people I was leaving behind, but I don't remember doing even that. All I know is that when the next plane left, I was on it, and when the clouds closed behind me over Easter Island, whatever future I could have had there vanished into mist.

Everything I have written since then has come from that decision. Leaving Easter Island broke my heart, but it also turned me into a travel writer.

It's a nutty way to live, really — a kind of paid homelessness, a career dependent on permanent exile: Go away, have experiences, find stuff out and then come back to tell it to the folks at home. It means always being on the outside looking in, longing to stay and never staying. I was perfect for it.

I still looked for "home" when I was on the road, and sometimes — on other islands, in tiny towns — I found it for a while. But never again with the same foreordained, consuming clarity I felt on Easter Island. I wasn't surprised: All acts have consequences, and you can't defy destiny without paying some sort of price.

I have never gone back. I can't. When asked, I say it's because I don't want to see how the island has changed (all those hotels, all those tours . . .)

But the real reason is that I don't want to feel like an outsider there. I don't think I could bear being just another tourist in a place where once, however briefly, I belonged. And I don't need or want another look at the path not taken; I've been seeing it, ever since I caught that plane.

Over the years, readers have asked me about what I do. One

question comes up again and again, usually from women in full stride, doing the great American juggling act — husband, children, home, career: "Aren't you afraid," they say, "traveling around the world alone like that?"

No, I tell them. Leaving home's a cinch. It's the staying, once you've found it, that takes courage.

Contributors' Notes

Notable Travel Writing of 2007

Contributors' Notes

Bill Buford is a staff writer for *The New Yorker*. Previously, he was the fiction editor of the magazine, from 1995 to 2002. Buford came to *The New Yorker* from *Granta*, which he edited for sixteen years. His book *Heat: An Amateur's Adventures as Kitchen Slave, Line Cook, Pasta-Maker, and Apprentice to a Dante-Quoting Butcher in Tuscany* (2006) recounts his experiences in a number of professional kitchens, beginning at Babbo, Mario Batali's flagship restaurant in New York City. He is also the author of *Among the Thugs* (1992), a highly personal nonfiction account of crowd violence and British soccer hooliganism. Buford lives in New York City.

Ian Buruma is the Henry R. Luce Professor at Bard College. He received this year's Shorenstein Award for writing about Asia. His latest book, *Murder in Amsterdam*, is available in paperback and was winner of the *Los Angeles Times* Book Prize for the Best Current Interest Book. He writes about a broad range of political and cultural subjects for major publications, most frequently for the *New York Review of Books*, *The New Yorker*, the *New York Times*, *Corriere della Sera*, the *Financial Times*, and the *Guardian*.

For his first book, the award-winning *The Final Frontiersman*, **James Campbell** made six trips to Arctic Alaska. *The Ghost Mountain Boys*, his story of the soldiers' grueling march and the subsequent battle for New Guinea, was released in October 2007. He lives in Wisconsin with his wife and three daughters.

Peter Chilson is the author of two books on Africa, *Riding the Demon: On the Road in West Africa* and the fiction collection *Disturbance-Loving Species*, which won the Bakeless Fiction Prize in 2006. His stories and essays have appeared in *The Best American Travel Writing 2004,* the *American Scholar, Ascent, Audubon Magazine, Creative Nonfiction,* the *Long Story, North American Review, Gulf Coast, High Country News, West Africa Magazine,* the *Daily Telegraph,* and elsewhere. He teaches writing and literature at Washington State University.

Simon Doonan is a style commentator with over thirty years experience in the World of Fashion. He is a regular guest on Vh1, *America's Next Top Model, Full Frontal Fashion,* and Sirius Satellite Radio. As creative director of Barneys New York, he is responsible for all aspects of the Barneys image. He is most known for his sometimes controversial windows, which have been a Barneys trademark since 1985, and for his provocative "Simon Says" column in the *New York Observer.* After the 1998 publication of Simon's memoir *Confessions of a Window Dresser,* New Line Cinema quickly grabbed the film rights for Maverick Films to produce and Simon to adapt. Simon's second book, *Wacky Chicks: Life Lessons From Fearlessly Inappropriate and Fabulously Eccentric Women,* was published in 2003. His memoir entitled *Nasty: My Family and Other Glamorous Varmints* was published in 2005. The rights were acquired by the BBC: A comedy series entitled *Beautiful People,* produced by Jon Plowman and based on *Nasty,* is scheduled to air in fall 2008. He lives in New York City with his partner, the ceramicist and designer Jonathan Adler.

J. Malcolm Garcia's essays and journalism have been published in the *Virginia Quarterly Review,* the *Missouri Review,* the *Alaska Quarterly Review,* and McClatchy newspapers, among other publications.

Karl Taro Greenfeld is the author of *Speed Tribes, Standard Deviations,* and *China Syndrome,* chosen by the *Village Voice* and New York Public Library as one of the twenty-five Best Books of 2006. A former writer and editor for *The Nation, Time,* and *Sports Illustrated,* he is currently a contributing editor to *Condé Nast Portfolio* and *Details.* His writing has also appeared in *GQ, Vogue, Outside, Men's Journal, Wired, Condé Nast Traveler,* the *New York Times,* the *Wall Street Journal* and the *Washington Post,* among other publications. His fiction has been published in the *Paris Review, American Short Fiction,* and *Asia Literary Review.* He is currently at work on a book about his autistic brother, Noah.

Peter Gwin is a staff writer at *National Geographic.* His assignments have led him to the Sahara's largest Stone Age graveyard, the oldest known tyrannosaur, and Nazi U-boats sunk in the Gulf of Mexico. A native of Fayette County, Georgia, he is based in Washington, D.C.

A native of Missouri, **Peter Hessler** arrived in China as a Peace Corps volunteer in 1996. He taught English in Fuling, a small city by Chinese standards (population 200,000). After that he moved to Beijing, where he became *The New Yorker*'s China correspondent; he also contributes to *National Geographic*. He is working on *Country Driving*, the final book in a trilogy that spans the decade he spent in China. The first two books are *River Town* and *Oracle Bones*. He now lives in southwestern Colorado, in Ridgway, a small town by American standards (population 700).

Melik Kaylan was born in Istanbul, grew up in England, and is based in New York. He has written for English and American publications since the 1980s. He now writes about culture for the *Wall Street Journal*. He has written about the smuggling of antiquities, scuba diving with the NYPD, and searching for Inca treasure in the Andes. He spends a lot of time trying to dodge who he was the day before. He has lived with Karen rebels in the Burmese jungle, dived with the Cousteau ship in the Red Sea, and survived in Baghdad's Red Zone with a lot of facial hair.

John Lancaster is a former Middle East and South Asia correspondent for the *Washington Post*. He lives in Washington, D.C.

Emily Maloney's first published essay, "Power Trip," was selected for *The Best American Travel Writing 2003*. After graduating from the University of Puget Sound in 2000, she spent a year in Japan, studying at Naruto University, and then another year in South America. She currently lives in Oregon, writes a regular column for *The Smart Set*, and is at work on a book about her travels.

Bryan Mealer is the author of *All Things Must Fight to Live: Stories of War and Deliverance in Congo*. He was the Associated Press staff correspondent in Kinshasa, Congo, and has reported from locations across the African continent, including Kenya, Somalia, and Togo. His writing has appeared in *Harper's* and *Esquire*, among other publications. He was born in Odessa, Texas, and graduated from the University of Texas at Austin.

Pankaj Mishra is the author of *The Romantics: A Novel* and three books of nonfiction, *Temptations of the West: How to Be Modern in India, Pakistan, Tibet and Beyond; An End to Suffering: The Buddha in the World;* and *Butter Chicken in Ludihiana: Travels in Small Town India*. He contributes regularly to the *New York Review of Books*, the *Guardian*, and *Travel + Leisure*.

Annie Nocenti is the former editor of *High Times* and the screenwriting magazine *Scenario*. She has written numerous comic books and graphic novels for Marvel and D.C. Comics, including *Daredevil, Spider-Woman, Kid Eternity,* and *Batman.* She is now a freelance writer.

Kristin Ohlson is a Cleveland-based writer whose work has appeared on *Salon.com* and in the *New York Times,* the *Walrus, American Archaeology, Wildlife Conservation, Tin House,* and many other publications. Ohlson is the author of *Stalking the Divine,* a memoir that won the American Society of Journalists and Authors' 2004 award for best nonfiction, and the coauthor of the *New York Times*–best-selling *Kabul Beauty School: An American Woman Goes Behind the Veil.*

David Sedaris contributes frequently to *The New Yorker,* and has also regularly contributed essays to *Esquire.* He is the author of *Barrel Fever* (1994) and *Holidays on Ice* (1997), as well as four collections of personal essays: *Naked* (1997), *Me Talk Pretty One Day* (2000), *Dress Your Family in Corduroy and Denim* (2004), and *When You Are Engulfed in Flames* (2008). In 2005, he edited an anthology of stories, *Children Playing Before a Statue of Hercules.* Sedaris and his sister Amy Sedaris have collaborated under the name The Talent Family and have written several plays, including *Stump the Host; Stitches; One Woman Shoe,* which received an Obie Award; *Incident at Cobbler's Knob;* and *The Book of Liz,* which was published in book form by the Dramatists Play Service. His original radio pieces can often be heard on the show *This American Life.* In 2001 Sedaris became the third recipient of the Thurber Prize for American Humor and, the same year, was named by *Time* magazine as "Humorist of the Year." In 2005 he was nominated for two Grammy Awards for Best Spoken Word Album (*Dress Your Family in Corduroy and Denim*) and Best Comedy Album (*David Sedaris: Live at Carnegie Hall*).

Gary Shteyngart was born in Leningrad in 1972 and came to the United States seven years later. His debut novel, *The Russian Debutante's Handbook,* won the Stephen Crane Award for First Fiction and the National Jewish Award for Fiction. It was also named a *New York Times* Notable Book, a best book of the year by the *Washington Post* and *Entertainment Weekly,* and one of the best debuts of the year by the *Guardian.* His second novel, *Absurdistan,* published in 2006, was named one of the best books of the year by the *New York Times Book Review* and *Time.* In 2007 he was named one of the Best Young American Novelists by *Granta.* His work has been translated into over twenty languages, and his fiction and essays have appeared in *The New Yorker, Travel + Leisure, Granta, GQ, Esquire,* the *New York Times Magazine,* and many other publications. He lives in New York City.

Seth Stevenson is a contributing writer for *Slate*. His work has also appeared in the *New York Times, Newsweek, New York Magazine,* and *Rolling Stone,* among other publications. He recently spent five months circumnavigating the earth using only surface transportation (including cargo freighters, bicycles, and terrifying Cambodian taxis). A graduate of Brown University, Stevenson lives in Washington, D.C.

Thomas Swick is the travel editor of the *South Florida Sun-Sentinel* and the author of two books: a travel memoir, *Unquiet Days: At Home in Poland,* and a collection of travel stories, *A Way to See the World: From Texas to Transylvania with a Maverick Traveler.* His work has appeared in numerous magazines and *The Best American Travel Writing 2001, 2002,* and *2004.*

Jeffrey Tayler is a correspondent for the *Atlantic* and a contributor to *Condé Nast Traveler, Harper's,* and *National Geographic.* He has published five books, including *Facing the Congo* and, most recently, *River of No Reprieve.* His next book, *Murderers in Mausoleums,* about traveling the back roads of empire between Moscow and Beijing, will be published in January 2009. An accomplished linguist, he is fluent in Russian, Arabic, French, and Modern Greek and can get by in Spanish and Turkish.

Matthew Teague is a native of the Mississippi Delta and now lives with his wife, Nicole, and two children in Alabama and Pennsylvania. He works in places as diverse as Algeria, Sri Lanka, Tonga, Egypt, and elsewhere, writing for *Philadelphia Magazine, National Geographic,* the *Atlantic Monthly, Men's Journal,* and others.

Paul Theroux was born in Medford, Massachusetts in 1941 and published his first novel, *Waldo,* in 1967. His subsequent novels include *The Family Arsenal, Picture Palace, The Mosquito Coast, O-Zone, Millroy the Magician, My Secret History, My Other Life,* and *Kowloon Tong.* His acclaimed travel books include *Riding the Iron Rooster, The Great Railway Bazaar, The Old Patagonian Express,* and *Dark Star Safari. The Mosquito Coast* and *Dr. Slaughter* have both been made into successful films. He was the guest editor of *The Best American Travel Writing 2001.* His latest book is *Ghost Train to the Eastern Star: On the Tracks of the Great Railway Bazaar.* He divides his time between Cape Cod and the Hawaiian Islands, where he is a professional beekeeper.

Calvin Trillin has been a staff writer for *The New Yorker* since 1963. His most recent book was *About Alice,* a memoir. His novels include *Tepper Isn't Going Out* (2001), which he claims is the first parking novel, *Runestruck* (1977), and *Floater* (1980). His other books include two books of verse on the Bush

Administration, a collection of reportage on murders, three books on eating that were republished as *The Tummy Trilogy,* and a travel book called *Travels with Alice.* He lives in New York.

Catherine Watson is the former travel editor of the *Minneapolis Star Tribune.* A writer, photographer, and writing instructor, she is the author of two collections of travel essays, *Roads Less Traveled: Dispatches from the Ends of the Earth* (2005) and *Home on the Road: Further Dispatches from the Ends of the Earth* (2007). She lives in Minneapolis.

Notable Travel Writing of 2007

Selected by Jason Wilson

Scott Anderson
  Afghanistan: Coming of Age at Band-i-Amir. *National Geographic Adventure,* May.

Mischa Berlinski
  Woman Marries Snake. *Harper's Magazine,* November.
Tom Bissell
  Up the Mountain Slowly. Very Slowly. *Play, New York Times Magazine,* November.
Jake Bogoch
  The Rock. *Skiing,* November.
Frank Bures
  The Lost World of Nigeria. *WorldHum.com,* July 30.
  Spirits in the Material World. *Washington Post Magazine,* September 16.
Colby Buzzell
  The Red-Hot, Pork-Stuffed, Corn-Wrapped, Blues-Flavored Enigma. *Esquire,* May.

Tim Cahill
  Death Valley. *National Geographic,* November.
Rich Cohen
  The Summer of Our Discontent. *Harper's Magazine,* September.
John Colapinto
  The Interpreter. *The New Yorker,* April 16.

Kevin Fedarko
  High Times. *Outside,* July.
Michael Finkel
  Bethlehem 2007 A.D. *National Geographic,* December.
Ian Frazier
  Outfoxing the Fox. *Outside,* October.
  "Yo, Frank!" *Outside,* May.
McKenzie Funk
  I Was a Chinese Internet Addict. *Harper's Magazine,* March.

J. MALCOLM GARCIA
  The White Train. *The Virginia Quarterly Review,* Fall.
  Lay of the Land. *The Missouri Review,* Fall.
STEPHEN GLAIN
  Truffles in the Sand. *Gourmet,* May.

TOM HAINES
  In a New Light. *Boston Globe,* January 7.
  Uncertain Terrain. *Boston Globe,* May 13.
  Twilight Time. *Boston Globe,* September 9.
  Solitary State. *Boston Globe,* November 18.
CHICO HARLAN
  Leap of Faith. *Washington Post Magazine,* October 21.
PETER HESSLER
  Walking the Wall. *The New Yorker,* May 21.
PAUL HOCHMAN
  Speaking Slovene. *Ski,* March/April.

PICO IYER
  A Life in the World. *Condé Nast Traveler,* September.

CHUCK KLOSTERMAN
  Futurama! *Esquire,* September.

JEANNE MARIE LASKAS
  Underworld. *GQ,* May.

EMILY MALONEY
  Crisis Is Magic. *TheSmartSet.com,* August 29.
PATRICIA MARX
  Emotional Baggage. *The New Yorker,* April 16.
ANDREW McCARTHY
  The Good, the Bad & the Ugly. *National Geographic Traveler,* April.
GREG MERRITT
  Roots of an Oak. *Flex,* July.
MARTIN MILLER
  House Broken. *Smithsonian,* August.
PANKAJ MISHRA
  Inland Empire. *Travel + Leisure,* February.
SETH MNOOKIN
  Secrets of the Dance. *Condé Nast Traveler,* November.
J. R. MOEHRINGER
  100 Hours of Solitude in Venice. *Food & Wine,* September.
MARIE MUTSUKI MOCKETT
  Letter from a Japanese Crematorium. *AGNI,* vol. 65.

CATHY NEWMAN
  Life on the Line. *National Geographic Traveler,* November/December.

THE BEST AMERICAN SERIES®

THE BEST AMERICAN SHORT STORIES® 2008
Salman Rushdie, editor, Heidi Pitlor, series editor

ISBN: 978-0-618-78876-7 $28.00 CL
ISBN: 978-0-618-78877-4 $14.00 PA

THE BEST AMERICAN NONREQUIRED READING™ 2008
Edited by Dave Eggers, introduction by Judy Blume

ISBN: 978-0-618-90282-8 $28.00 CL
ISBN: 978-0-618-90283-5 $14.00 PA

THE BEST AMERICAN COMICS™ 2008
Lynda Barry, editor, Jessica Abel and Matt Madden, series editors

ISBN: 978-0-618-98976-8 $22.00 POB

THE BEST AMERICAN ESSAYS® 2008
Adam Gopnik, editor, Robert Atwan, series editor

ISBN: 978-0-618-98331-5 $28.00 CL
ISBN: 978-0-618-98322-3 $14.00 PA

THE BEST AMERICAN MYSTERY STORIES™ 2008
George Pelecanos, editor, Otto Penzler, series editor

ISBN: 978-0-618-81266-0 $28.00 CL
ISBN: 978-0-618-81267-7 $14.00 PA

THE BEST AMERICAN SPORTS WRITING™ 2008
William Nack, editor, Glenn Stout, series editor

ISBN: 978-0-618-75117-4 $28.00 CL
ISBN: 978-0-618-75118-1 $14.00 PA

THE BEST AMERICAN TRAVEL WRITING™ 2008
Anthony Bourdain, editor, Jason Wilson, series editor

ISBN: 978-0-618-85863-7 $28.00 CL
ISBN: 978-0-618-85864-4 $14.00 PA

THE BEST AMERICAN SCIENCE AND NATURE WRITING™ 2008
Jerome Groopman, editor, Tim Folger, series editor

ISBN: 978-0-618-83446-4 $28.00 CL
ISBN: 978-0-618-83447-1 $14.00 PA

THE BEST AMERICAN SPIRITUAL WRITING™ 2008
Edited by Philip Zaleski, introduction by Jimmy Carter

ISBN: 978-0-618-83374-0 $28.00 CL
ISBN: 978-0-618-83375-7 $14.00 PA